RELIGIOUS TELEVISION AND PIOUS AUTHORITY IN PAKISTAN

RELIGIOUS TELEVISION AND PIOUS AUTHORITY IN PAKISTAN

TAHA KAZI

INDIANA UNIVERSITY PRESS

This book is a publication of

Indiana University Press
Office of Scholarly Publishing
Herman B Wells Library 350
1320 East 10th Street
Bloomington, Indiana 47405 USA

iupress.org

© 2021 by Taha Kazi
All rights reserved

No part of this book may be reproduced or utilized in any form or by any means, electronic or mechanical, including photocopying and recording, or by any information storage and retrieval system, without permission in writing from the publisher. The paper used in this publication meets the minimum requirements of the American National Standard for Information Sciences—Permanence of Paper for Printed Library Materials, ANSI Z39.48-1992.

Manufactured in the United States of America

Library in Congress Cataloging-in-Publication Data

Names: Kazi, Taha, author.
Title: Religious television and pious authority in Pakistan / Taha Kazi.
Description: Bloomington : Indiana University Press, 2021. | Includes bibliographical references.
Identifiers: LCCN 2020027326 (print) | LCCN 2020027327 (ebook) | ISBN 9780253052223 (hardback) | ISBN 9780253052247 (paperback) | ISBN 9780253052230 (ebook)
Subjects: LCSH: Television talk shows--Pakistan. | Television in religion—Pakistan. | Television broadcasting—Religious aspects—Islam. | Islam and politics—Pakistan.
Classification: LCC PN1992.8.T3 K39 2021 (print) | LCC PN1992.8.T3 (ebook) | DDC 297.6/1095491—dc23
LC record available at https://lccn.loc.gov/2020027326
LC ebook record available at https://lccn.loc.gov/2020027327

1 2 3 4 5 26 25 24 23 22 21

CONTENTS

Acknowledgments vii
Note on Transliteration xi

Introduction 1
1. A Background of Religious Programming in Pakistan 21
2. The Production, Ownership, and Control of Religious Television Shows 45
3. Doctrinal Activism and Religious Television 72
4. Religious Authority and Control over Religious Knowledge 99
5. Self-Styled Scholars and Religious Show Hosts: Emerging Sources of Religious Authority 118
6. Changing Viewer Assessments of Religious Authority 142
7. Redefining the Boundaries for Critical Deliberation in Islamic Public Debate 163
   Conclusion 186

Glossary of Arabic Terms 197
References 201
Index 219

ACKNOWLEDGMENTS

THE IDEA FOR THIS BOOK came to me on one of my earlier visits to Karachi. As I sat on a park bench on a pleasant winter evening to enjoy a book by one of my favorite fiction authors, an unfamiliar woman in her fifties approached me to randomly inquire about whether I had viewed the recent episode of the religious show *Aalim Online*. On learning that I had not, she proceeded to regale me with an emotional rendition of the momentous event that had transpired on the episode. A Christian boy, much impressed with the person of the popular religious show host, Aamir Liaquat Husain, had called in and expressed his desire to embrace Islam. The show host had responded by reciting the first *kalima*, the requisite verse for conversion to Islam, which the boy had then repeated after Husain in order to formalize his religious transformation. While listening to the woman tearfully extol Husain's virtues for making such an eventuality possible, I could not help but wonder why the event had affected her so deeply and personally. I was curious about how someone could be so exhilarated by an event that was essentially another person's spiritual transformation. Did the boy's conversion to Islam serve to reaffirm the woman's own faith, and if so, was this because prior to that incident she had been plagued with self-doubt regarding her religious conformance? I also wondered about the veracity and authenticity of the conversion itself. Had the event been staged deliberately to generate higher ratings for the show, or could it be that a religious show host as controversial as Husain had in actuality managed to inspire someone to such a degree that the boy was willing to relinquish his existing belief system in order to follow Husain more closely?

My curiosity about the park incident stayed with me for some time, so when one year later I embarked on my social science research, I opted to explore the impact of religious shows on the social, political, and religious lives of Pakistanis. This research has constituted the main thrust for writing this book. The completion and publication of this book owe to the cooperation and support of numerous people, all of whom I would like to acknowledge here. I would like to thank the people at Indiana University Press who helped me with the publication of this book and the two anonymous reviewers of this manuscript, whose insightful suggestions and feedback have made this book much better than it would have been otherwise. At SOAS, my PhD supervisors, Stephen P. Hughes and Mathew J. Nelson, offered me invaluable advice and encouragement for my research project. I am especially thankful to Stephen Hughes for acting as my primary guide, for reading innumerable drafts of each chapter, and for advising me on the organization of this book.

I would like to thank those journals that have allowed me to reproduce revised versions of earlier papers. Some of the material in chapter 2 has been reprinted here by permission of Taylor and Francis. The version of record of this manuscript has been published and is available in *Culture and Religion*, 2016, volume 17, issue 4, pages 468–85, https://doi.org/10.1080/14755610.2017.1296011. The material in chapter 7 has been reproduced by permission of the American Anthropological Association from *American Anthropologist*, volume 120, issue 3, pages 523–34, 2018, https://doi.org/10.1111/aman.13061. The material is not for sale for further reproduction.

In terms of my fieldwork, I owe immense gratitude to my extended family and friends, who agreed to participate in my research; allowed me privileged access to shared resources; permitted me to use their contacts to access religious producers, presenters, and religious viewers in the field; and helped me organize some of my field discussions. I could not have managed my fieldwork as well without their invaluable help and assistance. In Karachi, I thank my sister, Sharmeen Kazi, for allowing me to monopolize the family car and driver for the entire duration of my fieldwork. I am also indebted to my close friends Najia Ahmed, Nausheen Masud, and Faiza Shahid, who lent me their invaluable assistance for mediating my access to some of my interlocutors in the field. I am particularly grateful to my aunt Nasreen Bakar, who in her capacity as the headmistress of a kindergarten school permitted me to conduct group discussions with some of her school's teachers. She also played a central role in enabling my access to the otherwise-elusive and vastly popular religious show host Aamir Liaquat Husain. During the writing of this book, in London, my niece, Ansa Gohar, gave me her unending compassion and moral support, for which I am profoundly grateful.

I also wish to thank some of my interlocutors, particularly some religious presenters and producers who spent a great deal of time with me, patiently dealing with my research queries, in spite of their busy schedules. The immensely popular religious show host Aamir Liaquat Husain is foremost among those whom I would like to acknowledge here. I thank him for his hospitality on multiple occasions and for his willingness to candidly discuss with me the more controversial aspects of religious programming. His revelations have allowed me to present a more nuanced account of religious media in this book. Husain also extended his help in introducing me to other important religious presenters. I owe my acquaintance with the veteran religious presenter *Allama* Kokab Noorani Okarvi exclusively to Husain and his production team. I would like to take this opportunity to also thank the religious presenter *Allama* Noorani for contributing substantially to my knowledge of the key historical developments that took place in religious programming in Pakistan. His disclosures, which drew on his long-term association (almost fifty years) with televised forms of religion, have allowed me to present a more comprehensive overview of the history of religious programming in the country.

Lastly and most importantly, I would like to thank my parents for always backing me in all my life choices, regardless of how risky these may have appeared at the time. Their encouragement gave me the courage to abandon my earlier career and to reenroll in a university program to pursue a discipline that I found much more interesting and fulfilling. I thank my mother for always lending me her utmost support in all of my endeavors and for going to great lengths to ensure the fulfillment of my goals. I dedicate this book to my father, who while no longer with us nonetheless continues to act as a source of great inspiration for me in everything I do. His constant need to interrogate the normative assumptions governing Pakistani society, religiosity, and polity continues to resonate with me deeply and is very much part of the core analytical fiber of this book.

NOTE ON TRANSLITERATION

ALL ITALICIZED ARABIC WORDS IN the text have been transliterated by me according to the system of Brill *Encyclopedia of Islam*, 3rd ed. Some exceptions to this format are Pakistan's Islamic laws and the names of religious shows, all of which have an already established spelling in Pakistan.

RELIGIOUS TELEVISION AND PIOUS AUTHORITY IN PAKISTAN

INTRODUCTION

I ARRIVED AT THE PORT city of Karachi, Pakistan, in August 2013 to research the growing popularity of religious talk shows and their impact on Pakistani religiosity. Religious talk shows emerged as a popular genre of religious programming in tandem with the introduction of satellite television in Pakistan, following President Pervez Musharraf's media liberalization reforms in 2002. The first religious show of its type, *Aalim Online*, was broadcast on the privately owned satellite channel Geo Television Network in November 2002. The subsequent reproduction and adaptation of this programming genre by a number of competing private satellite channels is a testament to the genre's growing popularity within the Pakistani viewing public. As noted in the BBC News, the popularity of these shows is contrary to the ʿulamāʾs (erudite religious scholars, pl. of ʿālim) expectations regarding the potentially corrupting influence of "'obscene' foreign imports" on private satellite television channels, as it is not foreign content but rather religious programming that "dominates the airwaves" in the liberalized Pakistani media environment (Azhar 2012).

Pioneered by the popular anchor Aamir Liaquat Husain, religious talk shows mark some important transitions in the formal nature of religious programming in Pakistan. Prior to the liberalization of Pakistani media, it was customary for religious shows broadcast on the state-owned channel, Pakistan Television Corporation (PTV), to invite only one scholar, who would employ a didactic approach to sermonizing and restrict himself to providing exegetical commentary on select *Qurʾānic* verses and Prophetic traditions. Alternatively, contemporary religious talk shows follow a more viewer-centric and participation-based approach to religious programming. They entertain live viewer call-ins on the correct modes of Islamic comportment, the performance of obligatory rituals, the resolution of everyday family disputes, and so forth. Therefore, the task of the religious scholars invited is not limited to sermonizing but equally entails responding to viewer queries and issuing religious edicts on the different aspects of Islamic practice and conduct. The result is a reconfiguration of religious shows into *fatwā* (reasoned opinion) programs.[1] In addition, religious shows attempt to accommodate the diversity of religious thought in Pakistan and invite two to three male religious scholars of varying doctrinal (Shiʿa Ithna Ashari, Sunni Barelwi, Sunni Deobandi, and Sunni Ahl-i Hadīth) and educational (seminary-trained and self-styled celebrity preachers) backgrounds. All the religious authorities present are encouraged to debate among themselves and contribute their doctrinal viewpoints on the finer points of Islamic belief and practice. By including self-styled celebrity preachers, who lack the formal (*madrasa*-based) religious credentials generally ascribed to traditional Islamists, religious shows contribute to such preachers' expanding influence in religious public debate. These preachers inspire widespread adulation and trust in their audiences primarily on account of their appearances on religious talk shows.

Another key feature that sets contemporary religious talk shows apart from their predecessors is their novel presentation format. Within the new format, religious specialists predominantly do not address viewers directly. Rather, their rulings are mediated by religious show hosts, whose interventions are simultaneously premised on the hosts' role as show moderators and on their self-positioning as religious experts in their own right. In their capacity as show moderators and in their self-designated role as religious experts, religious show hosts represent the emergence of a new type of religious authority mediated exclusively by these talk shows.

In this book, I will examine the implications of these religious programming transformations for regnant conceptualizations of religious authority, orthodoxy, and religiosity and for the dynamics of religious power and Muslim politics in Pakistan. My analysis in this context has resonances with anthropological and religious media scholarship that has, in the context of the wider Muslim world, alluded to the significance of religious media movements in enabling the fragmentation of religious authority and in democratizing religious debate (e.g., Babb 1998; Hoover 2002; Eickelman and Piscatori 2004; Hefner 2005). In this context, much scholarship has implicated religion's media proliferation in expanding the scope for lay reflexive engagement (Hirschkind 2001; Meyer and Moors 2006; Mandaville 2007; Hoover 2008; Mahan 2012) and in creating opportunities for the emergence of "new" religious intellectuals who are "able to rethink religion outside traditional boundaries" (Eickelman 2018). Recent studies within the disciplines of religion and media have tended to favor a more balanced and nuanced approach, also acknowledging the role of "media outlets" in simultaneously "enhancing and/or challenging conventional religious sites, boundaries, organizations, and styles" (Hackett and Soares 2015, 6). The studies have convincingly postulated that "the opening up of the public sphere" can lead to "new forms of exclusion" and create opportunities for "intra-religious debates and public critique of religious 'Others'" (6–7).

Yet other academics have also attested to the role of religious media in enabling innovative modes of religious authority and Islamic thinking (e.g., Moll 2012; Hoesterey 2016). For instance, while attempting to explain the reasons behind the popularity of Egyptian celebrity preachers like Amr Khaled and Moez Masoud, Yasmin Moll has drawn attention to the significance of certain pedagogical attributes, such as the preachers' shared affinity with religious television viewers, in creating a preferred Egyptian regard for religious moderation over the severity of Salafi religiosity. Alternatively, James Hoesterey has noted the relevance of religious media in altering gendered configurations of religious power in Indonesia by rendering the authority of male televangelists such as Abdullah Gymnastiar contingent on their ability to sustain their popular appeal among their female followers (see also Kazi 2018).

I would like to push further in the direction opened up by these recent studies by also attending to the broader implications of the religious media, outside of their role in "improving individual piety" and popularizing Islam, albeit different understandings of it (Echchaibi 2011, 27). In particular, my propositions on the role played by Pakistani religious shows in prompting new ways of assessing, and thinking about, religious authority and changing the dynamics of religious power and authority in the country are indebted to Moll's (2010, 2012) and Hoesterey's (2016) analyses of the new modes of religiosity enabled by religious media movements. Yet, as it will become clear, my analysis also attempts to move beyond the emphasis prevalent in both Moll's and Hoesterey's scholarly works on the pious impulse of religious media movements. My deviation from these scholarly accounts on media is grounded in my broad-based analytical approach, which has entailed a joint consideration of the production and viewership aspects of religious programming and a sensitivity to the differences in people's religious orientation, including the multivalent significance of Islam in their lives. Drawing on this approach, I have been able to both demonstrate the instrumentality of religious shows for furthering particular commercial and political agendas and reveal their unintended and unanticipated ramifications for Pakistani religiosity.

Therefore, even as I emphasize the usefulness of certain religious programming transformations in allowing religious show producers to generate a wider viewership for their shows and simultaneously intensify the resonance of more accommodative and tolerant understandings of Islam in Pakistan, I also implicate these programming shifts in altering the dynamics of religious politics (see chaps. 3, 4, and 5) and provoking altered enactments of piety and religiosity (see chaps. 6 and 7). Especially in relation to the pluralistic emphasis of contemporary religious shows, I demonstrate how this programming development can enable more critically and expediently motivated lay engagements with Islamically prescribed social and ethical mores and with the religious authorities who uphold them. My propositions in this context are grounded in the dialectical nature of scholarly interactions on television and the corresponding significance of these interactions in drawing viewers' attention to the contested nature of Islamic belief and practice. I propose that as the viewers become more attuned to the disputed nature of religious knowledge, so too are they rendered more willing to oppose certain religious precepts, especially when they deem them to be irreconcilable they with their contemporary lifestyles and extant worldviews. It is from this perspective that I also implicate religious shows in instigating reevaluations of the fundamental nature of certain Islamic concepts and practices and in provoking a reconfiguration of religious knowledge.[2] On the basis of these findings, I emphasize throughout this book that to grasp the full implications of religion's proliferation of media, we must look beyond the revivalist impetus of this nexus.

FIELDWORK SITE AND RESEARCH METHODOLOGY

Of all the cities in Pakistan, Karachi appeared to me as the most conducive place from which to study the diversity of viewpoints in relation to religious programming. It is the largest and most cosmopolitan city of Pakistan, boasting a population of more than twenty million according to unofficial estimates. The city is home to two of Pakistan's primary ports and is a key hub of economic and industrial activity. For these reasons, it has attracted rural and urban immigrants from all over Pakistan, making it a microcosm of the entire country. It is home to people of different ethnic and religious sensibilities and affiliations. In addition, it is the city where I spent most of my childhood and adult life, and thus I already had a prior understanding of the workings of the city and an established network of friends and family at the time I initiated my research. However, what attracted me the most to the city was its relevance as the production site of popular religious shows such as *Aalim Online* and *Amaan Ramazan*, because of which popular religious presenters such as Aamir Liaquat Husain and *Allama* Kokab Noorani also reside in the city.

When I started my fieldwork in Karachi, I found the people of the city polarized over the role Islam should play in Pakistani society and politics. The diverse positions on Islam's public role were not particular to the city but were very much part of a wider national discourse on the ambiguities associated with Pakistan's creation as an Islamic state and the religion's exploitation by successive governments and various religiopolitical groups to extend their sphere of influence over Pakistani society and polity (see Cohen 2004; Iqtidar 2012). A prominent example of this exploitation is the political tenure of the military dictator General Ziaul Haq, whose facile attempts at Islamizing the country were more so directed at appeasing the religious right and perpetuating his military rule than at accomplishing *Sharīʻa* (Islamic code) compliance in Pakistan. Zia's instrumental deployment of Islam to sustain his military rule, together with the *ʻulamā*'s complicity in his political project, played a vital role in dividing the country on the matter of religion's incorporation into state affairs. Even as some people began to actively support Pakistan's conversion into a theocratic state, others began to view such a possibility as synonymous with the politicization of Islam and religious authority in Pakistan.

Some of the more recent events contributing to the polarization of the country along religious lines are 9/11, Pakistan's internally disputed participation in the United States–led "War on Terror," and the Western media's subsequent dichotomous representation of Muslims, as those who are radically driven and those who are moderately disposed, together with their vilification of the former category of Muslims. These events and representations also left their mark on Pakistan's already fractured religious psyche. Thereafter, a growing number of Pakistanis, eager to dissociate themselves from the more jingoistically driven, ideological aspects of their faith, began to identify themselves as moderate Muslims. Others, discomfited by Pakistan's participation in a morally dubious war that they viewed as strategically driven, rather than ethically motivated, became even more protective of their radical or conservative religious identities. Against this backdrop, General Pervez Musharraf's move to project himself as a vanguard of moderate and enlightened religious thought in Pakistan may have worked to earn him the favor of a section of Pakistani liberals, but it did little to endear him to the wider Muslim majority, who increasingly began to view the general's attempts at ideological maneuvering as akin to religious betrayal.

In Karachi—a city that had in the few years leading up to my research witnessed an unparalleled growth in Islamic militancy, sectarian violence, and religiously motivated crime—the polarization of people along religious lines was even more pronounced than in the rest of the country. This owed in part to the more recent political events affecting the city, such as the Pakistan military's anti-terrorism initiative in Pakistan's northern tribal belt, an initiative that had caused many Islamic militants to relocate to Karachi to escape the brunt of the military operation. "Operation Clean-Up," targeting various militant groups in the city and involving the country's paramilitary forces, the Pakistan Rangers, was initiated in the city in September 2013, and it was still underway when I returned to London after completing my fieldwork in September 2014. Therefore, at one end of the city's religiopolitical spectrum were those whose historical experience of Islamization under Zia, as well as their current experience of the deteriorating law-and-order situation and violent manifestations of Islamic militancy and sectarianism in the city, had made them strongly opposed to Islam's heightened role in the social and political affairs of the city.[3] On the other end were religious practitioners whose close ties with *madāris* (religious seminaries, pl. of *madrasa*), *masājid* (mosques, pl. of *masjid*), and centers of Islamic learning; their disillusionment with the present political system of governance; and their rising hostility toward the West, heightened by a perception of Pakistan's exploitation in the United States–led "War on Terror," had made them more sympathetic to those who offered Islam as a panacea to the country's political, social, and economic woes.[4]

These variations in perspectives regarding the religion's social and political role also informed my interlocutors' engagement with religious programming, so that its increased prominence in shaping contemporary religious thought in the country tended to garner mixed reactions. During my fieldwork in Karachi, I found people referring to these shows in both favorable and unfavorable terms. They would either acknowledge these shows as a better viewing alternative to secular, entertainment, and political programming content or emphasize their potentially deleterious implications for Pakistani religiosity. Those subscribing to the former view generally iterated their approval of religious programming in terms of its edificatory benefits and its usefulness for improving people's understanding of profound religious concepts. Alternatively, the majority of lay opposition to religious shows drew on a consideration of these shows in terms of their potentially radicalizing influence on Pakistani urban religious sensibilities.

People also expressed different opinions about the pluralistic format of religious shows. Some of my interlocutors felt that the representation of alternative religious viewpoints and the discussion-based format of contemporary religious shows would help neutralize sectarian tensions in the country.

Alternatively, others argued that these developments would, in fact, serve to further foment sectarian rivalries and exacerbate religious intolerance in an already fraught religious landscape (Murthy 2010; Azhar 2012; Walsh 2012). The latter sentiment was generally expressed in relation to the controversial religious content aired by some religious shows that featured discussions on doctrinally sensitive religious issues. For instance, on one episode of *Aalim Online*, broadcast on September 7, 2008, the show's anchor, Aamir Liaquat Husain, and two clerics had deliberately attempted to incite violence against members of the Ahmadīyā community by declaring all members of the community to be blasphemers.[5] Within forty-eight hours of the program going on air, two Ahmadis (people belonging to the Ahmadīyā sect) had been murdered. While the incident earned Husain much criticism and censure from members of the Pakistani general public and media, it did little to mitigate his popular appeal among his followers, who are largely among the middle class in Pakistan. Husain has since been lauded by *New York Times* journalist Declan Walsh (2012) as a religious "broadcasting sensation in Pakistan."

Events such as this one also provoked some people to assert that more official regulation was warranted in relation to the incendiary content of these shows and the provocative conduct of their hosts. Alternatively, some of my interlocutors demanded greater programming control in relation to the presence of celebrity preachers on religious show expert panels. Their contentions regarding these preachers as warranting greater official regulation contrasted markedly with an alternative and equally prevalent view of these preachers as creating opportunities for more practical and moderate incorporations of Islam in Pakistani society and politics. For proponents of the latter view, their opinion found expression in an iteration of these preachers as privileging ideas of Islam that were more easily incorporated into contemporary lifestyles than those espoused by traditional Islamists. Alternatively, for those espousing the former view, the willingness of these preachers to reconsider the "absolute" nature of certain established Islamic concepts came to represent a nefarious programming agenda aimed at promoting ethical and moral ideals and ways of living that were antithetical to the "true" spirit of Islam. This view of religious shows also derived credence from a consideration of other forms of religious programming, such as religious game shows, and was in keeping with the tendency of these shows to mix religion with entertainment and feature Islamically inconsistent programming. A popular adaption of religious talk shows, religious game shows, became the favored mode of *Ramaḍān* transmission on many private satellite channels soon after their initial airing on Geo Television Network in 2013. My interlocutors would generally employ both genres interchangeably when reflecting on the adverse impact of religious programming on pervasive forms of moral and ethical conduct.

It was in these varied invocations of religious programming that I first detected glimpses of a profoundly complex and fragmented Pakistani Muslim imaginary and found evidence of people's conflicting aspirations in relation to their viewing of religious shows. I came to realize that even as some people turned to religious shows to improve their piety, religious understanding, and observance, others were increasingly tempted to invoke these shows to justify their deviation from the more austere aspects of religious conduct. These distinct employments of religious shows corresponded closely with people's individually subscribed-to religious sensibilities—radical, conservative, moderate, or liberal—and their corresponding preferences for certain forms of religious authority over others. At the same time, they also impinged on people's varied engagements with the country's turbulent religiopolitical history and their corresponding notions of how much influence religion and, by extension, religious authorities should be allowed to exert over their everyday lives.

Since my fieldwork was conceptualized with these distinctions in mind, I opted not to restrict myself to a particular locality, as is characteristic of anthropological fieldwork. Instead, taking into account the diversity of perspectives on Islam's public and political role, and the ubiquity of television, which according to Armbrust (2004, 820) is "everywhere and nowhere at the same time, and hence maddening as an object of study," I attempted to approach the study of religious shows from multiple perspectives and locations. I included members of the viewing public in a wide range of social settings; religious show producers, presenters, and hosts, both within and outside the context of the production studios of *Aalim Online*; and religious scholars based in the city's seminaries and mosques.

My decision to locate myself in the producing studio for studying something as complex as television programming draws on two distinct types of media scholarship: one that foregrounds the usefulness of locating audiences in "less than obvious places" (Hughes 2011, 310; see also Ang 1991; Ganti 2002) and one that underscores the importance of uncovering the political, economic, and organizational contexts of media production (Carragee 1990, 84, quoted in Morley 1992, 34), with a view to glean insights into the dynamics of the "dominant power structure" (Curran, Gurevitch, and Woollacott 1982, 11, 18–19; see also Abu-Lughod 2005).[6] In addition, a production-based perspective allowed me to unearth the relationships of interdependence characterizing the production of religious shows. In line with these findings, this book neither presupposes the media as a tool for "mass" ideological domination (see Mulvey 1989;

Horkheimer and Adorno 2002; Powdermaker 2002) nor privileges the agency of audiences in appropriating dominant "media content" and using it "against itself, to empower themselves" (Budd, Entman, and Steinman 1990, quoted in Morley 1992, 28).[7] Instead, it considers the relationship between religious show viewers and religious programming to be mutually constitutive, one in which various social and political actors—including the state; religious scholars, media, and corporate institutions; and a highly diverse and fragmented lay population—jointly influence the content and format of religious shows and constitute the audiences for them.

MOSQUES AND SEMINARIES

Mosques and seminaries constituted a central feature for my study mainly because of my interest in exploring the types of transformations in religious authority enabled by religious shows. The types of seminaries I visited during my fieldwork ranged from those rooted in earlier models of Qurʾānic learning, such as the *kuttābs* (informal centers for Qurʾānic memorization and recitation located mostly in Karachi's working-class neighborhoods), to the more sophisticated and infrastructurally sound institutions of advanced Islamic learning such as the Deobandi *Dār al-ʿUlūm* and *Jāmīʿa ʿUlūm-ul Islāmīā*, located in the localities of Korangi and Banori Town, respectively. While most of the *kuttābs* I visited were affiliated with adjoining mosques, some also functioned independently and were informally housed in makeshift rooms in the resident *qarī*'s (expert in Qurʾānic Arabic diction), *muʾaddhin*'s (person who gives the call to prayers), or *imām*'s (prayer leader) living quarters. Given the emphasis on pluralism in my analysis of religious shows, I have been careful to include the perspectives of seminaries and mosques affiliated with all four key religious groups in Pakistan, including Shiʿa Ithna Ashari, Sunni Barelwi, Sunni Deobandi, and Sunni Ahl-i Hadīth.[8] In this context, some key concerns guiding my study are the shifting pluralistic focus of religious shows and the inclusion of "new" celebrity preachers on religious show expert panels. I was interested in examining the impact of both programming developments on doctrinal politics and traditional assertions of religious authority, respectively. Both programming developments, coupled with the commercial considerations underlying religious show production, tend to provoke a series of corresponding strategies that are closely aligned with the religious scholars' respective doctrinal affiliations and the dynamics of Muslim politics in Pakistan (chap. 3).

On the basis of my research conducted with all four doctrinal schools, I implicate religious shows in stirring the religious scholars' apprehensions in relation to the scholars' sustained relevance in people's lives. In this context, my analysis also cuts across doctrinal divides and sheds light on aspects of religious programming that affect all traditional scholars equally, irrespective of their denominational proclivities. One such programming aspect is the instructional focus of religious programming, which not only renders all scholarly rulings susceptible to greater viewer scrutiny and critical judgment but also puts pressure on the religious scholars present to at times sacrifice their doctrinal perspectives for the sake of generating wider viewership appeal (see chaps. 4 and 5). Moreover, I also highlight the relevance of this programming shift in alienating the scholarly majority, who tend to be confined to the seminaries and mosques, from their followers. This development is a corollary of religious shows serving as a more convenient alternative to visiting the seminary or mosque, for lay viewers interested in seeking resolutions to their everyday religious issues or in improving their knowledge of the prescribed forms of religious conduct.

With reference to the dangers religious shows pose expressly for "traditional" scholars, I would also like to clarify this book's framing of these scholars as distinct from self-styled celebrity preachers. I do not intend for these designations to allude to the "progressive" or "backward" tendencies of either category, nor do I seek to depict celebrity preachers as driven by a purely reformist orientation in contrast to traditional scholars. Rather, my employment of these terms is aimed at elucidating the distinction between religious scholars who have acquired their religious expertise through self-endeavor or through their enrollment in a religious study program at a secular institution and those who owe their religious erudition to the traditional institution of the *madrasa* and its affiliated institutions. References to self-taught scholars as distinct from the *'ulamā* were also made consistently by religious show viewers and presenters. However, these people's employment of both terms was extremely loaded and clarified a marked preference for one particular mode of religious authority over the other. This further implied that the status ascribed to both sources of religious authority varied greatly with the institutional or religious affiliation and orientation of those invoking these designations. I also want to point out here that my blanket employment of the term *'ulamā*, or traditional scholars, to denote a range of religious personnel draws on the colloquial usage of the term in Pakistan rather than on its official meaning. Strictly speaking, the term *'ulamā* derives from the Arabic word *'ilm* (knowledge) and is employed for religious scholars who can claim sufficient training and expertise in *Sharī'a* (Islamic code), *tafsīr* (exegetical commentary), *kalām* (speculative theology), *ḥadīth* (Prophetic tradition), and *fiqh* (jurisprudence), such as the *muḥaddith* (expert on the *ḥadīth*), the *muftī* (interpreter of Islamic law), and the *mutakallim* (expert on *kalām*). However, in Pakistan, the title tends to be loosely ascribed to all religious personnel who claim affiliation with a *madrasa* or mosque irrespective of their religious erudition, including the *imām* (prayer leader), the *khaṭīb* (person who addresses the prayer congregation), the *qarī* (expert in Qur'ānic diction) and the *mu'addhin* (person who gives the call to prayer) (see Khan 2012, 149).

With reference to the seminaries and mosques, I would also like to draw attention to the embodied aspect of my research methodology, which is linked to my efforts to negotiate my access to my scholarly interlocutors in the field, my status as a Muslim female, the fact that almost all of my *madrasa-* and mosque-based interlocutors were male, and the rules and restrictions surrounding male and female interactions in Islam. Because different doctrinal schools vary in terms of their rigidity regarding the rules of *'awrah* (covering up), for a Muslim woman, gaining access to religious personnel is often a matter of knowing how to dress adequately for different occasions.[9] While many middle- and upper-class women have adopted the *hijāb* (head covering) as the appropriate form of Islamic dress, the majority of Pakistanis continue to associate the *niqāb* and *burqa* (face covering and loose flowing cloak to cover the body) with working-class women. Thus, even covering up more and erring on the side of caution could have put me at a disadvantage, especially when negotiating my access to a more class-conscious religious scholar. By the end of my fieldwork, I became sufficiently proficient at identifying the appropriate mode of dress for different situations.

This also brings me to a consideration of some of the ethical and political dilemmas that an anthropologist, who is completely dependent on others for her fieldwork, has to contend with when negotiating her access in the field. For me, a key political issue that emerged from my position as a female involved the way that I was compelled to cover up for some of my meetings with religious scholars. To me this implied my own complicity in rendering myself and other women invisible in public life. At the same time, my covering up also posed an ethical dilemma. I was deliberately choosing to misrepresent myself to my more rigid scholarly interlocutors in order to secure their confidence. However, it is also a fact that many of my mosque- and seminary-based interlocutors would have refused to meet with me had I resisted this mode of representing myself. As Henry (2003, 234) notes, representation of "marital status, dress and gender behavior" have constituted key dilemmas for feminist ethnographers during fieldwork.[10] Günseli Berik (1996) provides a good illustration of this, while reflecting on her fieldwork conducted in rural Turkey. Berik (65) admits that her failure to conform to the widely prevalent "gender norms" would have hindered her access to her interlocutors. In my case, the cost of not conforming would have been my exclusion from one of my primary fieldwork sites—the religious seminaries. However, it is also true that despite my willingness to cover up, some religious scholars, particularly those of Deobandi persuasion, remained unwilling to meet with me on account of my status as a female.

RELIGIOUS VIEWERSHIP

Since a key aim guiding my research was to access the diversity of religious perspectives informing the Karachiites' engagement with religious shows, I approached my lay interlocutors from a sociological perspective, wherein age, gender, and socioeconomic class constituted the key bases for organizing my research. This way of envisioning television viewers is consistent with anthropological scholarship that has tended to link Muslim religiosity and understandings of Islamic tradition to economic and social class structures (Gilsenan 1982; Zubaida 2009; Ahmad 2010). In addition, my research approach was also inspired by Hall's (2003) encoding/decoding model, which foregrounds the significance of viewers' social realities in mediating their engagements with dominant power structures and cultural forms (see Morley 1980 for an illustration of this). More importantly, for me, incorporating a sociologically informed perspective into my study allowed me to explore the multivalent significance of Islam, and by extension religious shows for Karachiites.[11]

To reach individuals belonging to different social groups, I relied heavily on my established networks of family and friends. These networks gave me access to individuals from different socioeconomic backgrounds, such as housewives, working and retired men, students educated at Western universities, journalists, and writers. In addition, I also met with students from variously affiliated religious seminaries, secular schools, and colleges. I visited various types of schools and colleges, including those that were privately owned and that catered to the social elite, and others that were managed by the state and that catered primarily to students from working-class backgrounds. Even as conceptualizing my research more broadly in these terms facilitated my access to the diversity of religious thought and practice characterizing Muslim lives in Karachi, it simultaneously helped me recognize the importance of looking beyond these sociological categories to consider the part played by the political context and individual existential concerns in shaping people's engagement with religious shows. This methodological approach helped me realize the significance of televised Islamic pluralism in creating new affiliations and communities, where what connected my informants was not only their age, socioeconomic class, or gender but also their critical engagement with scholarly edicts on television.[12] This implication of pluralism is particularly manifest in my interlocutors' shared concern over the "mandatory" nature of certain religious beliefs and practices, regardless of their social affiliations (see chap. 7). Through a consideration of these shared concerns, I would also like to explain my decision to privilege the commentaries of women in the last two chapters of this book, where I evaluate the role of religious shows in transforming lay understandings of piety and religious authority. I primarily intend this emphasis to give women more of a voice in an otherwise male-dominated Islamic realm where, conventionally, women are excluded from religious public debate. Given that religious shows predominantly cater to, and are largely viewed by, women, this is one area where women get to speak for Islam and have a say in how the religion manifests in public life. However, even as gender constitutes a useful lens for analyzing my interlocutors' recourse to religious programming, I also highlight some of the issues inherent in focusing exclusively on gender, especially for evaluating my interlocutors' disregard for certain female practices backed by scholarly mandate.

In this context, I additionally reveal how some women's recourse to religious shows to justify their resistance to established Islamic modes of female comportment such as veiling did not only involve a consideration of their gendered status within Islam but equally implied a politically mediated distrust of religious scholars and a corresponding effort to limit such scholars' interference in state legislation, politics, and people's religious lives. These ways of engaging with religious television draw on a broadly perceived association of religious scholars with more extremist modes of Islamic thinking, sectarian violence, and Islamic militancy in Pakistan. Alternatively, for some women, a more critical appraisal of these practices corresponded with a culturally mediated Pakistani distaste for more prohibitive forms of female comportment, which these women perceived as more congruent with an Arab Islamic sociability than with the way Islam has traditionally been practiced by South Asian women. Moreover, the fact that many of the men I came across in the field also tended to associate these practices with the expanding influence of traditional male clerics over popular manifestations of piety and the consequent radicalization of Islamic thought in Pakistan further demonstrates that such concerns were not specific to Pakistani women but found resonance with all genders.

A key impetus guiding my research was to uncover what it is that people "do" (see Hughes 2011, 310) with religious shows, how these shows are integrated into people's everyday lives, how they influence understandings of Islam and religious authority, and more generally, why these shows matter to people.[13] For this reason, my research methodology has mainly focused on accessing the discussions and commentaries of people outside the immediate viewing contexts. Hughes (2011) has implicitly endorsed this approach, while acknowledging the difficulty of accessing the diversity of immediate viewing contexts.[14] Similarly, Wilk (2002) and Abu-Lughod (2005) have also implicated this approach in yielding more comprehensive insights into viewers' integration of media in their everyday lives.[15] In my case, a key reason for focusing on viewer commentaries outside the immediate viewing contexts was that the significance of religious shows for my interlocutors did not necessarily extend to their regular viewing of them. This was especially true for many of my seminary- and mosque-based interlocutors, who despite being extremely concerned about the subversive potential of religious shows nonetheless avoided viewing them and urged their followers to do the same. The same was also true for some lay viewers, who admitted that they did not follow these shows regularly. Instead, they mainly confined their access to religious shows to the more controversial and viral religious content on social media websites. Even in the case of Karachiites who did follow these shows regularly, their viewing patterns made it extremely difficult for me to access the immediate viewing contexts. Instead, I found the manner in which these shows animated everyday conversations on piety and "appropriate" forms of Islamic conduct, and the ways in which they elicited people's regard, conformance, condemnation, or apprehension more useful for my study. For me, it was equally important to understand why people avoided or rejected these shows as it was to understand why people viewed them and how they decided which religious personalities to follow on television. In the interest of my interlocutors' security, I have used pseudonyms for all of them, other than a select few such as Husain and *Allama* Kokab Noorani Okarvi, who gave their consent to being quoted directly.

THEORETICAL FRAMEWORK

Given that my interlocutors' engagement with religious shows was as diverse as it was complex, this book sheds light on two distinct dimensions of Muslim religiosity: one where "being" Muslim implies an activist or political commitment to Islam and a corresponding desire to expand the role of Islam into everyday life and state affairs, and one where the desire to be pious is relativized by other considerations, such as the perceived difficulty of incorporating Islam into everyday life, a fear of religion's exploitative and radicalizing potential, and a concern about its role in facilitating the social and political interference of its most fervent advocates, the *'ulamā* of Pakistan. Asad (1993,

2009b), Mahmood (2005), and Hirschkind (2001, 2006) are key proponents of the former understanding of Muslim religiosity, which is premised on an understanding of Islam as a "discursive tradition" characterized by its own hierarchies of power, rules of debate, and modes of reasoning and interpretation and a corresponding notion of Muslims as driven primarily by an activist or pietist commitment to the religion (cf. Gilsenan 1982; Zubaida 1993).[16] Within this notion of Islam, "orthodoxy" is at once the Muslim's ineluctable relationship with Islamic foundational texts and is a "relationship of power" (Asad 2009b, 21).[17] Asad (22) notes that in its latter manifestation "orthodoxy" implies "the power to regulate, uphold, require or adjust *correct* practices, and to condemn, exclude, undermine, or replace *incorrect* ones." I employ this scholarship's proposed understandings of Islam and "orthodoxy" to analyze the pious aspirations of lay viewers and to assess the traditional scholarly concerns over religious shows in terms of their role in destabilizing regnant forms of religious authority and Islamic thinking. This approach has also allowed me to examine the dynamics of religious power, the forms and limits of reasoned argumentation, and the nature of Muslim politics set into motion by religious television shows, especially with regard to doctrinal activism and its role in mediating the ʿ*ulamā*'s insecurities over, and struggle to sustain, their authority in religious public debate.

Notwithstanding the usefulness of the aforementioned scholarship in clarifying different elements of scholarly and lay engagements with religious television, some aspects of my discussions with lay viewers are too complex to be circumscribed to the modes of piety and Islamic reasoning outlined by Asad, Hirschkind, and Mahmood. In these instances, I draw on scholarship on everyday religious practice, which, while acknowledging the embedded nature of religious practice in "traditions, relations of power and social dynamics" (Schielke and Debevec 2012, 8; see also Schielke 2010, 2012; Debevec 2012; Simon 2014), additionally takes into account the complexity, ambivalence, and moral contradictions that characterize everyday religious practice.[18] In employing this scholarship, I aim to highlight aspects of Muslim life and "thought processes" (Marsden 2005, 23) where Islam and piety are not the primary concerns. In addition, I also find this scholarship's focus on everyday religious practice useful for analyzing aspects of lay faith where varying existential concerns and different socioeconomic contexts imply that, for Muslims, their religion may simultaneously constitute a source of hope and anxiety (Simon 2009, 265; also see Schielke 2102). It may both offer solace to them or manifest as a burden (Orsi 2005; Debevec 2012). However, while I employ scholarship on everyday religious practice to highlight aspects of my interlocutors' lives and engagements with religious programming where Islam and piety were not the primary concerns, I also move beyond this scholarship's insistence on the *uncritical* Muslim regard for Islamic values and foundational texts (Schielke 2009).

Schielke's emphasis on this aspect of Muslim faith is rooted in his fieldwork conducted among young men in the northern Egyptian village of Nazlat al-Rayyis, for whom the willingness to deliberate over the social and moral values defining their lives did not extend to a critical evaluation of religious values. Rather, for these men, declaring certain values religious often ended the debate (S32). By contrast, primarily in the last chapter of this book, I demonstrate that Muslim viewers in Karachi—prompted by the difficulties of reconciling certain elements of Islam with their lived experiences, the pressures of everyday life, and their existing worldviews—are increasingly willing to contest the privileged place of Islamic values over secular modes of living. I note the significance of religious shows in making these forms of Islamic engagement possible through their airing of doctrinally diverse and conflicting, liberal and conservative, religious discourses on television, all of which claim to be rooted in the *Qur'ān* and *ḥadīth*. The propensity of religious shows to represent multiple viewpoints, together with celebrity preachers' precedent of critically reevaluating the contemporary relevance of certain Islamic doctrines, has a profoundly individualizing impetus on Muslim belief, wherein the responsibility of gauging the legitimacy of Islamic provisions comes to reside increasingly with the individual viewer rather than with those claiming expertise in this task. Drawing on Jackson (2005) and his assertion regarding the "primacy" of existential concerns, I show how this development may not only preclude a rigid compliance to televised Islamic norms but also imply a more cautious engagement with piety, and a preference for values generally considered antithetical to Islam. This is a consequence of the ways in which the pluralistic impetus in religious programming provokes a rethinking of Islam from its earlier conceptualization as an all-determining discourse to a religion that increasingly depends on individual opinion for its continued relevance.

Within this reconceptualization, the prevalent idea of Islam is that of a religion that can increasingly be adapted to the contingencies of contemporary life. I suggest that the pervasiveness of such ideas simultaneously alters the forms and boundaries of Islamic public debate and paves the way for more irreverent and critical engagements with Islam. I became privy to these modes of Islamic engagement during my meetings with people whose recourse to religious shows both entailed a consideration of certain Islamic concepts in terms of their commensurability with modern ways of living and also reflected their privileged regard of modern, secular values, such as individual autonomy and gender parity, over and above what was Islamically ordained. These ways of engaging with religious programming were heavily imbricated in the country's historical experience of various religious and political figures' attempts to Islamize the country. At the same time, they also bore the impress of people's wariness regarding religion's constraining potential and their fear of the ʿulamāʾ's increased interference in state legislation and politics, given the ʿulamāʾ's widely perceived association with sectarian violence and Islamic militancy and their enhanced presence in people's lives by virtue of their regular appearances on religious shows.

In this context, I portray a third dimension of Muslim religiosity in this book, one that anthropologists and religious media scholars alike have tended to largely overlook despite its relevance: Muslims' critical and oppositional engagement with Islamic concepts and their consequent attempt to minimize Islam's pervasive influence over their lives. For Muslims prone to this mode of religious engagement, circumscribing Islam's role to the private domain of individual belief and conduct, and curtailing the role of religious scholars in the sphere of everyday life, constituted profoundly more compelling concerns than the prospect of leading Islamically conformant lives (see chap. 7). Following these revelations, two key normative themes that encapsulate much of the discussion in this book are the complexity of Muslim lives and the contradictory and ambivalent outcomes of religious media movements, including a consideration of their role in instigating Muslims to challenge emergent forms of religiosity in Pakistan. *Religious Television and Pious Authority in Pakistan* should, therefore, be considered as much an exposition on the complexity of Muslim lives in Pakistan as it is an elaboration of the effects of contemporary religious programming in the country.

NOTES

1. Fischer and Abedi (1990, 125–26) define a *fatwā* as "opinion reasoned through the disciplines of exegesis" by a "leading [Islamic] jurist of the day."

2. My use of the terms *Islamic concepts*, *norms*, and *principles* refers to what Shahab Ahmed (2015, 274) has termed the "authoritative, prescriptive and exclusivist" forms of Islamic thinking and reasoning.

3. I borrow Marsden's (2005, 9) definition of the term *Islamization* to denote "activities by Muslim organizations, movements and persons which seek to promote changes at both the collective and individual level in Muslim thought and behavior in line with their visions of the formal requirements and doctrines of Islam."

4. As Norris and Inglehart (2004, 4) point out, existential insecurity can lead to heightened religious observance. In the Pakistani context, Bano (2012, 110) alludes to a similar phenomenon while attributing the higher levels of *madrasa* enrollment in Pakistan to the "failing state structure, the insecurity of income and employment, . . . and the poor law and order conditions."

5. People belonging to the Muslim sect *Ahmadīyā* and followers of Mirza Ghulam Ahmad of Qadiyan, who claimed to be a prophet in the late nineteenth century (Faruqi 1991, 215). The *Ahmadīyā* sect "rejected one of the pillars of Islam—that Muhammad (PBUH) was the final prophet of God. After Parliament passed a law declaring the Ahmadiyya sect a non-Muslim minority, following the provisions in the 1973 Constitution which required that both president and prime minister be Muslims, the oath of office was amended to include an affirmation of the finality of Muhammad's (PBUH) prophethood" (Hassan 1985, 263).

6. Ganti (2002, 284), in a study of the Indian film industry, locates the value of analyzing media production in its capacity to generate useful insights about the audiences. For Ganti, decisions regarding Indian cinematic content include the "filmmakers' assumptions" about how their audiences will respond to a particular film. This aspect of production, to Ganti (289), "demonstrates how filmmakers themselves constitute an audience." See also Ang (1991), who similarly locates the audience in the production's analysis of viewer ratings.

7. Morley (1992, 7–9) and Askew (2002) have accused this approach, popularized by the Frankfurt School (Horkheimer and Adorno 2002), of leading to the rising popularity of text/content analysis as a tool for analyzing the influence of television, film, and radio. See Powdermaker (2002, 162), who views Hollywood films as privileging "one set of values over another" and deliberately underplaying the "real" economic causes of "modern-day" anxieties. The Frankfurt School's proposition on the ideological power of media texts foregrounds a critique of the "culture industry" based on the distinction between "high" or "traditional" and "low" or "mass" culture. For Adorno (1991, 2), a leading theorist within the school, the "effectiveness of the culture industry depends not on its parading an ideology, or on disguising the true nature of things, but in removing the thought that there is any alternative to the status quo." See also Benjamin for offering a functional perspective of "mass" culture as prompting the emergence of a more egalitarian society (in Scannell 2003). See Mulvey (1989) for an assessment of Hollywood films as privileging the "male gaze" and therefore as reaffirming the extant patriarchal ethos. For a critique of these approaches as abstracting media audiences from a consideration of media influence, see Morley (1992) and Carragee (1990). For a critique of reception studies, see Murphy and Kraidy (2003, 9), who suggest that a focus on "active" audiences was achieved at the cost of ideology. See also Morley (1992, 28) for the limitations of this approach in overlooking the ideological content of the encoded

message, as "decoding [always] comes to the rescue." Carragee (1990, 84) also argues against a sole focus on audience agency, which according to him results in a loss of economic and organizational contexts. Also see Radway's (1996, 244) argument that an emphasis on "reception" merely reinforces the notion of "media use" as a "linear process of reception and response."

8. While these groups have further subdivisions, for the purpose of clarity I do not consider them. For the emergence of the Barelwi movement, see Sanyal (1996) and Zaman (1998). Originally referred to as the Ahle Sunna, the name was later appropriated by the militant Deobandi Sipah Sahaba Pakistan, subsequent to the ban imposed on them by the Musharraf government. The group is now popularly referred to as Barelwi, primarily because of the geographic affiliation of its leader Ahmad Riza Khan, who hailed from Bareilly, a town in Uttar Pradesh, India. Sanyal elaborates how the Ahle Sunna movement emerged in the 1870s and 1880s in response to the reformist Deobandi and Ahl-i Hadīth movements. Whereas the Deobandi movement revolved around a commitment to the "reform of ritual practice and to an emphasis on *ḥadīth* scholarship," reform for the Ahle Sunna implied "reviving the Prophetic *Sunna* (path, way)," not individually but "with the help of saintly intermediaries" (Sanyal 1996, 8, 37). Zaman (2005) indicates that the movement was a response to the Puritanism espoused by Deobandi *madāris*. The Ahl-i Hadīth renewal movement emerged soon after the Deobandi movement. However, it takes a different approach to the "centrality of the Prophetic model" than the ones espoused by the Deobandi and the Barelwi ʿ*ulamā*, in that it rejects *taqlīd* (the authority of the four Sunni schools of Islamic jurisprudence) in favor of an exclusive focus on the Qurʾān and *Sunna* (Sanyal 1996, 8, 37).

9. The rules for ʿ*awrah* differ by Islamic school of thought. Some schools also include the female's voice as implying ʿ*awrah*. Therefore, they mandate the female employment of a harsher tone when addressing non-*mahram* men (in front of whom veiling is not obligatory).

10. Kondo (1986) and Abu-Lughod (1990) have made a similar proposition in the context of their respective research.

11. Abu-Lughod (1990) highlights the various ways in which age mediates understandings of tradition among Bedouin women in Egypt. Abu-Lughod focuses on the small acts of resistance that "younger" Bedouin women engage in, and in doing so highlights the relevance of age in mediating perceptions of tradition. See also Ahmad's (2010, 315–16) proposition on Pakistani middle-class women who subscribe to "High Islam," which is a more "sophisticated" and rationalized version of the "Low Islam" of the Pakistani majority. In making this claim, Ahmad clearly illustrates how differences in class account for variations in belief and practice. Also see Zubaida (2009) for the link between class and the instrumental deployment of religion, in which the impetus for religious

movements stems from the failure of socially disadvantaged groups to benefit from "*modernity*." My decision to look at differences in gender draws largely on feminist and anthropological scholarship that delineates women "as repositories of tradition" (Mahmood 2005, 118; see also Brenner 2011) and nationalism (Stowasser 1994; Ahmad 2010; Abu-Lughod 1986). According to Ahmad (2010, 305), because Islam in Pakistan is taken as the "raison d'être of the nation, religious ideology has intertwined itself with nationalist ideology, resulting in a hegemonic religio-nationalist discourse," in which women occupy a central position. Ahmad's observation mainly draws on Stowasser (1994, 5), who notes how women symbolize the key elements of the "Islamic struggle for the maintenance of indigenous values and 'cultural authenticity.'" Also see Abu-Lughod (1998, xxii), who argues for the relevance of gender as a lens for understanding the ways in which "moral systems are used to establish [social] hierarchies that not only disfavor women but make it difficult for them to defy the social system."

12. The tenuous link between social class and religiosity is also upheld by Bano (2012, 104), who maintains that 40% of her student interlocutors who were enrolled in *ḥifz* (rote memorization) programs at elite *madāris* in Karachi came from "financially affluent" backgrounds.

13. Like Hughes (2011, 310) my reference to "do" includes an analysis of "production, consumption as well as commentary, appropriation, indifference or avoidance."

14. Hughes (2011, 292) acknowledges that audiences are "located in many forms, ranging from a physical face-to-face gathering at a specific time and place to an abstract and dispersed collectivity linked in neither time nor space."

15. For Wilk (2002, 287), who focuses on the ways that people talk about the place of television in the everyday social and moral discourse in Belize, the benefit of studying television discourse emerges from the possibilities it offers in allowing anthropologists to understand the place of television "in social processes at a local and global scale." Wilk (289) argues that "the message of television is interpreted and absorbed socially, rather than individually." Abu-Lughod's (2005) emphasis on discussions and commentaries that occur outside viewing times derives from their potential in allowing an examination of the relationship between television shows and the everyday worlds that people inhabit.

16. These scholars have drawn on the notion of "invented tradition" (Hobsbawm and Ranger 1992) to show tradition's susceptibility to being used for achieving different religiopolitical ends.

17. Asad's (2009b) proposition on the study of Islam is rooted in MacIntyre's (1988, quoted in Haj 2002) work on Western philosophical traditions.

18. See Orsi (2012, 151), for whom the everyday religious is "improvised and situational" and therefore "not [always] performed in accordance with authority."

ONE

A BACKGROUND OF RELIGIOUS PROGRAMMING IN PAKISTAN

IN A GRIPPING ACCOUNT ENTITLED "It Fell from the Heavens," Paracha (2010) attempts to identify the defining moment in Pakistan's television history that instigated the trend of politically motivated religious programming in Pakistan. Paracha situates this moment in the sensational coverage from PTV (state-owned channel) of the events surrounding the imminent fall of NASA's (National Aeronautics and Space Administration) Skylab satellite, in July 1979. NASA had warned the Pakistani government of the possibility of the satellite falling into the Indian Ocean or onto Australia. According to Paracha, who recalls the "somber tone" and exhortations to prayer characterizing PTV's regular updates of the satellite's position, the state-owned channel's deliberate amplification of the danger the satellite posed to Pakistan provoked a rise in Pakistani religiosity as many viewers turned to their faith for solace. Haque and Zaidi (1981, 162) make a similar association in their study on the psychological ramifications of the Skylab incident, when they attribute the rising Pakistani concern for religious conformance, and the surge in number of mosque goers, to the widespread sense of "hopelessness and senselessness" that prevailed in Pakistan just prior to the satellite's crash. In Paracha's (2010) opinion, the heightened concern for salvation that PTV's apocalyptic imagery aroused in Pakistani viewers implicitly benefited the military dictator, General Ziaul Haq, by allowing him to enlist some support for his military coup against the democratically elected government of Zulfiqar Ali Bhutto in 1977. On account of PTV's sensational coverage, Zia's Islamization agenda suddenly held greater appeal for the distraught and more religiously inclined Pakistanis. Following these observations, Paracha speculates about the government's potential culpability in encouraging PTV to deliberately exaggerate the danger the satellite posed to Pakistan.

Even though the Skylab episode presents a compelling example of Zia's employment of religion for political propaganda, its role in paving the way for future manipulations of Islam by the ʿulamā and religiopolitical parties, and in rendering the Pakistani viewership more susceptible to religion-coated political propaganda, needs to be duly acknowledged. As Paracha laments, although the Pakistanis soon forgot the Skylab episode, "the apocalyptic outlook that it had triggered lingered." Moreover, instances of Islam's political manipulation in the region can be found even prior to Zia's leadership, during the colonial era, when the Muslim elite employed the discourse of Muslim nationalism to simultaneously justify the partition of the Indian subcontinent and precipitate Pakistan's subsequent creation in 1947. While Jinnah, the founder of Pakistan, was successful in garnering support for the creation of a separate Muslim homeland, he failed to elaborate the shape and form that Islamic ideology would take in the newly formed Pakistani nation. Many scholarly accounts since then have highlighted that Jinnah's failure led to equivocation regarding Islam's role in Pakistani society and polity (Iqbal 1984; Hassan 1985; Korson and Maskiell 1985; Faruqi 1991; Metcalf 2004; Mandaville 2007). The ambiguity surrounding Islam's role also influenced Islam's subsequent manifestations on television, as these came to vary greatly with the political agenda of successive governments. Therefore, even though General Ziaul Haq easily stands out as the most notable proponent of Islam's political manipulation in Pakistan, an exclusive focus on Zia's Islamization program may be limiting when examining contemporary trends in religious programming in Pakistan. What follows, then, is a history of religious programming in Pakistan, from its earlier configuration as a subject of state control to its subsequent reconstitution as a consumer good under the military regime of General Pervez Musharraf. I employ a historical understanding of religious programming in Pakistan to contextualize my subsequent analyses in this book and my claims regarding the contemporary aspects of religious programming in Pakistan.

THE PERIOD BEFORE MEDIA LIBERALIZATION

Virtually all scholarship detailing the history of Pakistani television, prior to the liberalization of Pakistani media, reads out as a narrative on Pakistan's political history (see Akhtar 2000; Hasan 2000; Shaikh 2007). These scholarly works cover little of the developments that took place within specific genres of television programming, such as within entertainment and religion. Instead, they emphasize the various instances when television's political instrumentality, or its control by various governments, became more manifest. In the following sections, I tease out some historical moments that demonstrate television's susceptibility to governmental influence. Because of the paucity of indigenous scholarship and official documentation on Pakistan's television history in general, and religious programming in particular, in many places in this chapter, I revert to my field-based interactions with religious television presenters in order to compensate for the gaps left by existing media literature. In these instances, the narrations of my scholarly interlocutors, which are rooted in their long-term association with religious broadcasting—starting from the introduction of religious programming on the state-owned channel, PTV, and leading up to the more recent appearances of these scholars on private satellite channels—have allowed me to present a more comprehensive overview of the key developments that took place on television under different Pakistani governments. In tracing these developments, I demonstrate how the differences characterizing the political agendas of various Pakistani governments favored the proliferation of extremely diverse and differentiated modes of religious representation on television.

AYUB KHAN (1958–69)

Television was first introduced to Pakistan in 1964, under the military dictatorship of Field Marshal Ayub Khan. The government envisioned that television would aid the ruling military elite in instituting social, economic, and educational reforms within Pakistan (Hasan 2000, 32). Hasan informs us that this move was part of a larger government plan to use the media to efface Pakistan's regional diversity, through the proliferation of images of unity and homogeneity (34). Therefore, while scholarly histories of television programming pay due credit to Ayub's government for introducing this "new" technology to Pakistan, they simultaneously also highlight Ayub's culpability in setting the stage for television's political manipulation by future Pakistani governments (see Hasan 2000; Shaikh 2007). The first instance of television's political deployment under Ayub Khan was PTV's celebration of the military government's decade of development. As noted by Shaikh (2007, 20), PTV deliberately highlighted this celebration at the behest of the military dictator in order to counter his waning popularity among the Pakistani masses. However, PTV's efforts in this context not only misfired but also generated widespread skepticism regarding the political neutrality of broadcast content. The Pakistanis' mixed response to PTV's initiative prompted an already vulnerable government to undertake substantive reforms regarding the autonomy accorded to television producers. On account of these reforms, in 1972, PTV was transformed into what ostensibly promised to be a more professionally managed and autonomous Pakistan Broadcasting Corporation. However, Shaikh notes that these reforms were primarily cosmetic in nature, and governmental influence and control remained a salient feature of PTV's transmissions throughout Ayub Khan's tenure in government (70).

While Ayub Khan was not averse to using television to further his political career, he was extremely wary of deploying religion for this purpose. Khan alludes to Ayub Khan's wariness of religion when comparing him to his successor, Ziaul Haq. Khan notes that, if "for Zia, *mullaism* was a desired state of being," for "Ayub Khan *mullaism* represented an ill that had to be wiped out" (2003, 55). Metcalf (2004, 223–24) makes a similar observation while noting that Ayub's preferred understanding of the economy was "wholly divorced from moral considerations" and entailed a view of it as "subject to its own laws." In Metcalf's opinion, it was not so much that Ayub did not use Islam to further his interests but rather that he conformed to a more "modernist" approach when it came to Islam's political deployment. For Ayub, therefore, unlike Zia, Islam did not so much act as the "blueprint" for state-mandated policies but rather constituted the ultimate interest that was served as a consequence of following state policies (Metcalf 2004). Metcalf's suggestion also sheds light on why the influence of religious leadership in economic and governmental policies remained marginalized under Ayub's governance.

ZULFIQAR ALI BHUTTO (1971–73 AND 1973–77)

The precedent of media control set by Ayub Khan's government was continued by the democratically elected government of Zulfiqar Ali Bhutto, which despite its popular mandate was not averse to enacting the "repressive press laws" introduced by the previous military dictator (Hasan 2000, vi). Hasan (123) reminds us how these laws were "mercilessly" deployed against several newspapers and their editors to curb the printing and broadcast of anti-Bhutto rhetoric. On television, Bhutto wielded his political influence mainly through his cronies, whom he placed in upper-level management positions at PTV (Hasan 2000). However, despite his political savviness, Bhutto, much like his predecessor, was also disinclined to employ religion to further his political career. When I met with the renowned Barelwi religious scholar and television presenter *Allama Kokab Noorani*, he confirmed to me that during Bhutto's term in government, religious programming had been severely neglected on the state-owned channel. This included PTV's deliberate disregard for the precedent set by the former Ayub government to initiate television transmissions with the name of Allah and the recitation of *khuṭbā* (a Qur'ānic verse used to mark the start of an event). While speaking of the more general measures undertaken by the government to tailor PTV's programming ethos to Bhutto's religious preferences, *Allama* Noorani, whose association with PTV dated back to the channel's fledgling run under Ayub Khan's governance, additionally drew my attention to the government-imposed ban on any mention of, or reference to, the word *sharāb* (alcohol) on the state channel. He was of the opinion that the ban had been mandated by the government to avoid drawing public attention to Bhutto's drinking habit. However, if the veteran religious presenter faulted Bhutto's government for not giving religion its due importance on television, equally he opposed giving credit to Ayub's government for promoting religious programming in Pakistan. This was despite the fact that *Baseerat* (Insight), the first religious program to air on PTV, in 1969, was initially broadcast during Ayub's time in government. Instead, the religious presenter firmly maintained that it was only during Zia's political tenure that religion had been accorded its proper place on television. *Allama* Noorani acknowledged Zia's role in this context in spite of his misgivings about the military dictator's dubious, and distinctly political, motives for promoting Islam on television.

GENERAL ZIAUL HAQ (1977–88)

In his book *Uncensored*, a revealing exposé on the Pakistani state's manipulation and control of the state-owned television channel, Hasan (2000) provides a detailed account of Zia's obsession with controlling television. Hasan cites many occasions when Zia's simultaneous fascination with, and wariness of, television manifested with his greater control over featured programming content. For example, when speaking of the *Khabarnama*, a name given to the news bulletin telecast on PTV every day at 9:00 p.m., Hasan recounts that a daily recording of the *Khabarnama* was sent to Zia for review. In fact, Zia was so concerned about his projected image that even minor deviations from the state guidelines would disturb him and provoke his censure. The president's "extraordinary interest" in the *Khabarnama* also included regular visits to PTV's National News Bureau by his information secretary to ensure that the channel complied with the president's wishes (199). Hasan also recalls that Zia's compulsion to deploy the state-owned channel to further his own agenda was not limited to news. In fact, Zia was equally open to employing religious programming as the means of countering his waning credibility. The general had made repeated promises to the Pakistanis to hold new elections within ninety days of his takeover of government from Zulfiqar Ali Bhutto. In his first address to the nation, on July 5, 1977, Zia declared, "I want to make absolutely clear that neither have I any political ambitions nor does the army want to be detracted from its profession of soldiering. I was obliged to step in to fill the vacuum created by the political leaders. I have accepted this challenge as a 'True Soldier of Islam.' My sole aim is to organize free and fair elections, which would be held in October this year. Soon after the polls, power will be transferred to the elected representatives of the people. I give a solemn assurance that I will not deviate from this schedule" (quoted in Hasan 2000, 167).

However, a change of heart intervened, in large part prompted by Bhutto's increasing popularity among Pakistanis. Thus, despite his repeated assurances to the nation regarding the interim nature of his government, Zia failed to deliver on his promise. The mantra of Islamization, for which PTV's support was also enlisted, aided Zia in averting his fall from grace. Hasan notes that Zia, with the support of "some hired Ulema from the Council of Islamic Ideology," was able to depict the democratic system of governance as un-Islamic (187). Islamization, therefore, in Hasan's view, simultaneously provided Zia a way out of holding the promised elections and the means by which to win back popular support. Zia's desire for political ascendancy, and his corresponding employment of Islam as a means to placate his primary supporters, the religiopolitical parties, also prompted a salient reconfiguration in PTV's goals, transforming its main purpose from providing entertainment to promoting Zia's political and ideological agenda (Shaikh 2007, 71). In tandem with this agenda, Zia also gave a "psy-war specialist of the army," General Mujibur Rehman, complete control of the Ministry of Information and Broadcasting, with a view of curbing free media expression and promoting journalists with "rightist" orientations (Hasan 2000, 183). Zia viewed the latter as more supportive of his regime and thus enlisted those journalists' aid in realizing his dream of a theocratic state, including the elimination of all "'un-Islamic institutions' such as the political parties and democracy" (183).

Zia's Islamizing mandate specifically extended to broadening the scope of religious programming on the state-controlled channel. According to the religious presenter *Allama* Noorani, prior to Zia's arrival, religious programming had been accorded limited transmission time (thirty minutes) and had been confined to a daily show and occasional references to specific Muslim occasions, such as *'Āshūrā'* (commemoration of the martyrdom of Ḥazrat Ali's [RA] family¹), *Ramaḍān* (the holy month of fasting), and *'Īd Mīlād-un Nabī* (the celebration of the Prophet's [PBUH] birth anniversary). However, under

Zia's leadership, PTV introduced three new religious programs and increased the duration of religious broadcasts. Two of the newly introduced programs, *Farman-e-Elahi* (Decree of God) and *Fahm ul Quran* (Understanding of Qurʾān), focused primarily on pedagogical content or exegetical commentary on select Qurʾānic verses. However, the third program, *Tafheem-e-Deen* (Understanding *Dīn*), also established a new precedent in religious programming in that it also incorporated audience participation as a central feature of its format. The producers did this by eliciting queries in writing from members of the viewing public. In *Allama* Noorani's opinion, the written queries elicited by the former show constituted a much better form of viewer participation than live viewer call-ins, which are the favored mode of viewer participation for contemporary religious talk shows. *Allama* Noorani's preference for written queries drew on his assessment of this mode of viewer participation as one that allowed producers and directors greater discretionary control over featured religious content. Alternatively, I demonstrate in the next chapter that despite the incorporation of viewer call-ins and the shift toward live broadcasting, production control remains a salient feature of contemporary religious programming. This is because the calls coming in during live transmissions are carefully screened by production assistants before being forwarded to the host and scholarly presenters.

On the initiatives undertaken by PTV at Zia's behest, such as the allocation of airtime to religious programming, *Allama* Noorani informed me that both *Tafheem-e-Deen* and *Fahm ul Quran*, which were initially broadcast biweekly, became regular Friday features on PTV during Zia's tenure in government. Hasan (2000) and Paracha (2010) have made similar observations, both acknowledging a substantial increase in the duration of religious programming subsequent to Zia's takeover of government from Zulfiqar Ali Bhutto. PTV's increased mindfulness regarding the promotion of Islamic values also extended to other avenues of programming and involved a concerted focus on the observance of important Islamic events and occasions such as *Muḥarram* (the mourning period for Ḥazrat Ali (RA), who was martyred during the Battle of *Karbalā*) and the Prophet's (PBUH) birth anniversary. In recalling the sobriety of PTV's transmissions, especially on the ninth and tenth of *Muḥarram*, Ali (1986, 2171) observes that the occasion was commemorated with the marked absence of comedy shows and the elimination of all musical content, including the removal of "signature tunes of regular" programs such as the *Khabarnama*. The visible observance of religious events was, on the one hand, aimed by the government at instilling in the minds of the viewers the importance of Islam to their everyday lives and, on the other, directed toward reminding the viewers of the restrictions Islam, and by extension the ruling government, imposed on their lives.

The government's interference in television programming was not limited to encouraging increased Islamic content on television. In this context, Ali reminds us that the government also sought to dictate the types of religious content that would be featured by the state-owned channel. One particular incident narrated by Hasan (2000) serves to illustrate Ali's argument. Hasan recalls that one of the many measures adopted by PTV in support of Zia's government included the daily telecast of a select quote from the Prophet (PBUH), which informed the viewers of their divinely ordained obligations in their quest for a heavenly abode in the afterlife. However, the Prophetic quotes to be broadcast were not decided on independently by the channel's producers but rather were dictated by the producers' expectations regarding the government's response. For instance, PTV, on the advice of the Ministry of Information, tactfully removed a frequently telecast quote (167). As the quote exhorted the believer to fulfill a promise, Hasan believes that it pricked Zia's conscience by reminding the military dictator of his unfulfilled promise to the nation. In Hasan's view, Zia may have been concerned that the quote's repeated telecast would draw attention to his suspect credibility and so attenuate his political appeal among the Pakistani masses. According to Hasan, the incident served as a further blow to PTV's autonomy, as the channel subsequently took particular care to tailor all its religious content to presidential preferences. While speaking of his personal experience as a religious presenter on the state-owned channel, *Allama* Noorani similarly recalled that, under Zia, all religious content featured by the channel had been subject to the advice and prior approval of the Ministry of Information. This entailed the government sending instructional press notes to religious producers prior to the recording of each episode. Moreover, since Zia's Islamization project favored the articulation of unified and monolithic understandings of Islam, doctrinally oriented representations of Islam were automatically excluded from religious programming.

Zia's control over televised religious content was also exercised through the selection of *ʿulamā* and scholars. Ali (1986) notes that under Zia's leadership, state-favored religious scholars became a regular feature on PTV. When I spoke to *Allama* Noorani about this development, he insisted that it was good practice as it allowed the government to prioritize scholars who had comprehensive knowledge of, and complete mastery over, Islamic texts and traditions. In addition, it implied that invitations to present on television would be extended only to those religious scholars who were mindful of fulfilling their Islamic obligations and who were strictly committed to conforming to the Islamic codes of dress and physical appearance. However, I suggest that the selection of religious scholars who were willing to endorse Zia's vision of an "Islamic" state also allowed Zia's military regime more control over the ideological articulations of Islam on television. At the same time, the emphasis on Islamic codes of dress and physical appearance also enabled the government to emphasize the more normative, "public," and visible aspects of lived Islam. For example, the government could highlight the necessity of visiting the mosque for *namaz* (prayers, *ṣalāt* in Arabic) or the idea that piety emanates from the length of one's beard or the donning of a turban. Such emphases implicitly favored "traditional" sources of religious authority, whose strict and visible adherence to Islamic codes of appearance and dress encouraged a perception of them as the true arbiters of Islamic tradition. Akhtar (2000, 65) implicitly upholds this observation when he suggests that Zia's influence on PTV manifested in portrayals of the *ʿulamā* as the "true spokesmen of Islam."

These incidents provide a compelling illustration of the political deployment of religious programming under Zia's regime. However, to fully appreciate the scale of Zia's engagement of television for the spread of Islamization, we need to look beyond isolated instances of religious programming and focus more broadly on the general aspects of programming on PTV. In the latter context, Ali (1986, 2171) notes that Zia's efforts toward proliferating a perception of Islam as the primary reason for Pakistan's creation and existence also involved an increased depiction of Islam as an "all encompassing faith" and therefore as relevant to all aspects of Muslim life. It thus became incumbent on PTV to reflect this belief in all genres of television programming. Hassan (1985) makes a similar point in his detailed analysis of the ostensible Islamic reforms undertaken during Zia's tenure. According to Hassan, these reforms involved a heavy emphasis on religious education and practice in daily television broadcasts (265). In Ali's (1986) opinion, because the ruling elite used Islam as the key weapon to perpetuate its rule, Islam also became the single most important denominator for gauging the suitability of featured entertainment content.

Considerations regarding the suitability of program content had an immediate impact on portrayals of Pakistani culture on PTV. The first manifestation of PTV's Islamization was a shift in the general culture portrayed on television, which, much like religious programming, also became visibly Islamic. The series of reforms undertaken by PTV in this context included the telecast of the name of Allah to mark the beginning and end of transmission. Moreover, the *adhān*, a call to prayer, became a regular feature and was broadcast at least twice a day. Ali (1986) observes how, ironically, these frequent telecasts of the *adhān* were aimed at reminding the viewers "that they should put their sets off (and miss their favorite program that follows) and go and say their prayers" (2171). Other Islamization measures undertaken by PTV involved ensuring that all female actors and presenters covered their heads. Furthermore, all forms of physical closeness between males and females were prohibited. Ali laments, "It is common for lovers to meet each other and just say hello, as it is for a husband and wife, after a long separation, not to even touch hands, lest the *mullah*s who determine what is right and wrong, ban them for life on grounds of immorality" (2171).

PTV undertook all these measures in conformity with the censorship rules promulgated by Zia's government. Niazi (1994, 3) confirms the all-encompassing nature of these censorship rules, which implicated "all dailies, periodicals, books, pamphlets, posters, handbills, photographs, motion pictures, dramatic and stage productions, phonographic records, radio and television programmes."[2] Because the Jamāʿat-i-Islamī was one of the few religiopolitical groups that supported Zia's military regime, the general rewarded them by giving them charge of the Federal Ministry of Information and full authority to impose their own Islamic ideals on television programming (Paracha 2013).

Other aspects of PTV's Islamization included a ban imposed on dancing. The ban also extended to singing in that it prevented singers from swaying to the beat of the music. Singers were asked to "either sit or stand still like statues" when rendering their songs (Ali 1986, 2171). As Ali points out, no programming on television could be anti-state or anti-Islamic. Niazi (1994, 9) provides an apt illustration of this policy while recalling the degree to which the ruse of an "undefined" Islamic ideology allowed Zia to curtail journalistic freedom. According to Niazi, as the self-appointed custodian of Islam, Zia could punish a journalist or writer with ten years of imprisonment, a fine, or lashes, without providing recourse to a court of law. Other measures Zia undertook to control the media included banning from PTV any "actors, . . . producers, and playwrights" whom Zia considered "pro-Bhutto" (Paracha 2013). The government's resulting list was exhaustive, containing the names of more than fifty writers, poets, and journalists (Niazi 1994). In Niazi's opinion, this ban was in stark contrast to the measures undertaken by the preceding Ayub and Bhutto governments. While both governments had favored their preferred artists, neither had taken such extreme measures to influence television programming. Paracha (2013) notes that the same list also contained the names of certain Pakistani films, songs, and PTV plays that were not allowed reruns because they were considered obscene, vulgar, or subversive. According to Ali (1986), portraying the ruling class's ideology in PTV programs helped the government keep the Pakistani people in their places. The restrictions Zia imposed on entertainment programming were in marked contrast to the freedom accorded to PTV, with respect to entertainment, under Zulfiqar Ali Bhutto. During an interview given to Tanya Anand for her book *The Game Changer: A Brief History of Television in Pakistan* (2014, 11), Sultana Siddiqui, a former producer on PTV and the president of a popular satellite channel in Pakistan, describes the period under Bhutto as the singular period in PTV's history when producers were given complete creative freedom and autonomy with respect to entertainment content. It is not surprising then, that at least in the context of entertainment, Siddiqui refers to PTV's run under Bhutto as the "best era" of PTV programming (11).

While these observations clarify the lengths to which Zia was willing to go to impose his will on the Pakistani masses, perhaps one of the most persistent consequences of Zia's Islamization program was the deliberate insinuation of religion in electoral politics. Hasan (2000) notes that all of Zia's political speeches and his addresses to the nation were preceded by *tilāwat* (recitation of the Qur'ān) and *na'at* (hymn in praise of Prophet Muhammad [PBUH]). In addition, the trend of inviting religious scholars to participate in current affairs and political shows became commonplace at PTV at Zia's behest. However, perhaps a more noticeable example of Zia's encouragement of the nexus between politics and Islam is provided by the events that followed Zia's dismissal of Prime Minister Muhammad Khan Junejo's government. Hasan (2000, 210) recalls that Zia's failure to get a popular mandate, as reflected in his failed referendum attempt, prompted him to hold nonparty elections in 1985. Zia felt that the move would grant him some legitimacy and at the same time offer some respite to Pakistanis, who had become increasingly disillusioned with the continued imposition of martial law in the country. Junejo's name as a potential prime ministerial candidate appealed to Zia mainly because of the latter's presumptions regarding Junejo's mild and unassuming manner. Zia believed that the docile candidate would not offer much resistance to Zia's continued dominance over governmental affairs. However, Junejo's unwavering posture toward the restoration of democracy, which was contrary to Zia's expectations, made the former a formidable opponent of continued martial law in Pakistan (185–88). To assert his superiority under the Constitution, the new prime minister dismissed Zia's trusted adviser and information secretary, General Mujib. Junejo's attempts at restoring democracy to Pakistan also extended to PTV, where Zia's tenuous hold on the state channel became increasingly apparent. Hasan (209) notes that one of the first examples of Zia's attenuating influence was a marked decline in the proportion of religious programming and a change in PTV's emphasis from religious scholars to political leaders. It is not surprising that Junejo's blatant opposition to Zia provoked the military dictator to dissolve the National Assembly, together with Junejo's government, in 1988.

Following Junejo's dismissal, Zia relaunched his Islamization program, which had lost its pervasive hold under Junejo's influence. However, Hasan observes that Zia's speech reiterating his commitment to *Sharīʿa* (Islamic code) was not accompanied by the televised fanfare that had been accorded to his speeches before Junejo became the prime minister. PTV's perfunctory treatment of the speech, which was followed by everyday programming, annoyed Zia, who felt that his speech should have been followed by the customary broadcast of national songs and detailed discussions by notable religious scholars and lawyers. In Hasan's opinion, PTV's lack of respect for the speech prompted Zia to order PTV to tailor its programming to promote Zia's Islamization project (110–11).

Zia's insistence on including religious scholars in the discussions following his speeches demonstrates the lengths to which the military dictator went to promote the nexus between religion and politics. As Hasan (187) observes, "with one master stroke Ziaul Haq changed the entire complexion of Pakistan from a 'modern' secular and progressive State to a theocratic one to be run by an all-powerful *Amirul Momineen* (that is himself), with the advice and consent of the same gang of Ulema who had opposed the creation of Pakistan as conceived by the *Quaid-e-Azam* [Jinnah]." As a result, the religious scholars, who despite their attempts to insinuate themselves in electoral politics had been disregarded as a serious threat, became a common feature on political and current affairs shows. Their regular television appearances both honed their political acumen and consolidated their political influence in the minds of Pakistani viewers, who increasingly accepted their participation in politics.

Other aspects of Zia's Islamization project and PTV's role in his agenda have also been highlighted by the political activist Pervez Hoodbhoy (2007), who locates the impetus for Zia's project in Pakistan's ideological conception and religion's susceptibility to political manipulation. Hoodbhoy reminds us that, in conformance with Zia's agenda, PTV went so far as to exploit the equivocal ideological references in Jinnah's persona and speeches. In Hoodbhoy's opinion, PTV's mission to project Jinnah as an "Islamic" rather than a "Muslim" leader prompted the channel to selectively feature "a steady stream of profound pieties [which] emanated from a stern, sherwani-clad [a locally worn long coat] man who filled television screens across the country. Gone were his [Jinnah's] elegant suits from Saville Row, as was any reference to his marriage with a Parsi woman. Jinnah had miraculously morphed into a deep-thinking Islamic scholar" (3300).

While these developments indicate PTV's success at promoting Zia's vision of Islam, the use of television for propaganda has its limits. Hasan (2000, 80) warns us that "projection on the media, particularly on TV, is like poison. If given in measured doses it helps but the overdose certainly kills." For instance, Shaikh (2007) informs us that Zia's military predecessor, Ayub Khan, made similar attempts to improve his image, also employing television for this purpose, and that such measures backfired badly and further attenuated Ayub's already waning popularity. Many authors have similarly opined that PTV's overemphasis of religion during Zia's tenure adversely affected its viewership and popularity (Hasan 2000; Page and Crawley 2005a; Shaikh 2007). As the prominent journalist Khaled Ahmed noted, the domestic audiences were fed up with the ideological underpinnings of television programming and increasingly craved entertainment (quoted in Shaikh 2007). A similar account of PTV's waning popularity is implicit in the following statement from Siddiqui (former director general of Pakistan National Council of Arts): "Tell me of any nation that does not have a taste, a liking, an urge for music, fine arts, for fun and laughter" (quoted in Shaikh 2007, 71).

Zia's own awareness of the limitations of television is apparent in two speeches in which he censured Pakistanis for their declining interest in PTV. In the first, Zia suddenly discarded his written speech and declared that he knew why most viewers had stopped watching PTV: "*Mujhey pata hai log ab PTV kyon nahi daikhtay. Chirian jo urr gain*" (I know why some people have stopped watching PTV. All the birds have flown [from the channel]) (Paracha 2013). Zia's reference to the birds having flown away suggests his awareness of PTV's declining entertainment value. Zia knew that the loss of entertainment was a direct consequence of his programming reforms. In his second speech, Zia chastised Pakistani viewers for their frivolous attitude toward the religious orientation of PTV programming:

> People think that they have cracked a big joke by branding Radio Pakistan and Pakistan Television as a religious school which will be greeted by peals of laughter by others. But alas, these people are a joke themselves. The people of Pakistan can discriminate between good and bad; they don't laugh at them but they only feel sorry for them. They say what kind of people are they who have a grouse against the ban imposed on Pakistan on the performance of vulgar dances, on night clubs and dancing houses? Lashes are administered for drinking. Films are probably pruned and edited before they are shown on television. The call for prayer reverberates from radio all the time. The *Maulvī* has got stuck on the TV screen; and let me tell you he will remain stuck there. (Ziaul Haq, inaugural address, Islamabad, October 9, 1982, quoted in Khan 2003, 64)

BENAZIR BHUTTO (1988–90 AND 1993–96) AND NAWAZ SHARIF (1990–93 AND 1997–99)

Zia's mysterious death in an air crash in August 1988 opened the electoral front for political parties whom Zia had banned from electoral politics. The November 1988 elections marked the entry of Benazir Bhutto, who won the people's mandate to become Pakistan's first female prime minister in December 1988. Hasan (2000) describes the period subsequent to Zia's sudden departure from politics as an ongoing tussle for power between Pakistan's two main political parties, the Pakistan People's Party (PPP) and the Pakistan Muslim League Nawaz (PMLN). Both governments' political terms ended abruptly because of their repeat dismissals (twice each) by President Ghulam Ishaq Khan. The president used the controversial article 58(2)(b) of the Constitution of Pakistan to dissolve all four governments. Hasan (2000, 233) refers to the initial period under Benazir as a "breath of fresh air" for PTV, a time when the station followed a more balanced approach in its coverage of politics and current affairs. On the political front, PTV's programming broadcasts included statements from members of opposing parties. As a result, many Pakistanis who had shifted their loyalties to BBC Radio's South Asian News Service during Zia's tenure felt they no longer had to turn to other channels for accurate coverage of national news and current affairs (Hasan 2000). However, Hasan laments that the initiatives taken by Benazir's government were ephemeral in nature, as within four months of Benazir's arrival, PTV had reverted to its one-sided coverage of current affairs (234–35).

The partiality of PTV's coverage was especially noticeable during Benazir's second term, when the press's allegations of her and her husband's corruption and nepotism provoked Benazir to threaten the press with the establishment of press courts (Hasan 2000, 264). On Benazir's encouragement, PTV also introduced programs such as *Muqabil Hai Aaina* (Face the mirror). In the program, Azhar Sohail, a PTV anchor of dubious journalistic repute, would go to great lengths to debunk all accusations leveled against the prime minster in print media (264). Therefore, although Zia's military dictatorship may constitute the most glaring example of PTV's political exploitation, many authors have since observed that even during Benazir's and Nawaz Sharif's tenures, PTV remained susceptible to government manipulation. For instance, in an interview given to Kamran Asdar Ali, Imran Aslam, the former director of PTV and the current president of the Geo Television satellite channel, recounts that both Nawaz Sharif and Benazir "attempted to buy or coerce journalists to report favorably" (Aslam and Ali 2009, 32). Aslam further reveals that both leaders exerted their influence through various government officials who regularly visited the PTV offices to closely monitor programming content. While speaking of the measures adopted by Sharif, Aslam narrates that journalists who were privately employed, and for whom government bribery did not hold much sway, were forced to contend with other forms of governmental persuasion, such as intimidation, blackmail, imposition of quotas, and cutbacks in government advertising (32–34). However, even though Benazir and Nawaz Sharif were not averse to using television to further their political ambitions, they were nonetheless wary of deploying religion for that purpose. In Benazir's case, the reticence was also due to her Shiʿa orientation, which meant that any deployment of Islam on television would have lessened her appeal within the Pakistani Sunni majority. Benazir's political standing as the female prime minster of an Islamic republic was already dubious, and her awareness of her vulnerability is apparent in her decision to don the *dupatta* (head scarf) as an integral part of her attire even before her election as prime minister. She may have decided to sport a *dupatta* not merely to placate the ʿ*ulamā* but also to appease the Pakistani general public, who had only recently come out of the oppressive impact of Zia's Islamization program.

It is not surprising, then, that Benazir's rise to political prominence was accompanied by a declining emphasis on religion in PTV transmissions. According to *Allama* Noorani, a notable illustration of PTV's changing ethos in this context was the establishment of NTM, the first television channel in Pakistan to broadcast a dedicated popular music program. The channel, which was a collaborative venture between the government and Shalimar Recording Corporation, was established in 1989 to encourage diversity in programming content (Anand 2014, 15–16). Moreover, it was also during Benazir's first term in government (1988–90) that the first fashion show aired on PTV. According to two male employees of a religiously organized charitable trust, the fashion show, which featured women modeling sleeveless outfits, had also set the tone for future displays of "immodesty and shamelessness" on private satellite television channels.

In Nawaz Sharif's case, particularly during his second term in government, his capitalist orientation, coupled with the more pressing political and economic concerns ailing his government, implied that he was diverted by matters other than religion. His government faced such issues as the nuclear tests conducted by Pakistan's armed forces and the subsequent imposition of United States–led sanctions. Moreover, his leadership also coped with the Pakistan Army's unsuccessful foray into Kargil, an area situated on the Indian side of Kashmir. As a result, the minimal insinuation of religion in televised content, characteristic of Benazir's political governance, persisted during Sharif's tenure in government. The declining importance of religion in television programming, first under Benazir Bhutto and later under Nawaz Sharif, demonstrates that the public face of religion in Pakistan has always been closely tied to the political agendas of successive governments. For Zia, religion was a political necessity, as it provided him with the justification for leading the Pakistanis in the absence of an electoral mandate. In contrast, his democratically elected successors, although wary of the religious right and also eager to appease them, did not rely on Islam as the raison d'être for their continued leadership of Pakistan. Therefore, their deployment of religion on television varied greatly from Zia's, in that they relaxed religion's hold over Pakistani society and polity.

THE RUN-UP TO MEDIA LIBERALIZATION

The political deployment of PTV by successive Pakistani governments contributed greatly to the state-owned channel's declining popularity among the Pakistani masses. This decline was exacerbated by the introduction of satellite television in Pakistan in the early 1990s. According to Page and Crawley (2005a, 242), the growing popularity of satellite channels was in large part a consequence of the general Pakistani apathy toward PTV's didactic programming content; Pakistanis bored with the monotonous and ideological content of PTV were quick to shift their loyalties to the newly introduced Indian Star TV and Zee TV channels. Alternatively, Shaikh (2007, 75–76) offers an equally plausible explanation for the growing popularity of Indian satellite channels, attributing this trend to PTV's waning credibility on account of the channel's employment by state institutions as a tool for political propaganda. Drawing on the results of a survey conducted by the English daily *DAWN* in the 1990s, Shaikh notes that the popularity of Star TV and Zee TV news and entertainment channels by far exceeded PTV's appeal.

The increasing popularity of Star and Zee networks had adverse consequences for PTV, which lost 10 percent of its advertising revenue to competing Indian satellite channels (Shaikh 2007, 78). The introduction of cable television in the 1990s and its regulation through the Pakistan Telecommunication Authority (PTA) in 2000 further exacerbated PTV's vulnerable position by enabling working-class access to previously unaffordable Indian channels. Whereas up until 1989 the penetration of cable television was minimal, access increased dramatically after its legalization in Pakistan. By 2006, cable television had permeated 50 percent of homes in urban cities and 30 percent of homes in the rural areas of Pakistan (Anand 2014, 39).[3] The spread of cable television was also precipitated by the changing broadcasting terms for Indian satellite channels, which included a shift in the transmission of Indian channels from free-to-air to decoder format in 1998 (23). Because the decryption of Indian channels was only possible with the aid of expensive decoders, local cable channels could infiltrate the satellite market by providing cheaper access to less affluent Pakistanis. These developments led to a further decline in the advertising revenue for PTV (Shaikh 2007).

Although there were no regulations in place prior to 2000, the need for regulating both satellite reception and the newly introduced cable television soon dawned on the Sharif government. The government became increasingly uncomfortable with the idea of a possible Indian cultural invasion by means of Star TV and Zee TV (80). The need to regulate the reception of Indian satellite channels became particularly pressing during the Kargil incident, when Pakistanis began to increasingly tune in to the Indian Zee News for regular updates on the event (Page and Crawley 2005b, 138). The Kargil conflict was instigated by the infiltration of Pakistan's armed forces into Indian occupied territory in the state of Jammu and Kashmir. Anand (2014, 28) notes how different accounts of the conflict by Pakistani and Indian news sources turned the conflict into "news propaganda." In Anand's opinion, the inconsistencies between local media and government accounts of the incident implicitly encouraged Pakistani viewers to tune into Zee News for a more comprehensive and cohesive account of the conflict (29). Whereas the Pakistani Army celebrated its small victories with regard to its infiltration of Kargil, the Pakistani state denied the army's role in Kargil, claiming that the infiltration was indigenous to the Kashmiris.

The Sharif government's concern regarding the Pakistanis' access to Indian news channels prompted it to impose a ban on the broadcast of Indian channels in Pakistan. Following Sharif's departure, the growing popularity of Indian news channels, and the consequent threat these posed to Pakistan's national identity, elicited a three-tiered response from Musharraf's government. First, to counter the implicit threat posed by Indian satellite channels, the government regulated the cable television business, continuing the ban on Indian channels (Shaikh 2007, 83). Second, the government undertook measures to strengthen state-owned channels, converting them into satellite channels. PTV World, the first state-run satellite channel, was launched shortly after Sharif's second departure from government, with a view to engender a positive image of Pakistan among satellite and cable television viewers residing inside and outside Pakistan (Anand 2014, 13). While Benazir had also initiated measures to put PTV's house in order by appointing a new managing director and giving her free rein over PTV's administration, it was the government-imposed ban on Indian channels, first under Sharif and later under Musharraf, that ultimately gave PTV the space it needed to win back its Pakistani viewership (Shaikh 2007, 84).

Earlier measures to restore the credibility of the media had also been proposed by the caretaker government of Malik Miraj Khalid (1996–97), which took over from Benazir after her second dismissal earlier that year, in November 1996. The EMRA Ordinance of 1997, proposed by Khalid, envisioned that all broadcasting would come under the control of an independent authority chaired by a retired judge of the Supreme Court of Pakistan. It is clear from the various sections of the ordinance that Khalid had already recognized the need for greater media autonomy to restore the credibility of Pakistani news (Anand 2014, 22). Moreover, the ordinance also aimed to provide greater choice and quality of broadcast content to Pakistani viewers (Shaikh 2007, 82). However, it was only after 2002, sometime after Musharraf's takeover from Sharif in 1999, that any substantive reforms were undertaken to deregulate the media and to thereby stall the growing popularity of Indian channels. In this context, the Musharraf government's third response to the onslaught of Indian channels was to open up the airwaves to private investors. The government believed that its initiative of media liberalization would both restore the credibility of Pakistani news and also provide Pakistanis with entertainment options that were more in line with Pakistani ethos and values (Shaikh 2007, 81). However, limited rural access to cable television in Pakistan, coupled with the Pakistan Electronic Media Regulatory Authority's (PEMRA) refusal to grant terrestrial licenses to private channel owners, has meant that PTV continues to be the favored channel in Pakistan's rural areas.

MEDIA LIBERALIZATION

The liberalization of media, which took place under the leadership of General Pervez Musharraf (1999–2008), led to the advent of several new private satellite channels (see Anand 2014). Initially the costs of setting up a channel and sustaining it were considerably higher and involved the added expense of uplinking from an overseas site, but this changed when PEMRA relaxed its criteria and opened up the airwaves for private channels (38). The resulting decline in cost led to the entry of several new players into the broadcast market. This development was further precipitated by the proliferation of cable television and the financial sector's extension of leasing facilities to media investors. While the former development allowed private channels to benefit from economies of scale on account of increased market size, the latter lessened the channels' expenditure on costly production equipment, which constituted a significant portion of their establishment costs (39). Against this backdrop, the declining prices of television sets and the additional expansion in market size further enhanced the attractiveness of the media industry for private investors. According to Anand (2014, 24), television viewership increased from sixty-three million viewers in 2004 to eighty-six million viewers in 2009. Out of these, eight million were cable television subscribers. The continued reduction in television costs also meant that by 2010 television had spread to 85 percent of urban households and 45 percent of rural households (104). However, if the declining costs of setting up a channel contributed to the attractiveness of the media industry for private investors, so too did they increase the competition between channels, on account of the unrestrained entry of new players in the private satellite market. By the end of 2006, more than one hundred channels were vying for greater market share and advertising revenue (24).

Within the newly liberalized environment, the difficulties inherent in maintaining the channels' commercial viability in the face of increased competition became quickly apparent to private broadcasters. Moreover, the introduction of several new channels meant that the prices of commercial spots sold to advertisers were considerably lower (43). This put a financial strain on private investors, and that strain was exacerbated by the loss of decryption fees from cable operators, some of whom began to disseminate pirated material to viewers. These operators illegally decrypted private channels, allowing them to avoid decryption fees (45). Such illegal decryption further meant that Pakistani channels had to compete with both Pakistani and Indian broadcast content to remain financially viable. In addition, some cable operators also started selling their own commercial time between program breaks, which resulted in a further decline in advertisement revenue for private satellite channels. Anand notes that all these factors placed a greater financial burden on private television channels, thus compelling some of them to exit the industry. For those who stayed on, the battle for commercial viability was mediated by attempts to align programming content with the preferences of television audiences and commercial sponsors.

The enhanced focus on commercialization also affected religious programming, which shifted its focus from disseminating Islamic ideology to attracting a broader viewership through the generation of novel and diverse programming content. According to Naqvi (2010, 118), the producers of religious shows felt increased commercial pressure to diversify and introduce new religious content, "transforming religious programming from an instrument of pedagogy to a more user-driven form 'infotainment.'" Naqvi's assertion is useful for understanding the reasons behind the introduction of religious talk shows and game shows, which aim to cater to the diversity of the Pakistani viewership and its entertainment needs, respectively. Both programming developments hint at producers' increased regard for viewer preferences in the competitive, liberalized media environment. However, an important claim over the form and content of religious programming is staked by multinationals, who by virtue of generating advertising revenue for private channels are also major power brokers in the mediation of televised religious content (Talat Hussain, quoted in Anand 2014). In this context, Anand (42) reminds us that "television broadcasters sell a dual product. The first being the content and the second being the audience that tunes in to watch that content." Talat similarly reaffirms media's susceptibility to the influence of commercial sponsors while noting that "the roaring giant that once took on the state and the army under Musharraf cannot even meow against the wrongdoings of advertising hegemons" (quoted in Anand 2014, vii). Talat's reference to the "roaring giant" is aimed at clarifying the might of popular private channels, such as Geo and ARY, that played a key role in Musharraf's ouster from government. While Talat makes this observation mainly with reference to political talk shows, it can be extended to consider the influence of multinationals over religious show content as detailed in the following chapter.

On the degree of freedom accorded to private channels by Musharraf's government, Naqvi (2010) notes that the entry of several new players into the broadcasting industry created unprecedented opportunities for the production and circulation of unofficial meanings. However, I propose that it would be a mistake to look at liberalization in terms of the complete absence of governmental control over television programming. In fact, in what follows, I elaborate that the government in the liberalized media environment has three formal options for maintaining its hold over television programming: (1) the Pakistan Electronic Media Regulatory Authority (PEMRA) Ordinances; (2) the selective issuance of licenses; and (3) its continued hold over the state-owned channel, PTV.

Musharraf's government established PEMRA in 2002, soon after the opening up of Pakistani airwaves. While PEMRA's mandate was to regulate the establishment and broadcast of all new entrants in the market, broadcast licenses were selectively issued by the government, subsequent to approval from the Ministry of Interior (Shaikh 2007, 83). In an interview given to Kamran Asdar Ali, Imran Aslam critically observes that, contrary to the tall claims made by Musharraf regarding the liberalization of Pakistani media, the government denied Geo's license to operate in Pakistan on some flimsy pretext (Aslam and Ali 2009). Aslam's claim is corroborated by Anand (2014, 38), who explains that the government's decisions on whether to issue licenses to private owners were contingent on the channel owners' favorable terms with Musharraf's government. Therefore, any hint of tension between the channel owners and the government implied that the affected channels had to uplink from UAE for their broadcasts. In Geo's case, the government's denial compelled the privately owned network to use Dubai as the launchpad for its news channel. Conversely, uplinking from UAE accorded private satellite channels such as Geo a certain degree of autonomy in relation to their programming content.

In terms of such autonomy, Naqvi (2010) observes that the initial period of media liberalization was characterized by a relationship of mutual tolerance and dependence between the government and private channels. If the private satellite channels depended on the military government for their continued broadcast, so too did the government depend on these channels to portray it as a vanguard of civil and media liberties. For Naqvi this meant that it was in both parties' interest to sustain the "myth" of media deregulation. The channels did so by selectively reproaching members of Musharraf's political party for their administrative lapses on the newly introduced political talk shows while avoiding any mention of Musharraf's equivocal political legitimacy. The government, for its part, kept the pretense alive by putting up with the criticism directed at its members, with ostensible equanimity. However, unfortunately for the government, the facade of media liberalization soon became apparent in the wake of Musharraf's politically motivated dismissal of the chief justice of Pakistan. Musharraf perceived the chief justice as a threat to his continued legitimacy as president. Naqvi (2010, 114) reveals how Musharraf's dismissal of the chief justice, and his government's adverse reaction to the media's substantive coverage of the following protests, exposed the "fragility" of Musharraf's deregulation initiative. Live broadcasts of injured lawyers and journalists who bore the brunt of government brutality left a lasting impact on the minds of Pakistani viewers, who had at long last been exposed to the "reality" of Musharraf's media "liberalization" reforms.

The government firmly and decisively responded to the media's candid coverage of the countrywide protests. Not only did Musharraf suspend the Constitution of Pakistan and declare a state of emergency, but he simultaneously issued a series of amendments to the PEMRA Ordinance (see DAWN 2007b). The latter measure was undertaken to curb the media's expression of anti-government rhetoric on private satellite channels. These amendments remained in force even after the state of emergency was lifted on December 15,

2007. While some sections of the amendment are exclusively aimed at curtailing free speech, other sections implicitly require television anchors to comply with state-mandated interpretations of Pakistani ideology. These amendments curb free media expression and mediate government control over channel owners, who have since been obliged to accommodate governmental preferences in their programming ethos. Moreover, one of these amendments particularly applies to religious television shows, effectively prohibiting extreme expressions of doctrinal activism. According to the amendment, the media will "ensure that all programs and advertisements do not contain or encourage violence, terrorism, racial, ethnic or religious discrimination, sectarianism, extremism, militancy, hatred, pornography, obscenity, vulgarity or other material offensive to commonly accepted standards of decency" (PEMRA Act No. II 2007, §20c). Therefore, even with regard to the impact of media liberalization on religious programming, it would be a mistake to see the public face of religion on television as wholly divorced of governmental influence.

Musharraf's claims to have rejected the orthodox and politically aligned Islam of his military predecessor, together with his media reforms and his participation in the United States–led "War on Terror," were all packaged by his government under the all-encompassing discourse of "Enlightened Moderation" (see Naqvi 2010). According to Naqvi (115), the discourse of "Enlightened Moderation," put forward by Musharraf, envisioned "the possibility of creating a modern (rational, flexible, historical) interpretation of religious scripture that nurtures personal conviction and supports the individual and collective integration of Muslims into a global liberal political order." We should draw on this perspective to move beyond a consideration of the channels' decision to invite celebrity preachers, such as Javed Ahmed Ghamidi, as solely driven by the channels' regard for commercial appeal. Rather, we should also analyze this decision from a political lens, by considering the significance of these preachers in facilitating Musharraf's agenda. In Ghamidi's case, his appearances on religious shows during Musharraf's tenure in government were enhanced not only because of his usefulness in allowing religious programmers to elicit a broader viewership but also because of his willingness to challenge the "conventional" rulings espoused by traditional male clerics and to consider alternative interpretations of Islamic scripture, in tandem with Musharraf's secular agenda and support of the "War on Terror."

In addition to these notable shifts in religious programming, Musharraf's secular vision for the nation, not unlike the all-encompassing nature of Zia's Islamization reforms on PTV, also manifested in multiple genres of television programming. For instance, the intimate love scenes featured by private satellite channels subsequent to the liberalization of media had no precedent. Another noticeable transformation in television programming was the visible separation of religion from politics. Private broadcasters and religious show producers facilitated this separation by limiting the participation of traditional scholars on political talk shows and simultaneously placing prohibitions on political discussions on religious television shows (see chap. 2). However, these transformations also problematize a straightforward conceptualization of media liberalization as effectively marking the end of the government's ideologically oriented sermonizing in favor of a more "upbeat, more 'modern,' youth-oriented menu" (Shaikh 2007, 85). My proposition here is also partly indebted to Mahmood's (2006, 323) analysis of the secularism project undertaken by the US State Department in line with their effort to "reshape and transform Islam from within" in the aftermath of 9/11. According to Mahmood (326), the secularization project was less about banishing religion from public life and more about reshaping religion's form and circumscribing its role in public life. Mahmood's assertion regarding the normative nature of the secularizing project is also relevant for understanding the ideological underpinnings of Musharraf's project of "Enlightened Moderation." After 9/11, the realization of this project favored a more flexible and moderate implementation of religion on television. It is from this perspective that we can also view Musharraf's project as "the ideological armature of a military-comprador state" (Naqvi 2010, 117). Therefore, while Musharraf ostensibly diverged greatly from Zia in his treatment of religion in the media, his holistic approach toward using religion to disseminate his political ideology was similar to Zia's. However, if for Zia this approach involved the utilization of tools of state control and censorship, for Musharraf it entailed the management of political consciousness through "the sedentary and visual pleasures of consumerism" (Naqvi 2010, 113). The leaders' treatments of Islam on television had distinct implications for religious programming. Whereas Zia's Islamization agenda encouraged a more unified and monolithic approach to Islam on television, Musharraf's liberalization of media, in line with his secular agenda, enabled the articulation of multiple and competing discourses on Islam. In this book, I mainly concern myself with the latter, and more specifically with identifying the transformations in religious orthodoxy, authority, and politics that Musharraf's liberalization of media enabled.

NOTES

1. Ḥazrat is an honorific title.
2. See also Shaikh Aziz (2015). Also see section 2 and 3 of Martial Law Regulation No. 49 (Government of Pakistan 1979), which gives the "Chief

Martial Law Administrator, or a Martial Law administrator" the authority to scrutinize or ban "the publication or propagation of any matter" considered "prejudicial to Islamic Ideology or the sovereignty, integrity and security of Pakistan or morality and maintenance of public order, or the purposes of Martial Law, by order addressed to a printer, publisher or editor or to printers, publishers and editors generally." The punishment for contravening the order is "rigorous imprisonment which may extend to 10 years" and "fine or stripes not exceeding 25." See also amendments to Sections 499, 500, and 502 of the Pakistan Penal Code (PPC) on Defamation, which includes "words either spoken or intended to be read," "signs," "visible representation," and "publications intending harm, or knowing that such imputation will harm, the reputation of such person." Section 502 of the Pakistan Penal Code also forbids the sale of "printing or engraving defamatory material." The punishment for defamation according to section 500 of the PPC is "imprisonment for a term which may extend to two years, or with fine, or with both" (Qadri and Anjum 2015, 493–503).

3. These figures are debatable. A BBC survey cites satellite and cable penetration in rural areas as limited to 11% of the population, in contrast to 69% penetration in urban cities (Yusuf and Schoemaker 2013).

TWO

THE PRODUCTION, OWNERSHIP, AND CONTROL OF RELIGIOUS TELEVISION SHOWS

ONE OF THE FIRST TASKS I undertook on reaching Karachi for my fieldwork was to enlist the aid of my media contacts to arrange a meeting with Aamir Liaquat Husain, the host of the popular religious show *Aalim Online*. I was four months into my fieldwork when I met with Husain, who turned out to be very obliging. Not only did he tirelessly entertain my endless research queries, but he also introduced me to some religious presenters and permitted me to observe the recordings of *Aalim Online* from within the production studio.

Before meeting with Husain, I had considered donning the *dupatta* (head scarf) in line with his religious sensibilities. However, in the end I decided not to do so, after taking into consideration the nature of his profession. I assumed that in his capacity as the host of a popular religious show, Husain would be used to dealing with all sorts of people of differing religious sensibilities. Therefore, I chose to represent myself more honestly, although this did not extend to my opinions. I often held back on how I truly felt about certain religious issues. It was somewhat acceptable for me to not be appropriately covered as long as I did not explicitly state my distaste for that mode of dressing. My decision to reserve my religious opinions was mainly on account of my desire to not offend my host. However, there was also an underlying fear that I would be labeled a heathen if I were to express myself freely.

During my visits to the studio, I usually spent some time with Husain and the invited scholars prior to the recording of an *Aalim Online* episode. While attending these sessions in Husain's office, I was always fascinated by how the different scholars would (or would not) interact with me and how that varied with their educational backgrounds and doctrinal leanings. Because

I was already used to interacting with scholars of differing persuasions, I had become well versed in the differences between religious groups, especially when it came to their interactions with women and what they deemed as appropriate modes of conduct and dressing for them. For instance, I knew that traditional Deobandi scholars, especially those who had received their training at *Jāmīʿa ʿUlūm-ul Islāmīā*, Banori Town, or *Dār al-ʿUlūm*, Korangi, tended to be more rigid than scholars of other religious denominations. I could also tell that Husain was aware of these differences, as he would take special care to introduce me only to select scholars: mainly those who he felt would be more open to interacting with me. Even as some scholars preferred to ignore my presence in the room, they would often engage in passionate discussions among themselves prior to the recording or airing of an episode. During these moments, I would often feel like a voyeur, getting to peek into an otherwise covert world of religious programming.

This chapter draws on my firsthand observations of the recordings of the popular religious talk show *Aalim Online* and my numerous interactions with religious show producers and popular television-based religious personalities, both inside and outside the production studio context. In examining the nexus between Islam and media, much scholarship has focused mainly on the implications of this nexus for lay engagements with religious authority. As I have noted in the introduction of this book, a large corpus of anthropological and media scholarship has theorized about the relationship between religious media and religious authority. In particular, scholarship has focused on how this relationship enables the "fragmentation" of religious authority (Eickelman and Piscatori 2004, x) and democratizes religious debate by creating opportunities for more individualized engagements with Islam (Echchaibi 2011; Schulz 2006a). Others have implicated the proliferation of Islam in media technologies in the creation of a heightened regard for innovative expressions of religious authority (e.g., Hoesterey 2016). By contrast, this chapter pursues a somewhat different line of questioning. Rather than focusing on how religious talk shows alter perceptions of religious authority, I elucidate the changing terms of asserting religious authority made inevitable by the changing dynamics of religious show production, ownership, and control in the newly liberalized media context.

Borrowing from de Witte (2015, 208), who in the context of Ghanaian media argues for an understanding of "mass media" as entailing "specific formats, styles and modes of address," I posit the significance of religious shows both in altering the nature of scholarly participation in religious public debate and in subjecting featured scholars to nonscholarly interests and agendas. These insights into the nature of religious authority on television are only accessible from a production-based perspective, which is crucial for evaluating the wider implications of broadcast media for religious authority. Ganti (2002, 283), in the context of Indian films, has demonstrated the utility of this approach in yielding insights into how producers "think about and construct their audiences" and evaluate "the appropriateness" of certain concepts for their audiences. This approach is useful because it can potentially illuminate the key production considerations underlying the formal transformations in religious programming and the corresponding modes of editorial control guiding religious show production in the liberalized media environment. In this context, my analysis seeks to highlight the commercial imperatives binding contemporary religious show production and to identify the dominant ideologies and political considerations undergirding production decisions on the form scholarly discourse should take on television. At the same time, I also unpack the nature of the formal transformations characterizing contemporary religious programming, in terms of their implications for the authority of established religious scholars. By drawing jointly on my in-studio observations of religious show production and on my discussions with religious producers, presenters, and religious scholars, I have also been able to highlight the significance of contemporary religious shows in altering the terms of authoritative scholarly conduct and discourse in religious public debate.

My analysis in this context is also indebted to literature on the new modes of Islamic televangelism on the Qatar-based Al Jazeera channel (see Galal 2009; Moll 2010) and to Davies's (1998) observations on the Welsh *Eisteddfod* festival. I draw on this scholarship to evaluate the impact that changes in religious show format and content have had on perceptions of religious authority and modes of Islamic thinking. In addition, I draw inspiration from John Caldwell's (2008) *Production Culture* and from Hall's (2003) "Encoding/Decoding" model, which I find useful for examining the nature of production agendas. The model also clarifies instances when religious shows challenge dominant perceptions of Islam and religious authority or have unintended or unforeseen consequences.

As indicated in the introduction of this book, my analysis of religious shows neither focuses on dominant production ideologies (cf. Horkheimer and Adorno 1972; Powdermaker 2002) nor overplays the significance of audience reception (see Budd, Entman, and Steinman 1990; see Morley 1992 for a criticism of this approach) in determining popular understandings of Islam and religious authority. Instead, I argue for a perspective that accounts for the relevance of multiple players—religious show producers, presenters, audiences, corporate sponsors, and state institutions—and the religiopolitical context in the attempt to understand the form of televised portrayals of Islam and religious authority. On the basis of my interviews with popular television-based religious personalities and my analysis of the innovative formats and modes of editorial control characterizing contemporary religious shows, I propose that whereas previously the state and ʿulamā mainly controlled religious content on television, now channel owners, religious show producers, viewers, moderators, and commercial sponsors also control the flow of televised religious knowledge.

EDITORIAL CONTROL

Two of the largest private satellite networks in Pakistan, Geo Television and ARY, have tended to take the lead in introducing novel religious content as well as in featuring the most widely watched religious content in Pakistan's urban centers.[1] Both channels were formally established in 2002, and both are family-owned media conglomerates that operate a mix of entertainment, news, and sports channels in Pakistan. ARY Network operates Pakistan's most popular dedicated religious channel, QTV. Alternatively, Geo Television Network introduced two of the most watched religious shows in urban Pakistan—*Aalim Online* and *Alif*—and furthered the careers of popular religious personalities such as the religious show host Husain and the controversial and subversive celebrity preacher Javed Ahmed Ghamidi.

As indicated earlier, Aamir Liaquat Husain emerged as a popular religious personality in Pakistan, primarily because of his appearances as the anchor of *Aalim Online*. The show, which was introduced on television on Husain's initiative, was conceived for the purposes of religious edification, including the facilitation of the general public's access to "authentic" Islamic knowledge and the proper form of Islamic practice. On account of Husain's great success as the host of *Aalim Online*, Geo Television Network invited the anchor to conduct many other religious shows, including the *sahar* (start of fast) and *ifṭār* (breaking of fast) transmissions, featured by the network in *Ramaḍān*, and the *Ramaḍān* game show *Amaan Ramazan*. The game show style of religious broadcasting is currently the preferred mode for the month of *Ramaḍān* on many private satellite channels in Pakistan. According to Husain, a key motivation underlying the conceptualization of religious game shows is to entertain ordinary Pakistanis while allowing them to sustain the sanctity of their fasts in *Ramaḍān*.

Geo Television Network helped to enable the popularity of the celebrity preacher Javed Ahmed Ghamidi by frequently hosting Ghamidi on the religious talk show *Alif*, where he appeared alongside other traditional religious scholars and shared his religious views on different subjects. Subsequently, the network gave Ghamidi his own show, in which the celebrity preacher appeared exclusively, alongside the show host, Owais Iqbal. In the words of the channel's management, the show, which was entitled *Ghamidi* and which targeted the urban youth of Pakistan, was aimed at directing "the audience away from conflict and extremism towards what can be termed as [the] true path" (Geo Television Network 2016b). In addition, the network's management also envisioned the show as serving to create "a balance between two extremes (liberal and religious)" (2016b).

Since both Geo and ARY dominate popular televised religious content, they also hold considerable sway over popular modes of Islamic thinking. Their influence over popular religious content also renders them proxies for instituting state and corporate interests. Channel owners and religious producers influence authoritative religious discourse on television by various means, including the selection of featured topics, the selection of scholars, the contractual obligations of scholars, the allocation of airtime, and decisions regarding whether to broadcast live or prerecord episodes. In what follows, I consider the significance of all these variables in the subjection of religious shows and religious presenters to state and corporate interests.

TOPIC SELECTION

During my time in Husain's office, I discovered that scholars were mostly given their topics in advance so that they could prepare adequately for televised discussions. Whereas some of the television scholars I had met with outside the recording context had already stressed to me the practical merits of this practice, I also came to recognize its potential from an editorial control standpoint. I realized that determining the topic in advance implied greater production control over the issues raised on religious talk shows. Husain permitted me to observe the *Aalim Online* recordings from both the studio itself (I would be stationed next to the cameraman in these instances) and from the production control room (PCR), where I would sit either next to the producer or with the production assistants tasked with managing the call-ins for the show. As Husain had no qualms about acknowledging his motive for allowing me access to the PCR, I knew that my invitation was intended to impress upon me the popularity of *Aalim Online* and the transparency of the viewer call-in procedure. During the live transmission of an episode, the production assistants would meticulously prescreen all calls before forwarding them to Husain and the invited religious scholars. In these instances, Husain made few allowances for production team slippages. Thus, when during a live broadcast a production assistant accidentally forwarded a less pertinent call to the religious presenters, Husain severely castigated her at the end of the transmission for her lapse in judgment. Alternatively, for prerecorded shows, the call-in audience would be selected from a list of callers maintained by the production team. This list consisted of past callers whose questions, while not relevant at the time, were put aside, together with the callers' contact details, for later use.

All of the recordings of *Aalim Online* that I attended were marked by an absence of studio audience. This was primarily due to what I observed to be a shifting focus of religious programming. Channels were more interested in holding debates on the broader issues plaguing Islamic understanding in Pakistan, such as on the (im)practicability of imposing an Islamic system in Pakistan, the Islamic standing of Taliban insurgency, and the rights and status of women under Islam. Confining live audience participation to call-ins implied that religious show producers could prioritize discussions on these issues. Thomas (2005, 87) highlights television's propensity to focus on what "is (a) interesting (b) at the moment," which according to him is also what renders "television cosmology so compelling." For Thomas (87), a central feature of this cosmology is therefore "not substance, but time (actuality); not the unchanging but that which creates resonance (the interesting)." Thomas's focus on both time and interest allows us to contextualize the shift in religious programming focus from "public service television," centered on correct Islamic practice, to "agenda setting" TV (Galal 2009, 154). In Galal's (155) view the shifting focus on "agenda setting" implies that more relevance is placed on larger Muslim issues than on "small issues, too narrowly related to private daily life." Specifically with regard to Pakistani religious shows, this shift becomes easier to understand when we consider the context in which these shows are featured, wherein the rising Muslim conflict in Pakistan, both sectarian and Taliban instigated, has raised many questions about the extent and type of influence Islam, and by extension the *ʿulamā*, should be permitted to exercise over state politics and legislature.

On the importance of topic selection in subjecting religious scholars to state and corporate interests, a pertinent consideration is the relevance of certain topics in facilitating the Pakistani state's initiative to tackle the more extremist manifestations of Islam in Pakistan. While observing a live discussion between two scholars of differing persuasions—Deobandi and Ahl-i Hadīth—on the Islamic status of terrorism, I noted Husain's fervent attempt to elicit a consensual ruling from both scholars against terrorism and its main proponents in Pakistan, the Taliban. While the Pakistani *ʿulamā* had previously resisted proffering their opinion on the issue, the nature of the discussion, coupled with the presence of the two scholars on a widely broadcast religious show, succeeded in putting pressure on both scholars to either declare their unequivocal opposition to the Taliban or risk being seen as complicit in the Taliban project. During the transmission breaks, Husain continued to alert the scholars about the damaging implications of the latter on their institution's image.

When driving home from the recording, I could not help but speculate on the convenient timing of the topic, setting the stage for military intervention against the Taliban in North Waziristan. This thought subsequently prompted me to pose to Husain the question regarding the possibility of state intervention in televised religious content. Husain fervently debunked my proposition, instead insisting that the topics were selected on his own initiative. However, another way to analyze this issue, one perhaps more useful in the liberalized media context, is to broaden our understanding of how outside influence can manifest in televised content. Moll (2010, 4), notes that even though satellite media channels may not be controlled by state fiat, there are many instances when the channel owners' own affiliations with state institutions may render the state "a vocal participant by proxy."[2] Further, the channels may be alert to the dangers of stirring up discussions where they expect state reprisal. Thus, to the extent that the state features in production decisions, it also constitutes a potential audience for religious shows and plays an important role in determining popular religious content and the form of religious public debate.

The level to which considerations regarding the state dictate religious content on channels like Geo, which was well known for toeing the official line, becomes clearer when we examine Geo's *Zara Sochiye* (Think a little) initiative (Mir Khalil ur Rahman Foundation 2016). The channel undertook the initiative during the political tenure of the military dictator Pervez Musharraf (2001–8). A central component of the initiative was Geo's deliberate recourse to it to provoke a reconsideration of Pakistan's controversial Islamic laws, such as the Zina Ordinance. The Zina Ordinance (VII) is an especially controversial feature of the Hudood Ordinances, which were introduced in 1979, during General Ziaul Haq's tenure in government. The ordinance deems adultery and fornication to be criminal offences, punishable under the law by lashes or stoning to death, and holds the victims of rape guilty of fornication or adultery, unless they can produce four adult Muslim male witnesses to testify to their innocence. Up until the featuring of *Zara Sochiye*, the Zina Ordinance had remained largely excluded from public reconsideration. Despite the ordinance's potential for misuse against women, the ʿulamā had remained impervious to the protestations of women's rights activists, labeling all those who opposed the Zina Ordinance as blasphemers. Against this backdrop, religious talk shows such as Geo Television's *Alif* played a key role in provoking a reconsideration of the ordinance.

Because Geo's initiative was undertaken soon after the 9/11 attacks in the United States, at a time when President Musharraf's government was actively supporting the "War on Terror" and busy proliferating an agenda of religious moderation (under the mantra of "Enlightened Moderation"), it aroused much speculation regarding Geo's complicity in furthering Musharraf's political agenda. This was despite Geo's categorical denial of any state involvement or influence in prompting the initiative. While it is difficult to directly implicate Musharraf's government in sponsoring *Zara Sochiye*, some recent developments make it possible to claim that Geo at the very least obtained the government's consent prior to launching the initiative. These developments involve Imran Khan (the leader of the political party Pakistan Tehreek-i-Insaf and current prime minister of Pakistan) and Mubashir Luqman (a popular political anchor on ARY News), both of whom previously accused Geo of launching *Zara Sochiye*, with American and Israeli complicity, to undermine the significance of Islam in Pakistan. To acquit itself of these charges, Geo admitted to obtaining consent from both the state and senior members of the military establishment prior to launching *Zara Sochiye* (Geo Television Network 2016a). Geo's admission clarifies the nature of state control in the newly "liberalized" media environment, which is less about direct intervention and more about channels regulating themselves in line with perceived civil and military leadership objectives. A major consequence of Geo's initiative was that soon after the televised debates on the Zina Ordinance, the National Assembly, despite protests from prominent religious scholars and religiopolitical parties, passed an amendment to the ordinance in the form of the Women's Protection Bill (DAWN 2006). While many legal activists have since then critiqued the superficial nature of the bill, its significance cannot be overstated in a religiopolitical landscape where fairly recently (in 2011), the ex-governor of Punjab, Salman Taseer, was assassinated for opposing another Islamic law (blasphemy). All these developments attest to the political significance of topic selection in furthering particular agendas. It is from this lens that we also need to evaluate the shift from practice-related questions to "agenda setting" as grounded in multiple deliberations, including the private broadcasters' acknowledgment of their personally held religious sensibilities, political affiliations and interests, and consideration of outside pressures, such as from the state and military.

SCHOLAR SELECTION

Religious producers selecting religious scholars need to consider the intended audience of their show. As Horsfield (1984, 120) suggests, religious broadcasters "choose their audience by the content, format and marketing of their programs" and "maintain the specific structure of their audience because it is the most financially supportive for them." Horsfield's view is useful for understanding the commercial underpinnings of scholar selection, which from the perspective of religious producers involves a consideration of their intended audiences. From a purely commercial standpoint, religious shows that exclusively invite the celebrity preacher Ghamidi are aimed at members of the more intellectual Pakistani elite, who are less interested in gaining practical knowledge and more driven to challenge, or at the very least question, the age-old assumptions governing contemporary religious belief and practice in Pakistan. Alternatively, Husain's primary market is mainly people comprising the lower- and middle-income groups in the country. Husain has also tended to focus largely on female audiences, as is evident from the morning placement of one of his religious shows, *Subhe Pakistan* (Morning Pakistan), which by his own admission is strategically placed to compete with the women-oriented morning shows. However, *Ramaḍān* forms the exception to this rule, as do some of Husain's more recent *Aalim Online* transmissions that deal with the broader political and social issues plaguing Islamic understanding in Pakistan.

Since the casting of religious shows is closely linked to the types of discussions featured, a major consideration driving scholar selection is the sort of religiopolitical impact intended by producers. As Dayan (2005, 173) argues, "imagining the social consists not only of highlighting themes or issues ('agenda setting') but of casting those who are concerned by, or involved in these issues." It is from this perspective that we can also appreciate the political relevance of jointly casting both traditional and self-styled religious scholars. Since both religious authorities are associated with distinct Islamic viewpoints and, therefore, appeal to very different viewers, selecting one over the other has consequences for the way that people engage with televised religious debate. For that reason, Husain would generally invite a mix of self-styled and traditional scholars for discussions on more sensitive topics, such as the implementation of an Islamic system in Pakistan. I came to realize the effectiveness of this strategy, as both types of scholars have distinct appeals. Whereas self-styled scholars usefully provoke reconsiderations on extant Islamic beliefs and practices, traditional scholars, by virtue of their established credentials, are indispensable for enlisting broader support, especially for less-established religious ideas. However, individual factors such as the scholars' willingness to acquiesce to production requests could also mediate their future prospects with channels, as producers could then privilege their own religiopolitical sensibilities and simultaneously cater to external interests, agendas, and pressures.

During my time in Husain's office, I frequently witnessed religious scholars fawning over him and deferring to his authority in religious matters. From the profuseness of their remarks, I could tell that their apparent regard for Husain was prompted more by a desire for repeat appearances on *Aalim Online* than by the faith these scholars may have had in Husain's religious erudition. This was especially true for the less recognized scholars who were accorded considerably less opportunities than their more influential counterparts to defend their personally held opinions on television. Producers gave the latter considerably more leeway because the producers had gone to considerable lengths to woo these popular scholars, who were immensely coveted, especially for *Ramaḍān* transmissions.

The degree to which the selection of compliant scholars can serve production interests was repeatedly stressed to me by many of my scholarly interlocutors who were familiar with presenting on television. One scholarly narration that stands out in this context is that of *Muftī* (Islamic juris consult) Umair's, a Barelwi religious scholar who presented regularly on the ARY QTV channel. As per his narration, *Muftī* Umair was once invited on a private channel to present his views on the Islamic standing of interest-based banking. The Barelwi jurist recounted how he had, in line with his knowledge of Islamic law, denounced the practice as ethically and morally proscribed. His ruling, however, had not elicited a favorable response from the show anchor, who had summarily cut off *Muftī* Umair's condemnation of the practice by resorting to a commercial break. During the commercial break, the anchor had pressured *Muftī* Umair to reconsider his position. *Muftī* Umair believed that the channel feared reprisal from an important commercial sponsor—a multinational bank. When *Muftī* Umair refused to oblige the anchor, the producers had asked him to leave the show. The program had continued with the other scholars present, who had all agreed to issue statements in favor of the practice. *Muftī* Umair's narration raises a very important point about the economic considerations underlying religious shows that are financed by "advertising or subscription fees" (Pink 1998, 129). It is only from a behind-the-scenes perspective, which allows us to discern the "manufactured" (Herman and Chomsky 2010) nature of religious shows, that we are also able to catch a glimpse of how access to particular Islamic perspectives "is [also] regulated by money" (Pink 1998, 129). Moll (2010, 5) makes a similar argument in the context of Egyptian religious programming when she argues for a consideration of the founders as "not inexperienced entrepreneurs bent on an idealistic project of staking a 'voice' for Islam on air, but rather [as] seasoned industry players managing multimillion dollars investments across a variety of domains, not all 'pious' in the conventional sense of the term."³ What Moll (5) observes in the Egyptian television context can also be applied to religious shows on Geo Television, which similarly involve "big dollar budgets and high-stake investments" and are also like entertainment shows "deeply enmeshed in processes of commodification." However, even though Moll (5) regards the commercial impetus behind Egyptian religious shows as "not at all at odds with their ethical impulse," *Muftī* Umair's narration indicates that, in the Pakistani context, there may be instances when the broadcasters' (and scholars') commercial interests supersede their religious considerations.

Muftī Umair also informed me that scholars were additionally made susceptible to production directives through the financial incentives offered by channels. However, *Muftī* Umair's emphasis on this aspect of scholarly vulnerability was also aimed at distinguishing himself from other scholarly presenters, especially those who participated in religious shows featured by the commercial Geo Television Network. In this context, the scholar also tried to impress upon me that his decision to align himself almost exclusively with the dedicated religious channel, QTV, reflected his ability to rise above such corporeal concerns while performing his scholarly duties on television. QTV, unlike its more commercialized counterparts, had a policy of only compensating select scholars—those who constituted permanent members of its religious panel. Since *Muftī* Umair was part of a body of scholars whom the channel did not compensate for their participation, he claimed that he could remain truer to his religious ideals. According to *Muftī* Umair, QTV's policy to only compensate select scholars allowed the channel to minimize its production costs, thus conferring on it the wherewithal to withstand pressure from its commercial sponsors. *Muftī* Umair's revelation is useful for noting that, while financial compensation may work as a powerful motivator for some religious scholars to relent to production requests, this is not the case for all scholars. In the latter instance, a key option available to religious producers' for ensuring their control over televised religious content is to select more accommodating scholars.

CONTRACTUAL OBLIGATIONS

A foremost option available to channels for sustaining their control over religious content is binding all featured religious personalities to contracts. Many of the *'ulamā* who appeared regularly on television informed me of the stringent terms of their contractual obligations, which incorporated the channels' concerns for abiding by the regulations of the Pakistan Electronic Media Regulatory Authority (PEMRA). In what follows, I offer a perspective into how the state-imposed regulations on religious programming, together with the commercialization of religious shows, may limit the usefulness of television for doctrinally motivated religious propaganda. For this, I revisit my discussions with two Barelwi religious scholars who presented regularly on religious shows—Professor Rahman and *Muftī* Umair.

My meeting with Professor Rahman came about completely by chance. Sakina mosque, where Professor Rahman regularly addressed the Friday prayer gathering, was located on my route to an older part of the city that I frequently visited to access my non-Deobandi scholarly interlocutors. The mosque, which I identified as a Barelwi one, was a recent addition to the Defence Housing Authority (DHA) landscape, and given the paucity of Barelwi mosques and seminaries in DHA, it immediately piqued my curiosity. I was particularly struck by the mosque's impressive facade and contemporary architecture, even as I wondered about the mosque's location right across the road from an equally impressive and newly constructed Deobandi mosque. My curiosity prompted me to visit the mosque one day and request a meeting with the Barelwi *imām* presiding over the mosque. The *imām* was very obliging and asked me to return on Friday for an introduction to Professor Rahman, a Barelwi scholar who presented regularly on the QTV channel. The *imām* felt that given the nature of my research, Professor Rahman would be better able to respond to my queries. Professor Rahman turned out to be very cordial, and despite his busy schedule, he spent considerable time with me, patiently responding to my queries on three successive Fridays. During my initial meeting with Professor Rahman, our discussion mainly revolved around the production aspect of religious television shows. While elaborating on the preconditions for presenting on religious television shows, Professor Rahman informed me of a contract that all scholars were required to sign prior to presenting on QTV. The professor explained that the contract made it mandatory for religious scholars to refrain from any radical preaching that involved personal or ideological attacks on the beliefs of competing doctrinal groups and their practitioners. This included the avoidance of any provocative speech that had the potential to either stir doctrinal rivalries and cause agitation between different religious groups or cause hurt to, or offend, the adherents of competing religious groups. Moreover, channel management also barred presenting scholars from initiating any discussion on current affairs, politics, or foreign policy. This included staying clear of any anti-West or anti-American rhetoric and of any explicit statements against the state leadership or the Pakistani armed forces. The attempt to dissuade religious specialists from engaging in any political discussion represents a major departure from PTV's mandate under the leadership of President Ziaul Haq

(1978–88), when religious authorities' participation in matters of government and politics was actively encouraged. While the strict and binding nature of these scholarly contracts is consistent with the channels' concern for abiding by PEMRA regulations, their broad scope simultaneously reflects the degree of control private broadcasters and religious producers exercise over televised religious content, which includes their ability to tailor all such content to match their own political, religious, and commercial preferences. For religious scholars presenting on religious talk shows, this development can also imply the need to accommodate interests and concerns that lie outside the purview of their individual religious beliefs and perceived responsibilities.

We need to view the prohibition on radical doctrinal speech as also motivated by the private broadcasters' commercial interests and their corresponding fear regarding the shows' otherwise-diminished popular ratings. Hoover (2003, 12) outlines a similar tendency in religious programming in the United States, where televangelists like Billy Graham and Jimmy Swaggart frequently employed references to "angels and talk of God" in their televised sermons yet were careful to avoid "reference to the specificity of Christianity." In the case of Billy Graham, Hadden and Swann (1981, 22) note the preacher attempts to downplay denominationalism despite his own Southern Baptist leaning. Hoover (2003, 12) grounds this tendency in a broader evangelical attempt to be "more broadly accessible to spiritually autonomous audiences." Alternatively, in Pakistan, the religious producers' concern for the commercial success of their shows does not only entail ensuring that religious scholars stay clear of doctrinal activism but also involves making certain that the scholars abstain from making any derogatory references about non-Pakistani or non-Muslim religious groups. This becomes apparent when we consider *Muftī* Umair's revelation that the same rules that applied to anti-American rhetoric on QTV also extended to anti-Indian or anti-Hindu propaganda. The fact that *Muftī* Umair admitted that the latter measure was primarily undertaken by QTV at the channel's own behest to ensure the continued telecast of its programs in India reinforces the point that in the liberalized media environment, the channels' commercial interests play a particularly important role in shaping religious content on television.

DECISIONS TO BROADCAST LIVE OR PRERECORD

Most religious shows are broadcast before or after prime time, which in Pakistan falls between 8:00 p.m. and 10:00 p.m. However, it is not uncommon for some very popular religious shows, such as *Aalim Online*, to be allocated prime-time slots. While decisions regarding the allocation of airtime mainly depend on the popularity of a religious show, they are also influenced by seasonal factors. For instance, during the month of *Ramaḍān*, prime-time slots are increasingly allocated to religious game shows and talk shows. In fact, the airtime extended to Husain's *Ramaḍān* game show, *Amaan Ramazan*, has tended to exceed the usual one-hour slot allocated to most other religious programs. In 2014, *Amaan Ramazan* was transmitted live for more than three hours daily in *Ramaḍān*. On select *Ramaḍān* days—those associated with the revelation of the Qurʾān and therefore considered especially auspicious for Muslims—the transmission time for Husain's game show went up to twelve hours. Furthermore, decisions regarding the allocation of airtime are not merely undertaken in line with commercial considerations. At times, these decisions are also strategically motivated to incorporate the Islamic agendas of religious show hosts, producers, and private broadcasters.

Two aspects of airtime allocation are relevant to this consideration. The first is how religious show hosts and producers can use the selective allocation of airtime between those invited to privilege particular modes of Islamic thinking over others. Many of my scholarly interlocutors who presented on religious talk shows complained that they either were given less time than their religious counterparts or were cut off frequently by the show hosts, who demonstrated a preferential bias for the views espoused by scholars affiliated with competing doctrinal groups. A second aspect of the strategic usefulness of airtime is related to producers' decisions regarding when to broadcast their shows. As Husain admitted to me, he decided to broadcast *Aalim Online* in the mornings, between 9:00 a.m. and 10:00 a.m., to curtail the corrupting influence of morning shows, which tended to be very popular with middle-class Pakistani women.

Another central element of production control that emerged during my visits to Husain's recording studio comprised decisions on whether to prerecord shows or air them live. While these decisions were contingent on Husain's availability and work schedule (if he was expected to be out of Karachi, some shows were prerecorded), they also involved a review of the sensitivity of the topic to be discussed. As I often observed, the more controversial the discussion, the greater the likelihood that the show would be prerecorded. Prerecording also allowed producers to balance elements of sensationalism with the show's credibility. As Husain explained to me, while he was willing to highlight some problematic aspects of Islamic practice, his adverse past experiences had taught him to be more circumspect. As highlighted in the introduction of this book, Husain had already witnessed the fallout of one of his transmissions on the Ahmadīyā community, which had subsequently incited the killings of two Ahmadis (Walsh 2012). Even though the transmission had not cost Husain much of his fan following, it had nonetheless earned him much censure and criticism from members of the civil society and popular media. As a result, he now felt more comfortable prerecording shows when the topics were of a sensitive nature, as he could then edit out the more problematic aspects of the scholarly discussion. Many of my scholarly interlocutors who frequently appeared on religious shows confirmed to me the significance of prerecording. They recalled instances when channel owners and show hosts had deliberately excluded some of their statements to avoid instigating controversy and backlash. Only by accounting for these hidden aspects of production can we also conceptualize religious shows as staged performances (Turner 1969, 1990), wherein a key incentive underlying their production is to engender nationwide religious transformation.[4] Their utility from an institutional perspective arises from their potential to institute religious change and perpetuate more tolerant conceptualizations of Islam in a hostile and conflict-prone Pakistani religious environment. My proposition becomes easier to understand when we take a look at some of the changes in religious show format subsequent to media liberalization.

TRANSFORMATIONS IN SHOW FORMAT

As mentioned earlier, some notable shifts in production format distinguish contemporary religious shows from their predecessors on PTV broadcast prior to media liberalization: the shift in focus from didactic sermonizing to the emphasis on providing Islamic rulings; the increased prominence and participation of live, call-in, and studio audiences; the shift toward pluralistic representations of Islam, including the accommodation of doctrinally and educationally inspired differences on religious show expert panels; and the introduction of religious game shows. I analyze each of these transformations in terms of its role in reconfiguring conceptualizations of Islam and religious authority.

FATWĀ PROGRAMS

A novel feature of religious talk shows is that they encourage Muslim viewers to pose questions on specific aspects of Islamic belief and practice to the invited panel of religious experts comprising the *ʿulamā* and "new" celebrity preachers. The inclusion of live, call-in, or studio audiences represents a marked shift from the didactic style of religious sermonizing featured prior to media liberalization by the state-owned channel, PTV. The task of participating scholars is to mandate what is *ḥalāl* (permissible) or *ḥarām* (forbidden) in line with their interpretations of Qur'ānic injunctions and in accordance with their respective doctrinally or individually held viewpoints. As in the case of *Sharī'a wa 'l-Ḥayāt* (*Sharī'a* and life), featured on the Qatari Al Jazeera channel, Pakistani religious shows also mainly provide *tafsīr* (exegetical commentaries) in response to caller queries (see Galal 2009). These developments contribute to a widely prevalent notion of religious talk shows as *fatwā* programs, which in turn has important implications for perceptions of religious authority. On the significance of *fatāwā* (pl. of *fatwā*) in mediating religious authority, much scholarship on Islam has noted how a redeployment of *fatāwā* from settling contractual and technical disputes (in the "calligraphic state") to addressing the everyday practical concerns (in the "modern" state) acts to reaffirm, expand, and consolidate the influence of traditional religious authorities (e.g., Messick 1993; Skovgaard-Petersen 1997), which are the *madrasa* educated, religious scholars and Islamic jurists in Pakistan. This is achieved through the proliferation of standardized conceptualizations of "common good" (see, e.g., Hirschkind 2001; Ismail 2003; Salvatore 1998).

Up until the *madrasa*-educated religious scholars are asked to respond to viewers and impart advice on issues of Islamic practice, religious talk shows facilitate the transmission of "'traditional' discourses of Islam," under which questions on the "correct" form of Islamic practice are posed to a traditional scholar adequately trained in the exercise of issuing *fatāwā* (see Galal 2009, 152). To the extent that religious talk shows involve traditional scholars as a compulsory and majority presence on their panel of religious specialists, they actively reinforce a "preferred reading" of these scholars as religious experts (see Hall 2003; Caldwell 2008). Rothenbuhler (2005) elaborates on this concept, while arguing for a broader application of Goffman's (1976) thesis on media representations in advertising photography. According to Rothenbuhler (2005, 94), "in the media presentation of personal roles and performances ... the range of realistic possibilities tends to be reduced to iconographic representations of selected, and thereby preferred, types." Similarly, by enabling the "greater public presence" and consequently the "social authority" of traditional religious scholars, religious shows implicitly position these scholars as the "preferred" type of religious authority (94). In doing so, they both testify to and implicitly sanction their superior religious authority, thereby restoring "a broader view of [religious] public life" (Lule 2005, 109).[5] Such a preferential framing of religious authority on television also draws on the immersion of religious producers in a culture and society that traditionally associates Islamic authenticity with the institution of the *madrasa*. Caldwell (2008, 334–35) makes a similar proposition in the context of American production culture, noting that the "film/video makers are also audiences" who "fully participate in the economy, political landscape, and educational systems of the culture and society as a whole." Within this framework, the positioning of traditional scholars as the preferred type of religious authority, together with the shifting programming emphasis on dealing with the viewers' everyday practice-related queries, does not simply act to reinforce the control of traditional religious scholars over religious matters but also serves to insinuate their controlling influence over people's everyday lives.

Alternatively, if the scholars' deployment of religious television offers the prospect of their sustained influence in religious public debate, so too does it pose a risk to their influence. The latter consequence has been foregrounded by Eickelman and Piscatori (2004) as one of the drawbacks of appearing too frequently on television, because of which scholarly ideas can become more susceptible to enhanced viewer scrutiny and critical judgment. When this happens, it may also be, as Lewis (2007, 439) claims, that television messages are interpreted in ways that "the producers might not have imagined or intended." Lewis's observation allows us to account for those key instances when religious shows inadvertently encourage the relegation of traditional discourses and sources of religious authority to more "innovative" and critical forms of Islamic thinking. Crucially, religious shows provoke a critical evaluation of traditional sources of religious authority when they feature doctrinally and ideologically inspired debates between religious authorities. By enabling these debates and by granting equal legitimacy to celebrity preachers on panels of religious experts, religious talk shows trigger widespread uncertainty over the authenticity of varying scholarly propositions.

Davies's (1998) observations on the Welsh *Eisteddfod* can be effectively applied to consider how the shift toward the inclusion of new celebrity preachers on religious show panels can affect the religious authority of traditional scholars. While commenting on the relevance of broadcasting decisions in the context of the *Eisteddfod*, Davies suggests that the broadcasters' decision to jointly feature traditional and untraditional festival activities, taking place inside and outside the main festival pavilion, respectively, also popularizes "images at variance with" the viewers' "stereotypical expectations" (147–51). For Davies (158), the overall effect of television "is [thus] to legitimate alternative performances as also being part of the *Eisteddfod* and hence of any Welsh identity it might project." In Pakistan, religious talk shows that invite self-styled celebrity preachers to issue rulings on the correct performance of

Islamic practices implicitly both undermine the privileged place of the *madrasa* in conferring religious expertise and also attenuate the monopoly of traditional religious scholars in interpreting Islam for the general Pakistani public. Within this framework, the efficacy of scholarly rulings in enabling traditional modes of religious authority and collective enforcements of morality is compromised. Instead, the relevance of scholarly rulings mainly derives from their role in mediating alternative and contesting claims to religious authority. Thus, once perceived as a religious obligation by some Muslims, scholarly rulings are increasingly rendered open to contestation, resistance, and negotiation.

AUDIENCE PARTICIPATION

To fully appreciate the complexity of the audience's contribution to religious shows, and consequently to dominant modes of Islamic thinking, we need to first distinguish between two very distinct types of religious talk shows: those that seek to educate viewers on the correct modes of Islamic practice and those that are increasingly characterized by agenda-setting motives. Most shows of the former type feature discussions on everyday aspects of religious practice, such as the payment of *zakāt* (obligatory alms), the correct form of fasting, and so forth. The significance of viewers on these shows is a function of the part they play in determining which questions will be raised and which authoritative responses will merit greater compliance. To an extent, these religious talk shows can be viewed as a reenactment of the *dār al iftā'* (center for Islamic rulings), so that "the audience is part of the spectacle, is itself spectacle, and its ways of participating—audience performances—may reconstruct the nature and meaning of the spectacle itself" (Davies 1998, 144). Within this format, the viewers' prominence also accrues from their propensity to not restrict their queries to traditional scholars but to also direct their questions toward self-styled scholars and religious show hosts. In this way, the viewers legitimize multiple forms of religious authority. Alternatively, the emphasis in religious programming on featuring doctrinally inspired forms of pluralism and the controversial nature of some Islamic practices, such as the procedure for divorce, on which there is little consensus even among traditional scholars, implies that even viewers who direct their questions exclusively to traditional scholars can enable the fragmentation of religious authority. In such instances, the representation of doctrinal difference by religious talk shows goes a long way toward enabling the greater authority of religious show viewers, who are thus able to employ their own discretion when discerning between competing scholarly claims.

I have already noted that audience participation in shows that prioritize agenda setting is generally restricted to call-ins. Moreover, some religious talk shows—such as *Alif*, featured earlier on Geo Television—have deviated slightly from this format, in that, despite the presence of a studio audience, the questions are mainly posed by the show moderator (Aneeq Ahmed in the case of *Alif*). On both types of religious shows, the significance of audience members in guiding the format and content is limited to the extent to which they factor in production decisions. Ganti (2002), drawing on Ang (1991), underscores the relevance of the audience in this context while elaborating on the success of Indian films as contingent on the production team's ability to accurately preempt audience preferences and competencies. In this context, the viewing choices that audiences make, and the resulting production assumptions regarding them, contribute to the former's relevance in shaping the direction of religious talk shows. The fact that religious show producers continue to emphasize the multivocality of Islam on religious talk shows is primarily a function of the shows' popular ratings. From this perspective, the mere watching of religious talk shows constitutes a form of audience participation through which the plurality of Islamic thought and the multiplicity of religious authorities—"new" celebrity preachers and traditional scholars (sectarian and nonsectarian)—is effectively legitimated and reinforced.

REPRESENTATION OF ISLAMIC PLURALISM

As already stated, religious talk shows offer viewers more variety in terms of the forms of Islamic thinking represented. Instead of inviting one scholar, as was customary on religious shows broadcast on the state-owned channel, PTV, prior to media liberalization, contemporary religious talk shows accommodate the diversity of Islamic thought in Pakistan, inviting two to three scholars of competing doctrinal persuasions to represent their distinct viewpoints on television. Even when some shows continue to invite one scholar to respond to audience queries, this is usually limited to cases where the scholar commands substantial following and respect, such as in the case of the popular celebrity preacher Javed Ahmed Ghamidi or the Barelwi religious scholar *Allama* Kokab Noorani. On the shows that invite more than one scholar, generally at least one is affiliated with a Sunni-majority doctrinal school.

When I met with Husain, the host of *Aalim Online*, he elaborated that just as different varieties of mangoes were on display for customers to choose between, so too was the presence of multiple scholars aimed at providing viewers with more choices, in tandem with their differing Islamic sensibilities. From Husain's words, we get a sense of the significance of the commercial considerations underlying the production of contemporary religious talk shows, wherein the accommodation of Islamic diversity also reflects the production aim to generate wider viewership. However, once we start to consider the commercial impetus behind the pluralistic format of religious talk shows, we must simultaneously consider how this may influence the nature of televised messages. For Murdock and Golding (1977, 37), considerations regarding the maximization of audiences and revenues imply that producers avoid the "unpopular and tendentious and draw instead on the values and assumptions which are most familiar and most widely legitimated." In the context of American televangelism, Postman (2006, 116) notes how such considerations provoke televangelists like Jimmy Swaggart to adopt more ecumenical modes of sermonizing, owing to their growing realization that television is "not congenial to messages of naked hate." It is from this perspective that we can also make sense of the religious producers' instructions to religious presenters to tone down any radical professions of doctrinally inspired activism on television in Pakistan. However, this is where Pakistani religious shows diverge slightly from those featured in the United States: rather than supporting an ecumenical emphasis, they attempt to maintain a delicate balance between catering to a fragmented viewership and taking care not to offend the religious sensibilities of diversely affiliated adherents.

Further, while a privileged consideration of religious audiences may constitute a major impetus for the new pluralistic format, it is not the only one. When we met, Husain also expressed a desire to encourage peaceful dialogue and interaction between different religious groups as a major incentive behind his show's format. Husain explained that prior to the introduction of *Aalim Online*, "traditional scholars were not even prepared to sit with scholars of competing doctrinal affiliations. They were at each other's throats." For Husain, thus, a key benefit of *Aalim Online* and its subsequent adaptations was their potential usefulness in paving the way for peaceful resolutions to doctrinally instigated intra-Muslim conflict. On his show traditional scholars of competing doctrinal persuasions could sit together and participate in civilized debate on issues of mutual import. Husain's words betray an instance of agenda setting, whereby a key motive underlying televised pluralism is also to neutralize the confrontational aspects of Muslim politics. This agenda implicitly matches the military's and government's efforts toward defusing tensions between opposing religious groups and curtailing more violent expressions of Islamic thought on account of the threat they pose to the Pakistani state.

RELIGIOUS GAME SHOWS

The significance of religious game shows emerges from their tendency to provide both entertainment and religious instruction to viewers. This locates religious game shows within the genre of infotainment programming. Much like religious programming in the United States, the introduction of religious game shows in Pakistan also owes to an increased realization among religious producers that their shows are in "hot competition, not only with a lot of secular and few mainline religious programs... but with each other as well" (Hadden and Swann 1981, 19). Like their counterparts in the United States, religious show producers in Pakistan increasingly subscribe to the view that the entertainment quotient of their shows "can determine their success or failure" (19). Religious game shows are typically aired in Ramaḍān because of the sorts of discipline fasting enjoins on and seeks to inculcate in a Muslim believer, wherein abstinence from food and drink may be primary, but not the only, considerations. The believer also has to undertake other forms of self-discipline, whereby the "ethics of seeing and listening" are part of a larger program to bring about inner spiritual transformation. For Muslim viewers, a major benefit derived from watching religious game shows in Ramaḍān is that they can partake in entertainment without experiencing the customary pangs of guilt associated with viewing other types of secular entertainment. This benefit makes religious game shows a particularly popular viewing option in Ramaḍān. The ability of game shows to be at once instructive and entertaining implies that they can be "many things to many people" (Abelman 1990, 100). Their ability to attract viewers of differing motivations—those seeking spiritual gratification and guidance and those seeking entertainment—makes them more attractive to private broadcasters, whose motivation to produce these shows also includes a consideration of their financial viability.[6] Therefore, in Ramaḍān, even popular entertainment channels, such as Geo Television and ARY, shift their resources from other forms of secular entertainment to religious game shows, which constitute the greater portion of their daily broadcasts. As already indicated, in the Ramaḍān of 2013, Geo extended the broadcast time for Husain's game show, Amaan Ramazan, to twelve hours.

The participants on religious game shows are usually selected through a random balloting process, for which anyone with online access can enroll. Most shows feature a variety of segments and are essentially a "kaleidoscopic mix of prayer, preaching, game shows and cookery" (Walsh 2012). Thus, despite a question-and-answer (Q and A) segment in which the audience can pose questions to featured religious scholars, the goal of most of these shows is essentially to provide entertainment. For instance, the entertainment segments featured on *Amaan Ramazan* in 2013 included a cooking segment displaying Husain's culinary skills; a quiz segment, for which the prizes ranged from designer cotton suits and mobile telephones to pricey kitchen durables and motorbikes; a game segment, in which live audience members were invited to play onstage in return for expensive giveaways; a guest segment, in which the invited guests included singers, actors, and other notable personalities; and a charity segment associated with Husain's charitable foundation, the Mahmooda Sultana Trust. Since the duration of some game shows, such as *Amaan Ramazan*, extends beyond *ifṭār*, they also feature communal *maghreb* (evening) prayers and the breaking of the fast.

While examining popular forms of Muslim televangelism in the United States, Naggar (2018, 14) observes that the popularity of the American Muslim televangelist Baba Ali necessarily benefits from the preacher's recourse to "contemporary media aesthetics," including the featuring of "music, songs and colorful images" on his show. Alternatively, in Pakistan, a similar recourse to secular entertainment within the presentation format of religious game shows can at once facilitate religious producers in eliciting a broader regard for their shows and subject these shows to widespread criticism. The latter is a function of some viewers becoming increasingly skeptical about the ethical impulse undergirding the production of these shows. In the context of Egypt, Moll (2010, 3) convincingly argues that the entertainment value of religious shows is not necessarily irreconcilable with the ethical impulse of religious show producers, as long as the programs do "not displace the centrality of the pious message itself," which after all is "the most important aspect" of religious shows for Muslim viewers. However, this is where Pakistani religious shows diverge significantly from Moll's proposition in terms of the balance maintained (or not) between religion and entertainment. While on the one hand the mixing of entertainment with religion implies that ideas of piety can be inculcated in a noninvasive manner, it also implies that more liberties are taken with Islam's portrayal on television. Some problematic aspects of religious game shows have generated much controversy: the free mixing of men and women, the participating audience's lack of observance of the ʿulamā-mandated codes of Islamic dressing, and the trivializing of religion, which comes with juxtaposing more frivolous content (games, humor, and fun) with religious edification.

It is in relation to these religious transgressions that I would like to draw attention to an alternative consideration of this form of religious entertainment, one to do with its susceptibility to being employed by various stakeholders in furthering an agenda of tolerance and moderation. Religious game shows' implicit encouragement of a conception of Islam as open to multiple interpretations and diverse ways of Muslim "being" makes them complicit in a "progressive" agenda, within which Muslims are encouraged to accommodate more alternative religious viewpoints (Husain, quoted in Walsh 2012). This agenda has growing support from the Pakistani state and military, given the war being waged in Pakistan's Northern Tribal region, to curb incidents of extremism and sectarianism-inspired violence in the country. Many of my informants, especially those affiliated with Pakistani seminaries, alerted me to numerous rumors implicating religious game shows in the military's anti-terrorism initiative. Even if these rumors are not grounded in reality, they nonetheless make religious game shows a salient site for contesting extant notions of Islamic belief and practice. The inclusion of entertainment on these shows raises important questions about how Islam will be lived and which understandings of Islam (traditional, liberal, or moderate) will be privileged in religious public debate.

TRANSFORMATIONS IN RELIGIOUS AUTHORITY

One of the unintended consequences of a more pluralistic and therefore competitive religious show format is that Islam is made increasingly political as ideas of Islam and "being" Muslim become contested. Also contributing to the politicization of Islam is that religious talk shows don't simply offer choices. They compel viewers to take sides by making religious difference an important feature of the format. This becomes evident when we consider that what distinguishes contemporary religious talk shows from their unified and didactic predecessors is not their potential to offer their audiences choices, as even past shows that favored a more didactic format performed this function by allowing viewers to switch between different religious programs. Instead, contemporary religious talk shows differ in that they enable different religious authorities to appear together on the same show. Their novel aspect lies in encouraging debates between different schools of Islamic thinking. Within this emerging discursive space, the religious specialists invited are not simply required to offer viewers more Islamic practice-related options but also expected to defend their claims against competing notions of Islam. Thus, an alternative approach to religious talk shows is to view them as staged contests between religious experts. Within this framework, religious scholars, who are on the one hand encouraged by show producers to favor more generic and less controversial modes of Islamic representation, are conversely also compelled to stage their authority in terms of the differences between them and other scholars.

The audience must acknowledge these differences to address questions to the scholars present. In other words, viewers who direct their questions at particular scholars implicitly opt for a preferred mode of political identification with Islam—sectarian, traditional, liberal, or modern.

These developments mediate the greater prominence of viewers in determining how Islam will ultimately shape their lives. In the last two chapters, I focus on how the competitive and polemical format of religious programming renders the viewers the final authority over televised religious content, and in doing so, inadvertently provokes a critical reevaluation of extant Islamic values, by raising questions about what Islam is and how it is to be lived in practice. This contradictorily displaces a pluralistic conceptualization of Islam. Within the idea of Islam privileged by religious shows, what constitutes "proper" Islamic practice needs to be definitively determined and defended against perceived deviations. Therefore, rather than simply focusing on the way in which religious television shows accommodate pluralism, we need to additionally consider that these shows may equally foreground the inadequacies of pluralism by activating a notion of Islam as a monolithic concept. Such inadequacies can be seen in the confusion generated by Islamic pluralism and the occasionally confrontational and hostile nature of televised debates on religious shows that invite scholars of differing doctrinal persuasions. However, ultimately, whether religious shows are perceived by viewers as foregrounding the inadequacies of pluralism, reinforcing Islamic difference, or encouraging more accommodative forms of Muslim engagement is also a function of the viewers' idiosyncratic views regarding their faith. While these are considered in greater detail in chapters 6 and 7, suffice it to say here that the individualized and fragmented forms of Islamic engagement implicitly encouraged by religious shows pose particular difficulties for traditional scholars, whose authority in the contemporary religious context is mainly staged in sectarian terms. Irrespective of whether these scholars underplay their doctrinal proclivities or emphasize them on television, both modes of authoritative assertion can have adverse implications for their authority with different viewers.

Moreover, in addition to problematizing doctrinally inspired claims to religious authority, the commercial and political influences guiding contemporary religious show production have the overall effect of subordinating traditional religious authority to the needs and preferences of nonscholarly actors. Within the format of religious shows, the latter wield immense influence over the modes of Islamic thinking and forms of religious practice that will be privileged. Religious show viewers' ability to influence religious discourse on television, whether through direct intervention or by virtue of the producers' assumptions regarding their diverse religious sensibilities, is a direct corollary of the newly liberalized and competitive media environment. From this perspective, we can also view the shift in religious programming, toward featuring multiple Islamic perspectives, as inspired by the producers' considerations regarding their highly fragmented viewership.

The political influences shaping religious show production do not generally manifest in the form of the state or military actively and directly controlling everyday programming content (although some recent incidents have revealed the possibility of this also happening). Rather, these influences are more a product of the ways that channels regulate themselves in tandem with broader state and military objectives.[7] To this end, the airing of sensitive Islamic issues, the Islamic inconsistencies featured on religious game shows, the contractual conditions set by channels, and the shift toward Islamic pluralism, especially the inclusion of new celebrity preachers, are all aimed at proliferating more accommodative and tolerant modes of Islamic thinking that are in keeping with state and military agendas.

The resulting transformations in religious authority enabled by Pakistani religious talk shows are by no means limited to the fragmentation of authority. Instead, an established scholarly presence on Pakistani religious talk shows is often contingent on the scholars' willingness to concede their influence in religious public debate and to succumb to production directives and the authority of nonscholarly others. Within this framework, the invited scholars' willingness to participate in discussions on sensitive Islamic issues, their adherence to the contractual conditions set by channels, their agreement to tailor their rulings to production mandates even when these go against the scholars' individually held religious sensibilities, and their willingness to appear alongside scholars of competing religious affiliations all attest to the relegation of scholarly authority to nonscholarly, commercial, and political, interests and agendas. The scholars' susceptibility to various commercial and political influences by virtue of their presence on religious talk shows corresponds with Winston's (2002, 138) suggestion that "religious movements and organizations have always had to struggle between their motivation to 'use' the media and their fear of losing control over how they will be represented therein (Hoover and Clark 2002, 88)." Winston's suggestion is especially applicable to the regulatory and pluralized context of Pakistani religious programming, where important preconditions for scholarly participation are the accommodation of religious difference and the toning down of more radical Islamic and sectarian stances. Here, I would like to emphasize the usefulness of a production-based perspective in allowing me to clarify the otherwise unaccounted for transformations in religious authority, engendered by religious media. On the basis of the insights gleaned though my employment of this approach, I would also like to suggest a greater role for religious talk shows than what has been theorized thus far, regarding their significance for the institution of various commercial and political agendas.

NOTES

1. PTV is more popular in rural areas.

2. Kraidy (2010) makes a similar argument in his book *Reality Television and Arab Politics*.

3. Stout (2012, 86) similarly notes that "accelerating the fusion of entertainment and religion is the commercial market; today religious media are commodities. Not only are they sites of religious experience, but also sources of profit."

4. Turner's (1969, 96) work on ritual and performance draws on Van Gennep's conception of ritual as a process or a "rite of passage," albeit with more emphasis on the symbolic relevance of liminality and feelings of "communitas" in mediating social change. *Communitas* refers to community of "equal individuals who submit together to the general authority of the ritual elders" (96). According to Turner (1990), social dramas typically have "four main phases of public action": (1) "breach of regular norm-governed social relations"; (2) "crisis, during which there is a tendency for the breach to widen"; (3) "redressive action ranging from personal advice and informal mediation or arbitration to formal juridical and legal machinery, and, to resolve certain kinds of crisis or legitimate other modes of resolution, to the performance of public ritual"; and (4) "reintegration of the disturbed social group, or ... social recognition and legitimation of irreparable schism between the contesting parties."

5. On the role of television in passing down and sanctioning tradition in media anthropology, see Jack Lule (2005, 104–9).

6. Abelman (1990) makes this claim in terms of his categorization of religious television viewers into three types: ritualized, instrumental (goal seekers), and curiosity seekers. I am aware that Abelman's categorization of ritualized viewers as constituting 90% of "passive" viewers is problematic (see Grimes 2002, 225). However, I use it here only to highlight the differences in viewer sensibilities and motivations.

7. The unfolding of some recent events has clarified the limited degree of autonomy available to private channels. For instance, in the first half of 2018, a state institution forced one of Pakistan's largest television networks, Geo Television, to go off air in tandem with the directives issued to cable service operators within the country (see Masood 2018). The concerned institution

undertook this measure in response to the private channel's airing of defamatory content against the country's armed forces. However, it needs to be pointed out that no state institution has to date actively claimed responsibility for this event and, further, that such extreme measures are generally employed by the state when the material being aired is of a politically, rather than religiously, sensitive nature.

THREE

DOCTRINAL ACTIVISM AND RELIGIOUS TELEVISION

THIS CHAPTER EXAMINES HOW THE changing terms of scholarly debate on television and the programming shift toward accommodating multiple Islamic viewpoints inform doctrinally founded claims to religious authority. Historically, religious authority in the Indian subcontinent has been vested in the 'ulamā's "oppositional engagement" with competing doctrinal groups, "ranging from well-structured debates through to vicious sectarian struggles" (Robinson 2013, 10). It has involved traditional scholars asserting their doctrinal group's "greatest right to speak for Islam, a claim with particular resonance in the Islamic Republic" (13). However, as indicated in the previous chapter, the pluralistic emphasis of religious talk shows, together with the constraints imposed on radical professions of doctrinal faith, makes such claims to religious authority increasingly difficult to sustain. Within the newly pluralized environment of contemporary religious shows, traditional scholars are faced with the difficult task of paradoxically having to differentiate themselves from their competing doctrinal counterparts without critiquing their religious concepts and ideas. I explore the implications of this development for Muslim politics and traditional scholarly assertions of religious authority.

A large part of my fieldwork comprised spending time with local scholars, jurists, prayer leaders, and clerics from all four mainstream religious groups in Karachi—Sunni Barelwi, Sunni Deobandi, Sunni Ahl-i Hadīth, and Shi'a Ithna Ashari. While the Jamā'at-i-Islamī (Islamic movement) also constitutes a part of the Sunni majority in Pakistan, it is distinct from the other three Sunni religious groups in that it does not represent itself as a religious educational movement, instead opting to focus its Islamization efforts on political reform

(International Crisis Group 2005).[1] Unlike its predecessors, it presents itself as "supra-sectarian," which also relates to its participation in electoral politics (3). These differences between the Jamāʿat (movement), which emerged in 1940 under the leadership of Abul Al'a Maududi, and its predecessors are also reflected in the Jamāʿat's engagement with television. Scholars from the Jamāʿat mainly participate in political talk shows as opposed to religious talk shows. For this reason, my interest in the Jamāʿat for the purposes of this book is limited to two of its scholars: Javed Ahmed Ghamidi and Israr Ahmed. Both scholars have, since their defection from the Jamāʿat, become prominent faces on religious television.

My primary interest in meeting with scholars from all four major doctrinal schools was to gauge their varying concerns in relation to the formal transformations characterizing religious talk shows. My access to religious personalities affiliated with all four schools mainly came about as a consequence of my frequent visits to variously affiliated mosques and seminaries in Karachi. In most cases I would simply spot a mosque or *madrasa* while driving to meet up with one or more of my scholarly interlocutors. Later, I would visit the institution and ask to speak to the religious authority in charge. My driver, Saleem, would also arrange for me to visit a religious personality in his area. In other instances, my scholarly interlocutors would refer me to the religious specialists within their doctrinal groups. My discussions with religious personalities associated with all four religious groups made me constantly aware of the compromises and negotiations involved in presenting on religious television shows.

For instance, I learned that scholarly decisions regarding whether to appear on religious talk shows tended to be closely aligned with the scholars' doctrinal leanings and their respective group's standing—dominant or otherwise—in mainstream religious debate. While discussing the effects of televised pluralism with various scholars, I also learned to read between the lines and to discern the subtle traces of doctrinal activism, couched in what appeared to be the scholars' generic concern for piety. More often than not, the strategies implicit in different scholarly accounts of religious shows were jointly influenced by the scholars' doctrinal affiliations and the dynamics of sectarian politics in Pakistan. In the following sections, I outline some of the challenges that religious talk shows pose to different schools of Islamic thought. In this context, I also highlight the varying scholarly attempts to counter the challenges posed by the pluralism of religious television. A key point made in this chapter is that, despite all such scholarly attempts, the diversity of Islamic representation on religious shows threatens to fundamentally alter the dynamics of sectarian activism and politics in Pakistan. I would like to indicate at the very outset that at times my analysis in this chapter may appear to pay undue attention to the Deobandi mode of dealing with televised Islamic pluralism. My intention here is not to confer a privileged place on the Deobandi doctrinal school. In fact, when this happens, it is mainly because the scholars subscribing to this school of thought position themselves very differently from the scholars affiliated with other doctrinal denominations in terms of how they choose to relate to religious programming: they are the only ones who opt to limit their appearances on religious shows.

ISSUES OF REPRESENTATION

I first became aware of the issues associated with doctrinally inspired portrayals on television during my visit to the home of the prominent Deobandi scholar Amir *Sahib* (honorific title). Amir *Sahib* was very highly regarded in his middle-class neighborhood of Gulistan e Jauhar, located in the outskirts of Karachi. His religious influence extended to his membership of the *Roohat e Halal* Committee, a committee sponsored by the federal government, established for sighting the moon on auspicious Islamic occasions, such as *Ramaḍān*, *ʿĪd al-fiṭr* (Muslim celebration at the end of the month of fasting), and *ʿĪd al-aḍḥā* (sacrificial celebration to mark the performance of *Ḥajj*). Membership of the committee is usually confined to select scholars who wield considerable influence within their doctrinal group. I had decided to initiate my research with Amir *Sahib*, largely because he was well known to my family and therefore relatively easy for me to access. I believed that Amir *Sahib*, with his depth of religious knowledge, not only would serve as a useful starting point for conceptualizing my research but also would facilitate my access to other influential Deobandi scholars. From our initial discussion, I understood that Amir *Sahib* was not a fan of religious shows. When I pressed him on why this was so, he responded with the following clarification: "Now people watch television and visit shrines. They ask the dead, instead of praying to God."

Amir *Sahib*'s derogatory reference to the growing tendency of people to visit shrines, instead of praying directly to God, is an apt depiction of the general Deobandi concern about the potential role of religious shows in popularizing Barelwi modes of Islamic thinking. More broadly, his remarks hint at a highly volatile Pakistani religious landscape, one rife with sectarian tensions, within which the identity of each doctrinal group is constituted in opposition to all other schools of Islamic thought (see Nelson 2014). Within this landscape, the antipathy between different religious groups is particularly marked in the interactions between Deobandi and Barelwi scholars. Both groups "dominate

Pakistan's religious sector" and vie for ascendancy within the Sunni community (International Crisis Group 2005, 3). In contrast, the other two groups—the Shi'a and Ahl-i Hadīth—on account of their limited following, constitute a lesser threat to the persisting influence of the two dominant Sunni groups.[2] While this also explains why followers of the Deobandi school exercise more restraint toward those of Ahl-i Hadīth persuasion, the former's marked restraint toward the latter group is also a function of both groups' shared condemnation of Barelwi and Shi'a ritual practices.[3] The adherents of both schools regard the Barelwi recourse to *taṣawwuf* (intercessional practices) and the Shi'a veneration of Ḥazrat Ali (RA) and his successors, as *bid'a* (innovation in religion) and *shirk* (idolatry), respectively.[4] For the Deobandis, the Barelwi emphasis on *taṣawwuf* and tendency to be drawn to the Prophet's (PBUH) "auratic personality," as opposed to his "person and life" (Khan 2003, 24), signifies the latter school's "attachment to ancient customs" (Sanyal 1996, 5). Alternatively, the adherents of the Barelwi school do not view their ideological emphasis on *taṣawwuf* as denoting their backwardness. Rather, for them *taṣawwuf* constitutes an essential aspect of gaining *ma'rifa* (gnostic knowledge). These conflicting positions on Islamic ritual practice explain why Amir *Sahib*'s rhetoric against religious television shows mainly revolved around the widespread diffusion of Barelwi practices. While conducting my fieldwork in Karachi, I found other Deobandi scholars similarly wary of religious talk shows; however, the reasons they proffered for their wariness differed greatly from Amir *Sahib*'s and included a consideration of factors other than the role of religious shows in popularizing Barelwi modes of Islamic thinking.

I was introduced to *Mawlānā* (learned scholar) FM, a Deobandi scholar who presided over a small *madrasa* in a predominantly working-class neighborhood in Karachi, by my driver, Saleem. Saleem resided in the same neighborhood, which was contiguous with the affluent Defence Housing Authority (DHA) residential area in Karachi. In the recent past, this neighborhood had acquired a reputation for subscribing to a particularly rigid interpretation of Islam and for serving as a refuge for militant and extremist Islamist groups hailing from the remote tribal areas of Pakistan. In keeping with this perception, the neighborhood had become a popular target for the military and secret services operations being conducted in the city. Most seminaries situated in the neighborhood fall under the control of the Ahle Sunna wa Jamā'at (ASWJ), a movement that aligns itself with the Deobandi tradition.[5]

Mawlānā FM had acquired his moniker while broadcasting his religious views on an illegally operated FM channel in the city. His channel, like other illegal FM channels in the country, had been subsequently banned by

Musharraf's government. My meeting with the *Mawlānā* did not take place in the *madrasa* itself. Instead, his assistant ushered me upstairs, into the *Mawlānā*'s living quarters, where my unexpected arrival surprised his wife and children. They subsequently informed me that they had mistaken me for an intelligence agency official, as they had already been the victims of a secret service raid earlier that week. Once the *Mawlānā* arrived, the discussion took a more focused turn, with the *Mawlānā* explaining his reservations about the broadcasting of religious shows. Throughout our conversation, the *Mawlānā* kept trying to enlist my aid in renewing his FM transmission. This was despite my repeated insistence that I could not do anything to assist him in his endeavor. Since my visit to the *Mawlānā* was preceded by my meetings with several other Deobandi scholars, I was already well aware of the Deobandi position on religious shows. Therefore, it came as no surprise to me when the *Mawlānā* apprised me of the various Deobandi rulings prohibiting the viewing of religious shows. "They [religious shows] are against the teachings of Islam. In a *ḥadīth*, it is stated that one should not even listen to a woman's voice, but these shows continue to invite women. They have no regard for Islamic principles."

In addition to highlighting the failure of religious shows to abide by the Islamic rules on the public visibility of women, *Mawlānā* FM also found fault with the tendency of popular channels to feature religious content alongside sometimes lewd and promiscuous secular entertainment content. Deploring this tendency, *Mawlānā* FM maintained that if the Deobandis were to endorse these shows, it would be tantamount to implicitly encouraging people to partake in the corrupting influence of secular entertainment programming. Instead, *Mawlānā* FM felt that the Islamic message would be better served if disseminated through other means, such as face-to-face interactions, written statements, audio CDs, or the radio. When I pressed the *Mawlānā* on why both of the issues he had highlighted could not be resolved through the establishment of a dedicated religious channel, he could offer me no plausible explanation. While a dedicated religious channel may not have offered Deobandi scholars a captive audience of the scope enjoyed by popular entertainment channels, it would nonetheless have afforded them the opportunity to propagate their doctrinal ideology without having to compromise their religious ideals. Therefore, I was surprised that, rather than follow this course of action, most notable Deobandi scholars opted instead to avoid television altogether. Because of this decision, Deobandi representation on religious shows was limited to occasional appearances by the group's university-educated or less renowned scholars. My confusion regarding the Deobandis' blanket rejection of all religious shows was further compounded by *Mawlānā* FM's emphasis on the *'awrah* (women's public visibility) as a way of justifying this decision. I could not reconcile his professed concern for abiding by the rules of gender segregation prescribed under Islam with his willingness to meet with me. While I avoided drawing the *Mawlānā*'s attention to the incongruity between his statements and his conduct, I did pick up on his subsequent admission that he was an avid listener of the morning radio show featuring Farhat Hashmi (a popular female preacher). When I tactfully drew his attention to his earlier insistence on the sin involved in listening to a female voice, *Mawlānā* FM appeared uncomfortable. After reflecting on my statement for a while, he offered me a rather flimsy explanation: he explained that it was not really Farhat Hashmi's voice that he listened to, but rather the sound of the radio. While I could have probed him further on the tenuous logic of this explanation, I chose not to pursue this line of enquiry. It was not in my interest to annoy the *Mawlānā*.

My suspicions regarding the Deobandi motives for renouncing television were further aroused when I subsequently learned that, despite the Deobandi prohibition on viewing television, some influential Deobandi scholars—such as *Muftī* Rafi Uthmani, the president of *Dār al-'Ulūm*, Korangi, the largest and most influential Deobandi *madrasa* in Karachi, and *Mawlānā* Tariq Jameel, a member of the Tablīghī Jamā'at (the movement for spreading religion)— continued to make special appearances on popular television channels.[6] Not only did *Muftī* Rafi Uthmani regularly sanction the live broadcast of his mosque sermons, in the last ten days of *Ramaḍān*, but so too did *Mawlānā* Tariq Jameel share video recordings of his sermons with popular channels in *Ramaḍān*, for the purpose of *da'wā* (invitation to accept Islam) and *iṣlāḥ* (guidance). One way of approaching these apparent inconsistencies in the Deobandi position vis-à-vis religious talk shows is to contextualize them in the state of Muslim politics in Pakistan. Two analytical considerations are pertinent to this analysis: the degree of influence the Deobandis wield in Pakistani religious public debate and the form Deobandi activism generally takes outside the framework of television. What follows, then, is an exploration of the complex relationship between some Deobandi scholars' disavowal of religious television and these two factors.

DEOBANDI INFLUENCE AND ACTIVISM

I undertook most of my initial fieldwork in the affluent neighborhood of DHA, an area that is a relatively new development (initiated in the late 1970s) primarily consisting of reclaimed land from the Arabian Sea. The housing association comes under the administration and control of retired officers of the Pakistan armed forces. Since my aim was to meet with religious personalities from all four key religious groups in Pakistan, I soon realized that confining my research to DHA would be an issue, as the area is mainly populated by seminaries and mosques affiliated with the Deobandi ASWJ. Many of the Barelwi scholars that I visited during my fieldwork regarded the ASWJ's religious monopoly over DHA as evidence of the Pakistani military's patronage of Deobandis. Even with regard to the Deobandi presence in the older parts of Karachi, *Muftī* Naeem, the Barelwi scholar affiliated with the religious show *Aalim Online*, informed me that control of some of the most renowned centers of Islamic learning in Pakistan, such as the Deobandi *Jāmiʻa ʻUlūm-ul Islāmīā*, Banori Town, had been forcibly wrested from the Barelwis during Zia's term in government. A similar point is made by a report published by the International Crisis Group (2005, 3) on the "State of Sectarianism in Pakistan," which implicates the military leaderships of both army chiefs, Yahya Khan and Ziaul Haq, in supporting and favoring the Deobandi movement.

With regard to Yahya Khan's support of Sunni extremist elements, the report notes that opposition from Bhutto's Pakistan People's Party (PPP) and a fear of Bengali nationalism prompted Yahya Khan to turn to Islamic extremists for support (9). The report also acknowledges Zia's role in furthering Deobandi ascendancy in Pakistani Muslim politics. According to the report, Zia's deliberate propagation of "orthodox" Islamic values in print and broadcast media, his patronage of militant Deobandi groups such as the SSP, his reconstitution of the Council of Islamic Ideology (a federal body of religious scholars instituted for Islamic reform) to include conservative Sunni Deobandi religious scholars, and his appointment of Deobandi "*khateebs*" and "*imams*" in government-managed mosques served to exacerbate the rivalry between the Deobandis and Barelwis (11). Because of these measures, hundreds of Barelwi mosques came under Deobandi control. Nasr (2006, 2010) additionally informs us that Deobandi domination gained further impetus on account of the Saudi Iran rivalry in the 1970s and the Afghan war in the 1980s. While the former provided the Deobandis access to Saudi funding on account of participation in the Saudi Iran proxy war, the latter encouraged them to give rise to the Taliban, in conjunction with American money and the Pakistani Military Intelligence (Nasr 2006, 100–101). The Deobandis' "pre-eminence in the *madrasa* sector," their deployment of published religious literature, and their widespread dissemination of Deobandi teachings by proselytizing movements such as the Deobandi Tablīghī Jamāʻat all allowed the religious group to amass a substantial urban and rural following in Pakistan, at the cost of the Barelwi group's majority following (International Crisis Group 2005, 3). However, of equal import in sustaining Deobandi ascendancy in religious public debate have also been the religious group's efforts on the political front, wherein the religiopolitical Deobandi party Jāmīʿat i ʿUlamā e Islam (JUI) has played a prominent role in eliciting widespread support for the group's ideology.

Given the Deobandis' domination of mainstream religious public debate, which is in spite of the Barelwi majority following, it is easier to comprehend why the former's interests are best served by avoiding religious shows. As the Deobandis presently control the majority of mosques and seminaries in Pakistan, avoiding these shows exonerates the group's scholars from justifying the Deobandi perspective on a more level playing field. Instead, the Deobandi rulings targeting religious shows serve to contain the group's followers' access to alternative claims made by competing religious groups. This is especially important given that the Barelwis are more influential than the Deobandis on television. Since the owners of popular religious channels, such as QTV, as well as popular show hosts, such as Husain, are of Barelwi persuasion, representations of Islam on television tend to be skewed toward the Barelwi tradition. Moreover, the incommensurability of televised portrayals of Islam with the Deobandis' rigid understanding of the religion makes it especially difficult for the group's scholars to justify their presence on religious shows. As already highlighted by *Mawlānā FM*, within the commercialized format of religious shows, Deobandi scholars would be compelled to make compromises in such areas as the rules on gender segregation. As the Deobandi scholars preach a very strict version of Islam, a fact that I was repeatedly made aware of during my visits to Deobandi mosques and seminaries, it is understandable that being featured alongside female presenters and audience members would be especially problematic for their image.

The Deobandis are mindful of the deleterious effect their frequent appearances on television could have on their perceived sincerity, which explains both their hesitation to employ television for Deobandi activism and their prohibition on viewing television. However, there is an alternative way to make sense of the Deobandi disavowal of television: to view it as a performance of authenticity, by means of which the religious group is able to assert its greater regard for piety in contrast to the other three groups. The Deobandi claim that the commercial emphasis in religious programming undermines religious "authenticity" and makes a mockery of "true" religious devotion positions the group in a relationship of discursive dominance with other religious groups that have seemingly succumbed to the "corrupting" pull of commercialized television. Through such claims Deobandi scholars are able to present their group's practitioners as sincerer than the practitioners of the other three groups whose scholars make regular appearances on television. In such instances, it may also be that the Deobandi concern for sustaining the group's pious image may constitute a more pressing concern than the regard for piety itself.

To clarify my proposition, I will refer to one of my meetings with a Deobandi scholar who presided over a local *madrasa* in the same neighborhood as *Mawlānā* FM. My driver, Saleem, enlisted the help of a local intermediary to arrange my meeting with the scholar. When we arrived at the *madrasa*, my driver hurried in to alert the scholar of my arrival, in accordance with the requisite protocol for gender segregation. However, he soon came out looking very worried and upset, as the scholar had changed his mind about meeting with me. The scholar also came out shortly after, to reiterate and explain his refusal to me, which he claimed was mainly on account of my being a woman. On my pleading with him to reconsider his decision, the scholar reluctantly ushered me into the *madrasa* and asked me to sit around the corner from him, so that he could no longer lay his eyes on me. However, I could tell that he was perturbed by the fact that we were being observed closely by his students and the assistant *qarī*. This was despite the fact that I was fully covered at the time, in the customary black ʿ*abāya* (loose gown covering), *hijāb*, and *niqāb*. Five minutes into the meeting, he once again iterated that he did not feel comfortable answering my queries. Instead he referred me to his esteemed teachers at the *Jāmiʿa 'Ulūm-ul Islāmīā*, Banori Town, who he insisted had better protocols in place for managing their interactions with the opposite gender. I finally gave up and left the *madrasa*. Throughout this exchange, I could sense that the scholar's discomfort mainly arose from a sense of being observed by his staff and students. Despite his reservations on inviting me inside the *madrasa*, he had nonetheless come out to speak with me and explain the reason for his refusal, thus undermining the very rules he claimed to uphold. I therefore felt that the scholar may have been more forthcoming had others not been observing us. This incident also clarifies why the commercial format of religious television shows, especially the relaxation of gender segregation rules, can be problematic for Deobandi scholars. Within this framework, the Deobandi scholars' recourse to ʿ*awrah* for justifying their denunciation of religious shows also renders the ʿ*awrah* a "disciplinary practice," by means of which the more normative and rigid versions of Islam associated with Deobandi activism are made more central to the attainment of "happiness, purity, wisdom, perfection, or immortality" (Foucault 1988, 18; see also Asad 1993). One must consider how these discourses allow the Deobandi group to sustain its following and distinguish itself from competing groups while simultaneously eluding the restrictions on doctrinal activism imposed by the pluralistic religious show format. While I have already covered most of these restrictions in the previous chapter, I identify an additional one here that may further undermine the potential of television for Deobandi activism.

VIEWER BACKLASH

As previously highlighted, the channel owners' and producers' considerations regarding corporate sponsorship interests, a fragmented and diverse religious television viewership, and state agendas generally circumvent the employment of religious shows for radical assertions of doctrinal faith. However, religious scholars presenting on religious shows have an additional motivation for toning down their doctrinal activism: the possibility of viewer backlash. To explore this concept further, I revisit one of my visits to a government primary school for boys in Karachi. My visit to the school came about as a result of my broader aim to access informants from diverse socioeconomic and religious backgrounds, including those studying and teaching at secular educational institutions in Karachi. This school had been recently adopted by a charitable foundation as part of a larger initiative to improve the state of public education in the city. During my visit to the school, the administration assigned me to Asif, a male teacher in his early thirties who aligned himself with the Barelwi tradition. Despite holding a degree from a prestigious business school in Karachi, Asif had opted to pursue a more spiritually rewarding path by teaching those less advantaged than himself. Asif's long beard and the hem of his *shalwar* (trousers), which he wore above his ankles, attested to his conservative religious orientation. During our discussion, I learned that Asif was skeptical of all religious shows. He tended to view them as instigating doctrinally inspired politics in the country. To clarify his position, Asif gave me the example of a previously aired religious show on which the popular self-styled scholar Dr. Israr Ahmed had been invited to narrate the events surrounding the martyrdom of Ḥazrat Ali (RA).[7] Asif recounted how, instead of simply describing the events, Dr. Ahmed had resorted to critiquing the Shi'a practice of commemorating the incident of *Karbalā* with *ta'ziyas* (replicas of tombs of the martyrs of *Karbalā*) and *mātam* (beating of the chest and other forms of self-inflicted torture, such as self-flagellation with small knives or daggers and walking on fired coals).[8] Asif explained that Dr. Ahmed's provocative remarks had sparked a spate of Shi'a retaliation against the scholar, which had taken the form of street protests and abusive graffiti painted on city walls. The graffiti had declared Dr. Ahmed "a dog" and an "enemy of the nation." Asif recalled how, on account of the Shi'a reprisal against Dr. Ahmed, the self-styled scholar had been compelled to disappear from television for a while.

Asif's narration, while aimed at clarifying the inflammatory potential of religious shows, is also useful for exploring the limitations of television for the purposes of doctrinal activism. A pertinent consideration here is how a religious scholar's derogatory references to a competing group's practices can provoke widespread retaliation from the targeted group's adherents. Thus, for scholars presenting on religious shows, an anticipatory fear of provoking such instances of backlash can act as a powerful motivator for avoiding the vilification of alternative religious practices. When arguing against the designation of Islam as a coercive discipline, in Western, liberal theory, Asad (2003, 184) contends that even within the so-called liberal public domain the "enjoyment of free speech presupposes not merely the physical ability to speak but to be heard, a condition without which speaking to some effect is not possible." For this reason, Asad warns us that "the domain of free speech is always shaped by preestablished limits." Within the context of Pakistani religious shows, the restrictions placed on hostile and confrontational expressions of doctrinal activism are imposed not only by producers and the Pakistani state but also by the adherents of opposing religious groups. As acknowledged by one of my informants, Nina, who worked as a marketing executive at a popular local news channel, religious scholars appearing on television were now too savvy to openly indulge in sectarian politics on television.

The way that religious television implicitly compels those presenting on it to tone down their hostility toward competing groups and to adopt a more tactful approach is in stark contrast to Islam's propagation outside the framework of television—especially within the confines of religious seminaries and mosques, where no such limitations apply. Television's restrictions on religious scholars are especially constraining for the Deobandi group, whose activism is largely premised on a rejection of Barelwi and Shi'a intercessional practices and whose advantage in the mosque and *madrasa* sector could essentially be neutralized by the restrictive and pluralistic environment of religious shows. In contrast, religious shows have the opposite effect on the position of the Barelwi group, in that they allow scholars to revive the group's authoritative influence by winning back adherents through the diffusion of Barelwi practices and modes of Islamic thinking. These contrasting implications of religious television for different doctrinal groups also had a varying effect on the ways that these groups reflected on the Islamic status of televisual technology.

THE BATTLE OF *FATĀWĀ*

Not surprisingly, the majority of objections to the use of televisual technology for religious propagation came from scholars aligning themselves with the Deobandi group. These objections primarily drew on the Islamic prohibition placed on *taṣwīr* (picture) and its employment in televisual broadcasts.

During the course of my fieldwork, I came across many Deobandi scholars who argued that since *taṣwīr* had been declared *ḥarām* (forbidden) under Islamic law, this also applied to any technology that employed it. The first invocation of the un-Islamic status of *taṣwīr* to justify Deobandi absence from religious television came from *Muftī* Qadir, during my visit to the center for Islamic rulings at the Deobandi seminary, *Jāmi'a 'Ulūm-ul Islāmīā*, Banori Town. I was referred to the seminary by some of my Deobandi scholarly interlocutors, who had received their initial Islamic training at the seminary and held it in high esteem. There is a general perception in Karachi that *Jāmi'a 'Ulūm-ul Islāmīā* favors an extremist Deobandi orientation and has trained and produced some members of Islamist militant and extremist groups, such as the Taliban, the ASWJ, and the Lashkar e Jhangvi (Army of Jhangvi). My visit to the seminary's center for Islamic rulings came about as a result of my association with Muhammad, a practitioner of the Deobandi tradition. Although Muhammad officially aligned himself with *Mawlānā* Tariq Jameel's Deobandi Tablīghī Jamā'at, he frequently offered his prayers at the mosque adjoining the seminary. His consequent familiarity with *Jāmi'a 'Ulūm-ul Islāmīā*'s administration prompted me to enlist his aid when arranging my visit to the seminary. While I had also asked Muhammad to mediate my access to the seminary's *banāt* (female quarters), the administration summarily denied my request on some flimsy pretext. Prior to my planned visit, Muhammad came over to my house to apprise me of the requisite attire for entering the institution. In accordance with Muhammad's instructions, and despite the sweltering heat at that time of year, I donned the customary '*abāya*, *hijāb*, and *niqāb*, together with socks and gloves. The latter two sartorial choices were meant to ensure that my feet and hands, along with the rest of me, would be well protected from the gaze of the seminary's male staff. On my entry into the seminary's center for rulings, I was ushered into a small ladies' enclosure, separated from the male portion by means of curtains and a bookshelf. I was later granted an audience with *Muftī* Qadir, an Islamic jurist at the center, who responded to my questions from across the bookshelf.

While *Muftī* Qadir generally disapproved of religious shows, a key consideration mediating his disapproval was the "forbidden" status of television images. He argued that "if pictures of animate beings are shown in a place, angels don't tread there." For him, this also implied that no *rahmat* (blessing) could be derived from the use of television. Referring to the incorporation of the Islamically prohibited *taṣwīr* in television technology, *Muftī* Qadir insisted that the path of sin would not result in well-being for anyone. *Muftī* Qadir's ruling against television drew on a famous *ḥadīth* cited in Sahih-Al-Bukhari (7/833) and narrated by Abu Talha, in which it is stated, "Angels do not enter a house in which there are dogs or pictures." Subsequently, when I raised the issue of *taṣwīr* with my Barelwi interlocutors, many of them responded by pointing out to me the inherent contradiction between the Deobandi ruling on television and the conduct of some prominent Deobandi scholars, who continued to make special appearances on television despite their group's conflation of television images with the proscribed *taṣwīr*. By delineating this contradiction as evidence of Deobandi hypocrisy, my Barelwi interlocutors were thus able to call into question the sincerity of Deobandi scholars and simultaneously justify their own religious group's presence on religious shows. When I questioned the prolific Deobandi scholar *Mawlānā* Kamaluddin on the ostensible contradiction characterizing the Deobandi stance on religious shows, he responded by presenting me with a book that he had published on the subject. *Mawlānā* Kamaluddin taught at the renowned Deobandi *madrasa Jāmīʻa Clifton*. His book, which is a compilation of arguments and counterarguments by Deobandi scholars on the Islamic status of television, presents a clearer picture of the Deobandi position with regard to the employment of television. Primarily, the book highlights that, while there is general consensus among Deobandi scholars on the un-Islamic nature of *taṣwīr*, there is widespread disagreement on whether television images constitute *taṣwīr* (Mustarshid, n.d.). *Mawlānā* Kamaluddin explained that these differences in opinion, characterizing the Deobandi school's understanding of what constitutes *taṣwīr*, had grown even more marked with the increased prominence and popularity of religious shows.

Within this internal debate, the Deobandi scholarly arguments primarily revolve around the scientific analysis of the properties of an image produced by a camera. Some scholars claim that the image formed by a camera is distinct from the image transmitted by a television or computer screen. The Deobandi scholars who view both types of images as scientifically distinct hold that digital images on television or computer screens bear closer resemblance to a shadow, a collection of rays, or a reflection as it appears in the mirror. Further, they claim that such images, unlike camera images, are transient and, unless fixed through printing, do not qualify as *taṣāwīr* (pl. of *taṣwīr*). The perceived distinction between camera images and digital images, together with an understanding of the latter as mainly an amalgam of rays, has prompted some Deobandi scholars to take a more lenient (and, in some cases, expedient) approach toward the deployment of television. Moreover, even among scholars who hold a stricter view of television images as falling within the scope of the forbidden *taṣwīr*, there are those who argue that this rule can be bypassed if the use of television is considered beneficial for the spread of Islam. However, there remain quite a few scholars who do not subscribe to this point of view and who continue to regard television and its use for any purpose as proscribed under Islam. The following *fatwā* issued by a jurist affiliated with the prominent Deobandi *madrasa Jāmi'a Binoria*, SITE area, Karachi, in relation to the Islamic status of the internet, clarifies the latter Deobandi perspective. I have translated both the query and the response to it by the Islamic jurist *Muftī* Ilahi. The question was as follows:

> *Asalāmualaykum* (Peace be upon you). The *'ulamā* of Deoband believe that good and evil cannot collect in the same place. If TV is a collection of good and evil, so too is the internet such a collection, whereby the pornographic sites represent the evil and the Islamic statements represent the good. Please clarify this point. *Jazakallāh* (As per the will of Allah).

Muftī Manzoor Ilahi (2011) has issued the following ruling in response to this question:

> The contemporary shape that television has taken implies that its deployment for the dissemination of the Islamic message will have more costs than benefits attached to it, as the evil on it far exceeds the good. However, if such a situation prevails where legitimate Islamic shows can be purged of their evil focus, and of the deleterious influence of advertisements, even then, simply on the basis of depicting images of animate beings, television will not be regarded as Islamic. However, to compare television to the computer is not correct, as the utilization of the internet is subject to the will of user, which is not the case with television.

While *Muftī* Manzoor Ilahi's ruling raises many questions, especially in relation to the dubious distinction it draws between the agentive capacities of television viewers and internet users, what is important for our purposes is that it condemns the use of television, irrespective of the purpose. In his book, *Mawlānā* Kamaluddin similarly situates himself against the deployment of television, as according to him television images are not distinct from the forbidden *taṣwīr* (Mustarshid, n.d.). However, while discussing this issue with him, I got the feeling that he may have been inclined to take a more lenient view if he had been invited to present on a religious show.

With regard to the Deobandi scholars who are inclined to take a more lenient view of preaching on television, such leniency should not be perceived as implying their lesser regard for, or disregard of, the Prophetic tradition or as implying a view of the tradition as no longer applicable in the contemporary context. In the context of Egypt, Hirschkind (2001, 9; see also Zaman 2005) similarly notes how all Muslim debates on the Islamic tradition are grounded in a view of the tradition as stemming from a divine source and therefore as not subject to human will with respect to its implementation. For Hirschkind, therefore, it is the "correct" interpretation of the tradition that constitutes the discursive foundation from which "opposing viewpoints" emerge. Alternatively, in Pakistan, the differing scholarly opinions on the status of television reflect modes of engagement with the *taṣwīr* tradition that are less concerned with determining the "correct" interpretation of the tradition and more so with figuring out the tradition's "proper" application in the contemporary media context. When the disagreement on the status of television is confined to scholars within the Deobandi school, it can be seen as synonymous with a scholarly effort to determine how the Islamic tradition should be lived in practice (see Fischer and Abedi 1990). However, when the same debate involves a doctrinal component, in that it is employed by scholars of Deobandi persuasion to undermine the sincerity of competing doctrinal groups, it should be perceived as congruent with the attempt to position the Deobandi school in a relationship of discursive dominance with all other doctrinal groups, who continue to employ television for the dissemination of their ideology (see Asad 1993, 210).[9]

Alternatively, in contrast to the Deobandi school, within which some scholars disagree on the designation of television images, the three remaining major doctrinal groups have tended to display considerable clarity and cohesiveness vis-à-vis their decision to employ television for religious propagation. Especially with regard to Barelwi scholars, we also need to bear in mind that the decision to appear on television could also be expediently motivated, in that by employing television for the propagation of their school's ideology, Barelwi scholars can work toward reinstating their group's dominant position in religious public debate. The Barelwi scholar Professor Rahman alluded to this as being a major consideration guiding his group's decision to enhance its presence on religious television. According to Professor Rahman, prior to the introduction of these shows, the other Sunni *masālik* (doctrinal schools, pl. of *maslak*) were much more successful than the Barelwi school in eliciting popular support for their respective ideologies, despite the latter group's majority standing in Pakistan. In Professor Rahman's opinion, in the face of growing competition from the other schools, the only option available to Barelwi scholars was to make increased use of television to regain their group's influence.

Not surprisingly then, the majority of Barelwi rulings that I came across in the field also reflected Professor Rahman's view and condoned the use of television for the propagation of Islam. I learned of one such Barelwi *fatwā* during my meeting with the prominent Barelwi leader and television scholar *Allama* Kokab Noorani. The *fatwā*, which was in stark contrast to the Deobandi rulings above, not only endorses but even encourages the use of television for the spread of Islam. A key justification contained in the *fatwā* for encouraging the Barelwi deployment of television is that, if "authentic" (which in this case implies Barelwi) religious scholars do not use this medium, then the "wrong" people (other doctrinal groups) will take over the medium for the spread of their ideology. I have presented an understanding of the *fatwā* below, which also derives its "authenticity" from the scientific distinction between photographic and television images. The *fatwā*, which has been published in a *Daʿwat i Islāmī* magazine titled *TV awr Movie* (TV and movie), provides detailed justifications for the use of television for religious purposes (*Daʿwat i Islāmī* Organisation, n.d.).[10] It holds that a mirror image does not fall within the scope of *taṣwīr*, as laid out in the Prophetic tradition. At the same time, it establishes that an image formed through a collection of rays does not constitute a *taṣwīr*, even if it appears to be so. It similarly declares that a reflection that forms on a liquid or steel surface does not fall under the scope of the *taṣwīr* prohibition. Instead, the *fatwā* clarifies that, just as a mirror image is not prohibited because it does not in actuality constitute a *taṣwīr* in the Islamic sense of the term, neither then is the image on the television screen prohibited because this too, in reality, is simply a collection of rays. The *fatwā* thus concludes that it is incorrect to apply the Islamic prohibition on *taṣwīr* to television images. However, the *fatwā* contains a provision whereby if at some point in the future it is proven that television images do, in fact, fall under the classification of proscribed *taṣwīr*, then the same prohibition will also apply to them.

An interesting point highlighted by the distinction between the Barelwi and Deobandi rulings is how different groups can deploy the same religious tradition to support two very distinct positions with regard to the deployment of television (see Metcalf 2004; Skovgaard-Petersen 1997). When seeking to understand the variations in Muslim understanding of Islam, many past anthropological studies have conceptualized Islam in terms of the distinctions between the local and lived manifestations of the religion and a universal essentialized version of the religion found in Islamic scriptures (e.g., Geertz 1971; Bujra 1971).[11] This way of conceptualizing Islam draws on the model of religion proposed by Robert Redfield (1956), wherein he suggests that religion can be divided into "great tradition," which is "reflexive, orthodox, textual," and "consciously cultivated and handed down," (Redfield 1956, quoted in Lukens-Bull 1999, 4), and "little tradition," which is "heterodox, peripheral, local, popular, and unreflective" (see Anjum 2007).[12] However, as subsequently contended by el-Zein, in seeking a hierarchy of the different versions of Islam, these studies are guilty of essentially partaking in theology and not anthropology. What el-Zein argues in relation to these studies also holds true for the distinct Deobandi and Barelwi positions on televisual technology, where it is impossible to assign a "higher truth-value" to either doctrinal group's proposition (see el-Zein 1977, quoted in Eaton 2003).[13] Instead, these distinct positions foreground the creativity and reflexivity of different, doctrinally inspired, scholarly positions, despite the scholars' sustained adherence to the Prophetic tradition, and are in contrast to the passivity generally ascribed to traditional scholars.

Here we can usefully apply Asad's (2009b) proposition on Islam as constituting a "discursive tradition" to make further sense of the debate on the *taṣwīr*'s application.[14] Asad's proposition in this context is heavily influenced by MacIntyre's (1988) work on Western philosophical traditions. According to Asad (2009b), an anthropological recourse to conceptualizing Islam as a "discursive tradition" does not imply the essentialization of certain practices as more authentic but rather involves the recognition "that the authenticity or orthodoxy of these has to be argued for from within the tradition and embraced or rejected according to its own criteria" (Anjum 2007, 663). In fact, for Asad (1993, 195), "belonging to a tradition doesn't preclude involvement in vigorous debate over the meanings of its formative texts (even over which texts are formative) and over the need for radical reform of the tradition." Instead, Asad argues that "the selectivity with which people approach their tradition doesn't necessarily undermine their claim to its integrity. Nor does the attempt to adapt the older concerns of a tradition's followers to their new predicament in itself dissolve the coherence of that tradition—indeed that is precisely the object of argument among those who claim to be upholding the essence of the tradition." Asad's proposition works especially well to elucidate the terms of the Barelwi argument on the impracticability of applying the Prophetic tradition to television images. An important consideration here is that the Barelwis are only able to resist a particular application of the tradition so long as they do not actively deny the relevance of the tradition itself.

The differing employments of the Islamic tradition by different religious groups and scholars are also considered by Skovgaard-Petersen (1997) in the context of his research on Egyptian *muftīs* and the exercise of generating *fatāwā*. Drawing on the "hermeneutic enterprise," Skovgaard-Petersen (374) suggests that the exegetical exercise of deriving a *fatwā* involves more than a simple reference to religious tradition, as it is framed by traditional as well as present imperatives. Skovgaard-Petersen's observation is also relevant for understanding the differing instrumental considerations underlying the distinction between the Deobandi and the Barelwi points of view, in that whereas for the former group it is more beneficial to advocate a prohibition on television, for the latter it is more advantageous to encourage the employment of television. The contrasting doctrinal references to the tradition of *taṣwīr*, which are closely aligned with each group's distinct mode of activism and degree of influence in religious public debate, also clarify an understanding of Muslim politics as grounded in the continuous negotiation and contestation between what it means to be a Muslim or how Islam should be lived in practice (Mahmood 2005, 103). Within this framework, each group's employment of *fatāwā* for asserting its views on the tradition also renders the *fatwā* a discursive modality by means of which competing doctrinal groups assert their superior understanding of Islamic tradition (see Asad 1993). What is at stake in these different rulings is not the tradition or its "authenticity," or even its application to televised images, but rather the political standing of different doctrinal groups in religious debate.

DISCURSIVE STRATEGIES

While the Deobandis were the only religious group to actively resist employing religious shows for the purposes of religious propagation, they were not the only ones to invoke the commercial impetus of religious shows as a means of asserting their group's superior piety. A similar recourse also served the other religious groups in distinguishing themselves from their doctrinally distinct counterparts. As already noted in chapter 2, *Muftī* Umair's condescending references to scholars of alternative persuasions being financially compensated for their appearances on popular channels were aimed at distinguishing his group's scholars as above such corporeal concerns on account of the latter's closer affiliation to the Barelwi QTV channel. Similar claims regarding the commercial emphasis of religious shows facilitated Ahl-i Hadīth scholars in contesting the Barelwis' domination of mainstream religious media. Scholars belonging to the Ahl-i Hadīth school would often try to impress upon me how the televised commemorations of Barelwi occasions such as *ʿĪd Mīlād-un Nabī*, while in keeping with the commercially oriented format of religious shows, were not Islamically appropriate.

Moreover, an emphasis on the commercial underpinnings of religious show production was not the only discursive strategy that religious scholars employed to distinguish their group's ideology from competing doctrines. For Barelwi scholars, whose primary aim was to uphold their group's majority standing and sustain their group's control over religious programming, the pluralistic format of religious shows posed the greatest problem. With this issue in mind, some Barelwi scholars contended that the inclusion of the two minority groups—the Ahl-i Hadīth and the Shiʿa—incited "*intishaar*" (disconcertment) and "confusion" among the masses who had not been adequately schooled in gauging the "authenticity" of multiple conflicting doctrinal claims. The Barelwi contentions in this context reveal that "participation in a plural, multivocal world is not the same as acknowledging or even embracing it" (Eickelman and Anderson 1997, 61). Moreover, the very fact that these contentions are not founded in ideological differences, but are rather more concerned with the minority status of the two competing groups, indicates that a desire for Muslim homogeneity and "majority rule," rather than a concern for the "finer points of religious doctrine" and "ritual practice," inform much of the traditional scholarly engagement with Islam (Nelson 2009, 607).

In accordance with the Barelwi concern about the representation of minority groups on religious shows, some Barelwi scholars also advocated for religious shows to avoid featuring discussions on doctrinally sensitive and controversial issues. This suggestion was made by the renowned Barelwi television scholar *Mawlānā* Ahmed, who firmly maintained that the general public should not be privy to such sensitive discussions. My meeting with *Mawlānā* Ahmed came about as a result of one of my field trips to a prominent Barelwi *mazār* (shrine) that also served as a mosque for Barelwis residing in the area. On my visit to the shrine, I learned from the authorities that *Mawlānā* Ahmed frequented the place every Friday to lead and address the prayer congregation. I already knew about the *Mawlānā*'s association with religious programming, and I was eager for an opportunity to interact with him, on account of his forty years of affiliation with religious television and his regular appearances on popular religious shows such as *Tafheem-e-Deen* and *Fahm ul Quran*. *Mawlānā* Ahmed was very hospitable during my Friday visits to the shrine, and he spent considerable amounts of time with me, tirelessly entertaining my research-related queries. During these discussions, I learned that even though the *Mawlānā* was favorably disposed toward religious programming in general, he found it difficult to condone the pluralistic orientation of contemporary religious shows. Instead, he insisted that religious programming should focus on the more generic aspects of religion and draw content exclusively from the Qur'ān and *Sunna*. *Mawlānā* Ahmed's willingness to abandon his doctrinal perspective in favor of a more generic emphasis is symptomatic of his concerns regarding the diffusion of alternative ideologies in religious public debate. In the context of Mali, Zappa (2015, 55) notes that Sufi publications' willingness to self-censor "some of their perceived 'excesses,'" and thus concede to "some of the arguments of their opponents," is the price these publications pay for reasserting their ascendancy in televised religious debate. Alternatively, in *Mawlānā* Ahmed's case, a willingness to renounce his group's "esoteric episteme" and focus on the more generic content contained in the Qurʾān and *Sunna* should not be perceived as necessarily implying an outright abandonment of Barelwi activism on television. Rather, we should also consider how such calls by Barelwi scholars could reflect their group's resolve to employ subtler forms of persuasion on television for the dissemination of their ideology. The following narration by the literary scholar and journalist Moin *Sahib* serves to illustrate this point.

According to Moin *Sahib*, the Barelwi *Muftī e Aʿzam* (Grand *Muftī*), *Muftī* Muneeb ur Rahman, had been invited on a popular channel to narrate the incident of *Sulaḥ al Ḥudaybiya* (peace treaty of *Ḥudaybiya*). *Sulaḥ al Ḥudaybiya* was a truce negotiated by the Prophet (PBUH) and his companions, with the non-Muslims of Mecca, in order for the former to gain access to the *Kaʿba* for the performance of *Ḥajj* (holy pilgrimage). However, the non-Muslim Meccans not only retreated from the truce but also took *Ḥazrat* Usman (the Prophet's [PBUH] companion, *RA*) captive when he went to mediate with them on behalf of the Muslims. *Ḥazrat* Usman's (*RA*) capture led the Muslims to mistakenly believe that he had been slain by the Meccans. In Moin *Sahib*'s opinion, while narrating these events, the Barelwi scholar *Muftī* Muneeb had skillfully employed "journalistic *angling*" to subtly reinforce the Barelwi belief regarding the Prophet's (PBUH) divine gift of *ʿilm-i ghayb* (unseen knowledge). He had done so by associating the Prophet's (PBUH) ability to discern a sincere person from a *munāfiq* (hypocrite) with the Barelwi belief regarding the Prophet's (PBUH) gift of unseen knowledge.

> For instance, *Muftī* Muneeb ur Rahman said that there was a rumor that *Ḥazrat* Usman (*RA*) had been slain by the nonbelievers. The *Bayt-i-Rizwān* (vow of Rizwān) symbolized the Prophet's (PBUH) and his companions' promise to exact revenge for *Ḥazrat* Usman's (*RA*) murder. At the time of taking the vow, the Prophet (PBUH) had, instead of placing only his right hand in the vow, also extended his left hand. *Muftī* Muneeb claimed that the left hand symbolically represented the Prophet's (PBUH) belief that *Ḥazrat* Usman (*RA*) was alive. As it happened, it was later discovered by the Muslims that *Ḥazrat* Usman (*RA*) was indeed alive. *Muftī* Muneeb accounted for the Prophet's (PBUH) act of placing both hands in the vow as evidence of the Prophet's (PBUH) possession of unseen knowledge. According to *Muftī* Muneeb, this explained why the Prophet (PBUH) had extended both hands when taking the vow, as one represented *Ḥazrat* Usman (*RA*).

Moin *Sahib* then proceeded to give me his own interpretation of *Sulaḥ al Ḥudaybiya*. He voiced a key question: If what *Muftī* Muneeb claimed were true, then why would the Prophet (PBUH) have been obliged to take the vow to avenge *Ḥazrat* Usman's (*RA*) death in the first place? Moin *Sahib* was of the view that a well-versed religious scholar like *Muftī* Muneeb could skillfully manipulate the Islamic tradition with full authority. He worried that a common person would be unable to detect the flaws in *Muftī* Muneeb's logic and would thus blindly accept the scholar's interpretation of the events.

While analyzing *Muftī* Muneeb's narration of the Prophetic tradition, Moin *Sahib* made an important point about the susceptibility of the tradition to its varied deployment by different religious groups to support their respective beliefs and ideas about religion. According to Fischer and Abedi (1990, 146), the contradictions and fabrications inherent in *ḥadīth* literature imply that this literature must be approached "dialectically (i.e., aware of the range of counter arguments in a given period), hermeneutically (i.e., aware of the allusions and contexts, nuances and changes in word usage), and dialogically (i.e., aware of the political others against whom assertions are made)."[15] Further, Moin *Sahib*'s observations about *Muftī* Muneeb's narration are useful for noting how some religious scholars negotiate and resist the constraints imposed by television by employing subtler techniques of persuasion to promote their beliefs. However, such covert tactics, while useful for reasserting Barelwi ideology in the pluralized religious show context, can also be counterproductive. My proposition draws on Willis (1977), who views any form of resistance as reinforcing the domination of the very structure it seeks to resist. I propose that the Barelwis, much like Willis's (175) labor class, are "not passive bearers of [Islamic] ideology, but active appropriators, who reproduce existing structures [which in this case is an Islamic discourse that is seemingly without Barelwi ideology] only through struggle, contestations and a partial penetration of those structures." The covert nature of these Barelwi tactics on television thus confers on them a functionality in reaffirming a notion of "legitimate" Islam as devoid of the Barelwi emphasis on intercessional practices.

In contrast to my Barelwi interlocutors, the majority of Ahl-i Hadīth and Shi'a scholars, in line with their minority standing, welcomed the pluralistic trend in religious programming. Scholars from both groups confided in me that on account of this trend their scholars were more able to clarify their doctrinal perspectives to the Pakistani masses. Another advantage perceived by both groups was this trend's encouragement of a more peaceful resolution of doctrinal disputes, allowing scholars to debate their doctrinal differences in a calm and dignified manner. Scholars from both groups felt that this development was in stark contrast to the more confrontational modes of engagement employed by different religious groups outside the pluralistic context of religious shows. An appreciation of televised pluralism was especially marked in the case of my Shi'a interlocutors, who believed that this programming development would allow their group's scholars to dispel some of the general Sunni hostility toward the Shi'a sect. Their views in this context also indicate how vulnerable Shi'a Pakistanis feel in a religious landscape where members of their group have been increasingly subjected to an unprecedented degree of Sunni rhetoric and violence.

By contrast, my Ahl-i Hadīth interlocutors viewed the benefits of religious shows as emerging from their potential to allow their group to amass a greater following. For this reason, much Ahl-i Hadīth opposition toward religious shows was primarily focused on the Barelwi domination of televised Islamic discourse and the corresponding unequal representation of the Ahl-i Hadīth perspective. According to the Ahl-i Hadīth scholar *Mawlānā* Safdar Usman, Ahl-i Hadīth scholars were not invited to present on religious shows as often as Barelwi scholars, despite having similar or superior scholarly credentials. On account of this belief, some Ahl-i Hadīth scholars also viewed religious talk shows as reinforcing their group's marginalization in mainstream Islamic discourse. Some Shi'a scholars echoed this concern, feeling that the current representation of doctrinal groups on religious shows was far from democratic. Since time limitations do exist on religious television shows, it is natural that these scholars, particularly those belonging to the minority religious groups, would have been concerned about their unequal representation. However, the fact that similar accusations were also made by scholars belonging to the two majority Sunni groups helped me realize that all religious groups sought exclusive representation on television.

In *Mawlānā* Usman's case, his concern for his group's adequate representation also stemmed from a fear that the privileged presence of the two Sunni majority groups would encourage a greater regard for *taqlīd* among television audiences and thus undermine the importance of the Qur'ān and *ḥadīth*, the two most important prescriptive texts for Muslims. Sanyal (1996, 93) elaborates how debates among the Barelwis, Deobandis, and Ahl-i Hadīth have commonly revolved around the Barelwi and Deobandi insistence on the absolute necessity of *taqlīd* (four Sunni schools of Islamic jurisprudence). While Ahl-i Hadīth give preference to *ijtihād* (the exercise of individual reasoning, critical deliberation, and deduction), the Deobandis and Barelwis argue that there is no *mujtahid* (practitioner of *ijtihād*) alive today and therefore view *taqlīd* as the only route to the restoration of the Prophet's (PBUH) *Sunna* (Sanyal 1996, 12, 174–77). Only by accounting for these ideological differences can we also theorize about *Mawlānā* Usman's lament about the prominence of *taqlīd* in televised Islamic discourse as constituting a form of Ahl-i Hadīth activism by means of which Ahl-i Hadīth scholars can both undermine the beliefs and practices of the two majority Sunni groups and assert their group's ideological superiority.

TELEVISED PLURALISM AND TRANSFORMATIONS IN RELIGIOUS DEBATE

In facilitating a consideration of the conflicting ways in which scholars of varying doctrinal persuasions position themselves in relation to religious television shows, I hope to draw attention to the role played by both the formal qualities of television and the contextual realities of the scholars' institutional and doctrinal affiliation in shaping the scholars' engagement with these shows. For Barelwi, Ahl-i Hadīth, and Shi'a scholars, working within the constraints set by television is seen as useful for countering the Deobandi advantage in the mosque and *madrasa* sector. Alternatively, the fact that Deobandi scholars continue to refer to religious talk shows as a means of asserting their superior Islamic conformance indicates that, despite Deobandi claims to the contrary, religious talk shows remain very much susceptible to their myriad deployments by all four religious groups. However, the vulnerability of religious talk shows to their varied deployment by different groups does not necessarily render them unproblematic for doctrinal activism. In fact, the nature of pluralism enabled by religious talk shows, when combined with the ubiquitous nature of satellite television, is fraught with problems for all four religious groups, compelling key transformations in the ways Islam is represented and doctrinal ascendancy claimed in religious public debate.

The allowances that private television channels give to varied expressions of Sunni faith are particularly problematic for the propagation of Deobandi ideology, which otherwise dominates mainstream Islamic discourse. In his assessment of Islamic pluralism in Mali, Zappa (2015, 53), drawing on Soares (2005, 247; see also Soares 1999) notes that the need to reach some sort of consensus in religious debate may "exclude from the public sphere certain categories of social actors whose practices were more tolerated, or even valued, in the recent past." In the context of Pakistani religious shows, this category of excluded social actors comprises the Deobandi group, whose activism is mainly asserted in response to the Barelwi and Shi'a intercessional practices, which they term religious innovation and idolatry, respectively. I have noted earlier that such modes of radical doctrinal activism are increasingly difficult to accommodate in the contemporary, pluralized religious show context, where the emphasis is on articulating more conciliatory or generic Islamic perspectives. Therefore, in addition to perceiving the Deobandi absence from religious television shows as a strategy willingly employed by the group's scholars, we need to also consider it as a compulsion, necessitated by formal developments in religious programming. In the latter context, we also need to bear in mind that the Deobandi absence from television, while a useful strategy for asserting the group's sincerity, could equally negate the group's advantage in the mosque and *madrasa* sector. In refusing to capitalize on religious television's broad reach and its potential for the proliferation of Deobandi beliefs, Deobandi scholars essentially leave this avenue open for other religious groups to exploit. The Deobandi scholars are aware of the dangers of doing so, and they are mindful of the fact that many of their followers continue to watch religious television shows despite their exhortations to the contrary. It is perhaps for these reasons that some mainstream Deobandi scholars, such as *Muftī* Rafi Uthmani, are rethinking their rigid stance toward television and considering the introduction of a Deobandi exclusive channel.

Even for the other three religious groups who participate on television, their ability to work within the constraints imposed by television and employ religious shows to advance their group's aims needs to be evaluated more critically. Since the Barelwis currently dominate televised religious content, it is understandable that their employment of television is mainly geared toward countering the Deobandi influence in mosques and seminaries. However, the fact that Barelwi activism on television needs to be couched in an ostensible focus on the Qur'ān and *Sunna* is in fact also a tacit acknowledgment that the group's beliefs and practices fall outside the scope of "legitimate" Islam. Moreover, it is not only the Barelwis who are compelled to tone down their activism on television. A key problem that religious television poses for all religious groups who present on it is that it compels them to acknowledge the pluralism of Islamic thought. As Nelson (2009, 603) points out, sectarianism in Pakistan does not so much revolve around an "effort to highlight, or exploit, the terms of religious or sectarian difference" as it entails "a deliberate effort to emphasize, even exaggerate, the terms of religious (or doctrinal) uniformity." Thus, participation in religious shows that aim to accommodate Pakistan's religious diversity is fraught with issues even for the two minority groups, as to participate with scholars of competing persuasions is to also acknowledge the legitimacy of their claims. It is also akin to accepting that there may be different ways of engaging with and living Islam.

These developments have profound implications for religious public debate, which is increasingly characterized by the accommodation of different Islamic viewpoints. One major consequence of this development is that it alters the dynamics of sectarian politics, especially in terms of the diminished influence of the two majority religious groups. However, and perhaps even more importantly, the newly pluralized format of religious shows has adverse consequences for the religious authority of traditional scholars of all persuasions. Such religious authority for traditional scholars has typically been asserted in terms of monolithic conceptions of Islam, wherein these scholars, by virtue of their doctrinal affiliation, seek to depict themselves as sole defenders of "true" Islam. The very fact that religious shows favor more accommodative approaches to Islam renders such articulations of religious authority problematic, thereby making these shows a potential threat to traditional religious authority.

NOTES

1. While the Deobandis have also formed a political party (the Jāmī'at i 'Ulamā e Islam, or JUI), as have the Barelwis (the Jāmī'at i 'Ulamā Pakistan, or JUP), both groups have simultaneously focused their efforts on the educational front.

2. According to the International Crisis Group report (2005, 2), which draws on the Pakistani Census of 1998, approximately 96% of the Pakistani population comprises Muslims, out of which 15%–20% are Shi'a. The Shi'a population figures are contested. Zaman (1998, 689) places them at 14%–15% of the total population.

3. Sunni hostility toward Shi'as has centered on the issue of *Hazrat* Ali's (*RA*) succession of the Muslim caliphate after the death of the Prophet (PBUH). Shi'as believe that *Hazrat* Ali (*RA*), the cousin and son-in-law of the Prophet (PBUH), was the central religious figure and, as such, should have been made the first caliph. They therefore do not recognize the three caliphs who preceded Ali as legitimate successors of the Prophet (PBUH) (International Crisis Group 2005). According to the International Crisis Group report (2005, 2), what is commonly referred to as Shi'a Sunni violence reflects the conflict between the Shi'a and Deobandi, in which the Deobandi are supported by the Ahl-i Hadīth.

4. *Taṣawwuf* is an intercessional ritual practice linked to *sufi* faith, under which the help of a *murshid* (teacher) is enlisted for the acquisition of gnostic knowledge. Sanyal (1996, 173), notes that "any belief, idea, or practice that came into use after the Prophet's life became problematic," constituting *bid'a* for the Deobandis and Wahabis (Ahl-i Hadīth are condescendingly referred to as Wahabis by their Barelwi and Deobandi Sunni counterparts). Sanyal further informs us that, whereas earlier the term "applied strictly to religious beliefs and practices (*'ibada*), rather than to social customs in general," this is no longer the case. "Modern Wahabism" labels anything as *bid'a* if it cannot be proved to have existed during the Prophet's (PBUH) life. In contrast, Barelwis differentiate

between good and bad *bidʿa*. For them, innovation that does not contradict the Qur'ān, *Sunna*, *ijmā* (consensus), or *qiyās* (analogy) is not bad *bidʿa*.

5. The *Jamāʿat* aligns itself with the Deobandi tradition and is an anti-Shiʿa movement that, prior to the ban imposed on them by Musharraf's government, referred to itself as the Sipah e Sahaba Pakistan. The literal meaning of Sipah e Sahaba is "Army of the Companions of the Prophet (PBUH)." The name Ahle Sunna was first adopted by the Barelwis to refer to themselves as affiliates of the *Sunni* tradition. While most Barelwi *ʿulamā* still refer to their tradition as Ahle Sunna, the name has more recently been appropriated by the Sipah e Sahaba Pakistan. Lashkar e Jhangvi (LJ) is their militant offshoot.

6. The Tablīghī Jamāʿat is a proselytizing movement that operates at a local and international level for the spread of Islam. *Mawlānā* Tariq Jameel is a prominent preacher within the movement.

7. Nasr (2010, 334) refers to Israr Ahmed as a lay Islamist thinker who followed the example set by *Mawlānā* Maududi (founder of Jamāʿat-i-Islamī) and established his own network of *madāris* in Pakistan. Nasr (2006, 163) views Israr Ahmed as a "fundamentalist of a decidedly radical stripe, keener to condemn than to persuade," noting that Ahmed's ambition and his keenness to make himself "an influential voice in Pakistan's crowded Islamic scene" led him to engage in anti-Shiʿa rhetoric, "caustically denouncing them with a force and stridency that were new to Pakistani life."

8. Metcalf (2007, 58) has defined *taʿziyas* as "the replicas of tombs of the martyrs of *Karbalā*, taken in procession during the mourning ceremony of *Muḥarram*."

9. Asad (1993, 209–10) makes this claim in the context of Saudi scholars and their contentions regarding the introduction of radio and television in Saudi Arabia. Asad argues that we should view these contentions as the scholarly attempt to assert their discursive dominance in relation to the Saudi state.

10. The *Daʿwat i Islamī* Organisation is an offshoot of the Barelwi tradition. Its followers are popularly referred to as the *hari pagri* (green turban), by virtue of the green turbans they sport.

11. Bujra's (1971) study of Islam in Yemen highlights Islam as an "instrumental ideology" that is created by the elite and consumed by the masses (quoted in Anjum 2007, 657). Similarly, Geertz's (1971) study of Islam in Indonesia and Morocco conceptualizes Islam in terms of the binaries between scriptural (great tradition) and lived (little tradition) Islam.

12. Anjum (2007) attributes the origin of this dichotomy to Robert Redfield (1956, quoted in Lukens-Bull 1999, 4).

13. el-Zein's (1977) contribution to the study of Islam is that all Islams are equal, a notion that leads him to foreground the futility of searching for any unifying factors among the various local Islams (see Anjum 2007, 658). However,

the issue with el-Zein's work is highlighted by Launay (1992, 6), who recognizes that "Islam is obviously not a 'product' of any specific local community, but rather a global entity in itself." Launay astutely points out that "the problem for anthropologists is to find a framework in which to analyze the relationship between this single, global entity, Islam, and the multiple entities that are the religious beliefs and practices of Muslims in specific communities at specific moments in history."

14. Asad (2009b, 14) describes Islamic tradition as consisting essentially of discourses that seek to instruct practitioners regarding the correct form and purpose of a given practice that, precisely because it is established, has a history. As explained by Hirschkind (1996), the discourses constituting the tradition are "embodied in the practices and institutions of Islamic societies and hence deeply imbricated in the material life of those inhabiting it."

15. See Brown (1996), who observes that, despite the Muslims' ostensible preoccupation with the authenticity and continuity of religious tradition, the ḥadīth's reliability and its consideration as "absolute knowledge" has remained a contentious issue in Muslim communities.

FOUR

RELIGIOUS AUTHORITY AND CONTROL OVER RELIGIOUS KNOWLEDGE

ONE OF THE MOST PROFOUND implications of religious talk shows for traditional authority is the *madrasa*'s loss of control over religious knowledge. The full scope and dynamics of this loss can be better appreciated by first tracing the antecedents responsible for establishing the *madrasa* as the key institution for the transmission of religious knowledge in Muslim societies. Eickelman (1985, 50) and Hefner (2007) inform us that in the first three centuries of the Islamic era, the transmission of religious knowledge was confined to *kuttābs*, which provided elementary religious knowledge and focused on Qur'ānic memorization and recitation. In fact, it was only from the eighth century onward that the seminaries began to play a more formal role in the transmission of religious knowledge. This formalization was instigated by the growing corpus of religious knowledge and the corresponding need to prolong the period of Islamic study. In the reconfiguration of the *madāris* along more formal lines, the designation of a scholar remained fluid and essentially rooted in the scholar's tutelage under a reputable teacher whose chain of learning could be definitively established. While study under an established teacher remained an important feature of the scholar's religious authority, two major changes, mediated by the formalization process, contributed to a designation of religious authority as essentially rooted in the *madrasa*. These were the salience of *fiqh* "as a centerpiece of '*ulama* learning" and the growing importance of the "written canon" in a *madrasa* scholar's training" (Hefner 2007, 10). Berkey (2003) explains that both developments, which took place in the medieval Muslim world, contributed greatly to the *madāris*' increased prominence. They also enabled the "reorientation and disciplining of religious knowledge and authority" (Hefner 2007, 10).

According to Berkey (2007), the prominence and subsequent formalization of the *madrasa* as the center of religious education in the eighth century played a key role in diffusing perceptions of the *'ulamā* as upholders of Islamic orthodoxy. This was because the memorization of a written canon became a principal feature for claiming religious authority, thereby promoting the "hierarchical character of instructional relationships" (46). This enabled the *'ulamā* to defend and preserve "the transmission of knowledge as an authoritative system" (46). As a result, in addition to the ineluctable relationship between scholarly standing and learning from a master teacher, the scholar's knowledge of canonical texts became an easy yet essential means for identifying "just who did and who did not count as a legitimate religious scholar" (Hefner 2007, 10). Religious authority became essentialized in a scholar's "command of a written canon, learned under a recognized master, and demonstrated in textual and oral performance" (10). While Hefner (2007) acknowledges that the Islamic seminaries were not the only institutions responsible for the reorientation of religious knowledge and authority, he nonetheless asserts that they were vital to it.

Both Berkey (2003, 2007) and Hefner (2007) also note that the formalization of the *madāris* in the eighth century did not definitively translate into a reconceptualization of religious education as rooted in the model of the Western university. Contending with Makdisi's (1984) comparison of tenth-century *madāris* with medieval Western universities, Hefner (2007, 8–9) argues that despite the introduction of classrooms, professorships, and endowed properties, the *madāris* of the tenth century "operated without the benefit of examinations, formal curricula, degrees, or college governance." Instead, the "pursuit of religious knowledge in Muslim societies" remained an "individual" or "networked undertaking" and entailed a continued emphasis on "personalized instruction" from a master scholar (9). However, despite the ostensibly informal quality of religious education, religious knowledge remained essentially conservative. This was manifest in the growing opposition to religious innovation and as characterized by a growing focus on *taqlīd* (imitating the four schools of Islamic thought), the desire to replace the "polyvocality" of Islamic tradition "with a univocal understanding of Islam" (Berkey 2007, 50).

These developments were all part of a larger effort to "re-center and standardize" the extant plural traditions of religious knowledge (Hefner 2007, 12). Hefner (21) notes that these efforts were particularly prominent in the nineteenth and twentieth centuries and were contemporaneous with the advent of mass education and "movements of Islamic reform." Central to these transformations were the *madāris*' focus on Islamic law and their reconfiguration in accordance with Western education models (21). The *madāris'* reconfiguration included a shift from the informal quality of religious education in the medieval ages to the standardization of Islamic knowledge and a renewed emphasis on classical Islamic texts. In South Asia, the Deoband schools were the first to initiate their institutionalization along more Western lines (Berkey 2007). The Deobandi *madāris* conceived on this basis had a regularized curriculum and boasted a "permanent and salaried" academic staff (49). Within these *madāris*, the students' progress also came to be a function of their performance, as gauged in a "series of carefully calibrated examinations" (49). Berkey (51) refers to this development as a shift toward a "scripturalist" orientation, a term that he borrows from Geertz (1971). In this move, the *madāris* were assisted by the growing importance of print Islam, which contributed to what Eickelman (1985) and Starrett (1998) view as the "objectification" of Islam.[1] According to Berkey (2007, 50–51), this development undermined the flexibility of traditional Islam, and as a result, Islam increasingly came to represent "a precise set of beliefs, values and practices" that took on an essential, "normative," and "timeless" character. The *'ulamā*, as the self-proclaimed masters of Islamic knowledge, thus became central to the determination of popular Islamic discourse.

By contextualizing the impact of contemporary religious programming on the *madrasa*'s historically significant role in controlling the flow of religious knowledge, we can also move beyond the implications of religious shows for doctrinal activism and understand the wider implications of these shows for traditional religious authority. In what follows, I examine the problems that religious shows pose for the *madrasa*'s sustained control over religious knowledge and for the religious authority of those affiliated with this institution. I draw on both the edificatory benefits of religious talk shows and their tendency to emphasize pluralistic conceptions of religious authority to argue that what appears to be the role of electronic media in extending the influence of traditional religious authorities (see, e.g., Soares 2004b; Galal 2009; Zaman 2002) needs to be more critically evaluated, while bearing in mind the changes in knowledge control and processes of knowledge transmission enabled by religious shows.

RELIGIOUS TELEVISION AS DISPLACING THE *MADRASA*

An important component of my research was gauging the popularity of religious shows among lay Karachiites. This often involved asking people questions about the benefits they derived from watching these shows, especially those shows that imparted religious advice and accommodated the viewers' diverse religious sensibilities. To many avid religious show viewers, such shows simply offered a more convenient alternative to visiting the seminaries. On one occasion, I had arranged to meet with the students of a prestigious business school, Shaheed Zulfiqar Ali Bhutto Institute of Science and Technology (SZABIST), situated in the elite neighborhood of Clifton, Karachi. The meeting came about because of my affiliation with the business school, which extended to more than fifteen years of teaching there as a member of the school's adjunct faculty. One of the teachers, Ayza, agreed to let me conduct a group discussion with her students after she had completed her lecture. The class was a small one, and even fewer students, around five, stayed for the discussion. Two of the five students acknowledged their affiliation with the Deobandi tradition. Both students regularly attended Qur'ān classes at their neighborhood Deobandi seminaries. By contrast, Ayza and the other three students, although also of Sunni persuasion, did not, like many other Karachiites, align themselves with any particular doctrinal tradition within their sect.

Religious shows, especially those favoring a pluralized format, such as *Aalim Online*, held little appeal for the two Deobandi students, whose main access to religious knowledge came from the Deobandi seminaries they frequented. While both students acknowledged a casual interest in Tariq Jameel's online sermons, they explained that the absence of esteemed Deobandi scholars on television undermined the appeal of religious shows for them. Alternatively, Ayza and the other three students did not share this disregard for religious programming. As Ayza candidly admitted, the academic and professional demands on her time made independent Qur'ānic study, or regular visits to the neighborhood seminary, exceedingly difficult for her. However, because of the instructional orientation of these shows, she could now be more attuned to the intricacies of Islamic practice without having to visit a seminary. For Ayza, therefore, the prescriptive value of religious talk shows contributed to their appeal and made them a favorable viewing alternative. She confessed to me, "We are too busy with our lives. We don't visit the *madāris* and we don't have time to read religious books. When we pick up a translation of the Qur'ān, we are not sure of the contextual relevance of a particular chapter, so these programs help us understand the Qur'ān better. We get easy access to religious knowledge without having to leave the comfort of our living rooms."

Ayza's recourse to religious shows as a convenient means for accessing religious knowledge indicates that religious shows can intervene in the process of religious knowledge transmission by allowing traditional religious authorities to access a larger audience than would otherwise be possible. This development can be especially beneficial for religious scholars who maintain that their face-to-face interactions with women will undermine their religiosity. By allowing religious scholars to access the wider Muslim community, religious shows can be viewed as facilitating the widespread diffusion of traditionally mandated discourses on Islam (see Soares 2004b; Galal 2009). This development, in turn, reaffirms a general understanding of religious authority as essentially vested in traditional religious scholars. However, there is an alternative way to approach religious talk shows: to regard them as conversely undermining the significance of the traditional institution of the seminary for everyday religious guidance. Ayza's statement explains how this can happen by indicating the significance of religious shows in serving as a more convenient option to the religious seminary for people interested in seeking religious guidance. To the extent that religious shows redirect the flow of individual Muslim queries from the seminary to religious presenters on television, they also contribute toward alienating the general public from the scholarly majority confined to the seminaries. By enabling this trend, they problematize a straightforward conceptualization of religious authority as vested exclusively in the traditional institution of the religious seminary. The resulting relocation of religious authority from the religious seminary to religious television is thus a direct function of the former's loss of control over the flow of religious knowledge.

Moreover, the capacity of television to confer greater legitimacy on those who appear on it contributes to the greater relevance of religious shows in people's lives. To clarify my proposition, I revisit my meeting with a group of students enrolled in a religious study program at a prestigious Ahl-i Hadīth seminary, located in the older part of the city. I had been referred to the seminary by one of my Ahl-i Hadīth scholarly interlocutors, who held the institution in high esteem. During my visit to the seminary, the administration agreed to let me conduct a group discussion with select students, provided that I did not include the seminary's name in my citation. My subsequent discussion took place in the institution's library. During that time, a student named Ziad drew my attention to an important implication of religious programming while recounting his recent interaction with a friend, in relation to a televised religious debate on the Islamic standing of *ribā* (financial interest, usury). Ziad detailed how his friend had completely discounted Ziad's proposition on the impermissibility of financial interest under the rules of *Sharīʿa* and had instead assigned greater credence to the proposition made by a television scholar, whose knowledge the friend regarded as superior to Ziad's *madrasa* education. The friend's partiality to the proposition made by a television scholar had provoked Ziad to sarcastically conclude that in the contemporary environment,

"Television is Islam. They [the common people] only believe what is on television. They see the knowledge on television as more reliable."

Ziad's remarks suggest that any evaluation of the implications of religious shows must also entail an examination of exactly whose authority is mediated by these shows. Even when religious shows appear to mediate the increased relevance of traditional religious scholars, this may not necessarily hold for all religious scholars, particularly those whose authority draws exclusively on their affiliation with a religious seminary. My interlocutors, many of whom similarly expressed a greater regard for television scholars than for their *madrasa*-based equivalents, constantly reinforced the need for such considerations. One such person more open to learning from television-based scholars was my friend Farha, a middle-class housewife in her midforties. When I questioned Farha about her higher regard for religious scholars on television, she explained that she found these scholars more relatable and less "extremist" in their religious orientation than the scholars based in the city's religious seminaries. "I believe that the religious scholars confined to the seminaries are fanatics, and even though I may be wrong about them, I do not want to know what they have to say about religion. I only follow the religious scholars on television as they tend to be more moderate." Farha's clarification is useful for noting the relevance of another variable in mediating a preferred regard for television scholars: the propensity of these scholars to espouse more moderate ideas about Islam. This propensity frames television scholars in contrast to their *madrasa*-based counterparts, who, by comparison, come to be associated with the more backward and retrogressive modes of Islamic sociability. Both Ahmad (2010) and Khan (2003) allude to the widespread diffusion of such stereotypes in relation to *madrasa*-based scholars in Pakistan. For instance, while analyzing the popularity of Al Huda, a female-oriented center for religious training, Ahmad (2010, 309) observes that Islam in Pakistan has historically been associated with the lower classes on account of its domination by "clerics or maulvis" whose understanding of Islam is perceived as "backward" and anachronistic by middle- and upper-class Pakistanis. Khan (2003) makes a similar observation while tracing the genealogy of the *mullah* in Pakistan. Khan (45) reminds us that measures to undermine the *'ulamā*'s authority were initiated by the colonial administration in pre-partition India in the nineteenth century. According to Khan (45), the colonial state painted a "caricature of the *mulla*" that depicted traditionally educated religious personalities as "historical relics, harbingers of a redundant learning who were obstructing the community's progress." Khan (45, 59) astutely observes how, in the Pakistani state, the term *mulla* was extended to delineate *mullaism* as a "societal condition" that afflicted "backward"

Pakistanis. The resulting caricature, according to Khan (84), blurred all distinctions between religious personalities, including the differences in "education, specialization, experience and status," instead positing the *mulla* as "a figure stuck in time."

By contrast, the scholars appearing on religious shows, with their "high-tech, tastefully decorated television studios," appear to "occupy spaces of cosmopolitan modernity" (Moll 2010, 17).[2] For many middle- and upper-class Pakistanis, this implies that religion is no longer perceived as something "vulgar," mainly "for the poor"; rather it is viewed as "something chic" and "something 'wow'" (17). In Farha's case, her increased openness to learning from television scholars on account of their association with a more "moderate" Islamic perspective is also a function of the production-imposed limitations on featuring radical speech and the channels' commercially motivated emphasis on more diluted and subtler forms of doctrinal insinuation. Moreover, even as religious shows play an important role in eliciting such comparisons between on- and off-television traditional scholars, these comparisons are also reinforced by the former category of scholars themselves, whose attempts at broadening their educational base, together with their willingness to explain the rationale underlying their rulings, is aimed at proliferating an image of themselves as more progressive, knowledgeable, and qualified than their off-television counterparts (see also Zeghal 1999).[3] One scholarly testimony that stands out in this context is Professor Rahman's acknowledgment of the changes he had made in his preaching style, in accordance with his enrollment as a religious presenter on QTV. According to the scholar, he was now more willing to defend his authoritative claims on television with rational arguments, as this facilitated his on-screen popularity among the more educated members of the viewing public, who were less inclined to be drawn to the dogmatic preaching style generally adopted by *madrasa*-based scholars.

In the context of the wider Muslim world, Asad (2009b) notes that religious scholars commonly employ reason as a way of defending their authoritative claims within Islamic public debate, wherein the establishment of any Islamic practice also entails a subject's willing conformance to the practice and requires that the subject is aware of the point and proper performance of the practice. However, the fact that scholarly television presenters in Pakistan employ such modes of argumentation, specifically with the intent to distinguish themselves from their *madrasa*-based counterparts, suggests that, at least in Pakistan, such employment of reason and argument is a relatively recent phenomenon, mediated primarily by the emergence of religious talk shows. By considering religious shows as enabling these transformations in religious authority, we can also interrogate various academics' arguments in relation to the enabling impact of electronic media on traditional scholarly influence (e.g., Zaman 2009). For traditional scholars, the adoption of a preaching style that entails a more rationalist mode of scholarly engagement with divine texts allows them to reach otherwise impenetrable sections of middle- and upper-class Pakistani Muslims but also has a steep cost attached to it. It perpetuates a notion of religious authority as no longer predicated on a particular religious group or institution's mastery over divine knowledge. Rather it is the rationale underlying authoritative claims that becomes a precondition for the subject's obedience. Viewed from this perspective, the television scholars' attempts at distinguishing themselves from *madrasa*-based scholars can in effect also be considered a relinquishment of the *madrasa*'s control over religious interpretation and the consequent relegation of traditional religious authority to public opinion and popular ratings. However, television scholars not employing this mode of preaching seem to surrender their religious authority to other scholars who are more willing to defend and elucidate their authoritative claims on religious shows.

While speaking of the popularity of the Nigerian cleric Sheikh Abubakar Gumi, Larkin (2015, 64) notes how his reformist measures partake in a "logic of rupture" that draws on a false dichotomy between "traditional" and "reformist," wherein the latter is portrayed as a "break with the past" (for examples of this, see Meyer 1998; Larkin and Meyer 2006).[4] In Larkin's (2015, 65) opinion, the temporal and moral foundation of such distinctions is problematic, as "one movement comes to [falsely] represent a backward past and another a modernizing future." Larkin (65) contends that the binary framing of such movements is "cohesive, bounded, and mutually separable, homogenizing what are internally diverse movements, and rendering them static." The neat application of such binaries is also problematic in the context of Pakistan, where the reforms undertaken by traditional television scholars such as Professor Rahman are more aimed at insinuating the past into the present than at provoking a rethinking or reconstitution of established Islamic practices. As Ahmad (2010, 316), drawing on Benford and Snow (2000, 619), aptly theorizes, in relation to Al Huda scholars, it is essentially the same message articulated through a "new angle of vision."

Conversely, my interactions with *madrasa*-based scholars, some of whom I found to be perfectly at ease with more contemporary understandings of Islam, also made me wary of subscribing to wholesale views of them as backward and ignorant. However, I did feel that the strict dress codes prescribed for women, together with the expressly male-dominated *madrasa* environment, acted to discourage female visitors. Therefore, for some women, it was not so much the negative stereotypes associated with *madrasa*-based scholars, but rather the lack of access to them, that mediated their preferential regard for television scholars. The sensitive nature of some of their issues, taken together with the anonymity accorded by the call-in format of religious shows, made other women more likely to seek guidance from television-based religious specialists. However, Wuthnow (1990, 88, 90) highlights another reason for people to turn to religious shows as opposed to the *madrasa* for religious guidance, arguing that the very fact that people have access to multiple scholars on television allows for a more "eclectic" and "idiosyncratic" engagement with religion. In the Pakistani context, this implies that whereas visiting the *madrasa* may allow for more individualized solutions to people's everyday religious dilemmas, some people are increasingly willing to forgo this benefit in favor of a more agentive engagement with Islam. In chapter 7, I note that religious shows, with their multiple scholars and wide range of rulings, make it possible for viewers to opt for understandings of Islam that are more closely aligned with their individually held religious sensibilities and lived realities, and in so doing mediate important transformations in the nature of Islamic knowledge.

MIXING ENTERTAINMENT WITH RELIGION

One facet of religious programming that has profound implications for the *madrasa*'s control over religious knowledge is the mixing of religion with entertainment on religious game shows. This trend encourages an understanding of fun and entertainment as consistent with Islamic culture, a consideration that directly conflicts with the modes of Islamic conduct prescribed by the scholarly majority in Pakistan's religious seminaries. In offering alternative modes of living Islam that are in stark contrast to the Islamic lifestyle espoused by traditional religious scholars, religious game shows also undermine traditional scholarly attempts at standardizing Islamic belief and practice. When I asked the Deobandi scholar *Mawlānā* Kamaluddin about his views on religious game shows, he understandably expressed his concern about the elements of fun and entertainment in contemporary religious programming. The religious scholar felt that the overall message conveyed by religious game shows was at odds with "true" Islamic culture. However, when I posed the same question to the religious show host Husain, he drew my attention to some of the practical benefits of incorporating these elements into the format of religious game shows: "If the people prefer a more conventional way of learning they can visit the religious seminary. My purpose is to draw in the less religious viewers to, and elicit their interest in, religion. I feel that this viewership will be turned away from religion if I employ the same style that is employed by the scholars sitting in the religious seminaries."

Husain's justification for employing an entertainment-oriented format as a way of popularizing Islam is not very different from the justifications offered by the religious producer Abu-Haiba in the context of the Egyptian Islamic entertainment channel Al Risala (Wise 2005). Abu-Haiba maintains that his primary objective is to "attract an audience" and make his channel competitive with other forms of secular entertainment. At the same time, he also aims to edify viewers and to offer them something that they can watch without forgoing their Islamic values. According to Abu-Haiba, other Islamic channels such as "Iqraa and Al Magd are 'too dull'" and secular entertainment channels "like MBC are 'too liberated' for conservative Arab society" (in Wise 2005). As Abu-Haiba explains, "I'm promoting [moral, Islamic] ideas in the first places," but "if I lose money, that means I'm not appealing, that means I don't have my viewership, that means I'm not promoting my ideas" (in Lindsey 2006). Husain's and Abu-Haiba's remarks indicate that neither the religious message nor the commercial considerations of channel owners are epiphenomenal in the production of religious television shows (see Moll 2010). The fact that many Karachiites continue to opt for game shows, as opposed to more serious religious content, as their favorite pastime in Ramaḍān is in effect an implicit endorsement of Husain's and Abu-Haiba's views.

One important consideration mediated by the commercial impetus of religious game shows is their impact on general understandings of piety. Both Moll (2010, 5) and Husain note that the commodification of televised sermons does not necessarily have to be "at odds with their ethical impulse" but may, in fact, aid in the proliferation of the Islamic message. For Moll (2010, 9), "it is precisely the association of television with entertainment ... that makes it such an attractive medium for these televangelists," in that it allows them to present "Islam as a viable (entertaining) alternative to secular and potentially immoral media." Moll's observation can be usefully applied to understand why the traditional forms of knowledge transmission employed by the religious seminaries, while suitable for the more devout practitioners, hold little appeal for the less religiously driven or piously motivated Muslim practitioners. This is perhaps one of the key reasons why religious game shows in Pakistan manage to attract even those viewers who would otherwise be disinclined to partake in the more serious religious content on television.

Even though the entertainment format of religious game shows makes it easier for religious producers to elicit the interest of less devout Muslims, traditional scholars still do not view these shows very positively. Bayat (2007, 454) clarifies the reasons for the scholarly objection to these shows by highlighting some of the issues involved in assimilating entertainment and fun into religion. In an attempt to uncover why both secularists and religious practitioners are "so apprehensive of expressions of fun," Bayat argues that their aversion to fun reflects "anxiety over loss of their paradigm power" (434). According to Bayat, who deems it necessary to transcend the "physicality" of fun, it is the potential of fun to subvert "presumptions about self, society and life that might compete with and undermine the legitimizing ideology of doctrinal power" (455). For Bayat, this potential of fun renders it a potential threat to the "moral-political authority" of Islamists (455). I would like to extend Bayat's argument to draw attention to how the assimilation of fun into religious television shows could be similarly perceived by Pakistani religious scholars as subverting the centrality of Islam to Muslim life. When combined with Islam, fun, which according to Bayat is "free-form, ad-hoc, spontaneous" and "unpredictable," also imprints these attributes onto Islam and in doing so renders Islam, and therefore the ʿulamā, as superfluous to mainstream life (454). Alternatively, borrowing from Mahmood (2005), who acknowledges the relevance of distinct pedagogical styles for claiming religious authority, I would also like to draw attention to fun and entertainment as alternative and unconventional pedagogical styles that owe their emergence exclusively to the format of religious game shows. Insofar as religious anchors such as Husain employ these alternative pedagogical styles to elicit wider interest in religion, "having fun" and "being entertained" also constitute key means by which religious practitioners can cultivate a pious disposition.

CONCERNS REGARDING SCHOLARLY IMAGE

If the incorporation of entertainment into religious game shows contributes to their enhanced viewership, so too does it generate widespread skepticism regarding the sincerity of all featured scholars, irrespective of their participation in the more controversial game show format. It was especially in connection to their colleagues' participation in religious game shows that many of my scholarly interlocutors also voiced their concerns about the potentially deleterious consequences of these shows for their institution's perceived credibility. The religious scholars believed that their colleagues' participation on these shows would undermine their institution's image and credibility within the wider Pakistani Muslim community. Moreover, these concerns were also voiced in relation to scholarly appearances on shows that featured more serious religious content. My scholarly interlocutors worried that even minor lapses on the part of the presenting scholar would expose their entire institution to widespread criticism, as viewers had a tendency to generalize the mistake of one scholar to the whole institution.

During my discussions with lay Karachiites, I often noted that the scholars' concerns in relation to their colleagues' television appearances were not unfounded. Many of my lay interlocutors confirmed to me that these shows frequently generated doubts regarding the 'ulamā's sincerity toward Islam. Even viewers who partook in televised religious content primarily for the purposes of entertainment overwhelmingly felt that it was not appropriate for religious scholars to appear on the game shows. Their resulting skepticism in relation to the scholars' appearances on these game shows was often generalized to the entire institution. Some religious show viewers also found it problematic that religious scholars appearing on television were financially compensated for their presentations. A perception of these scholars as economically motivated not only generated doubts about the scholars' supposed sincerity toward Islam but also engendered a general notion of these scholars as susceptible to other unsavory influences, such as the state and multinational corporations. Many Karachiites who engaged with religious shows asked, "Those who give *dars* [sermons] on television get paid for it, so how do we trust them?"

While describing to me the distinctive attributes of an ʿĀlim e Dīn (scholar of religion), Professor Rahman explained that the task of becoming a scholar entailed more than the simple acquisition of religious knowledge. The scholar was also required to practice what he preached as proof of his spiritual elevation. During my fieldwork, I often noted that stricter codes of conduct generally applied to religious scholars as opposed to common practitioners, as the former were held more accountable by their followers for minor transgressions. For instance, while meeting with two male employees of a charitable trust, I observed that both had especially high expectations of religious scholars, not only in relation to the latter's religious observance but also on the matter of their propensity to abide by the legal framework governing everyday life in Pakistan. As one employee remarked, "If you see an ordinary person violating a traffic signal, it does not carry the same negative connotation as when you view a religious scholar doing the same." The two employees also maintained that because every religious scholar was widely perceived as representative of his institution, his fallibility would also undermine the spiritual standing of his more learned and esteemed counterparts. These comments suggest that perhaps the greatest threat to the traditional scholar's authority is participation on religious game shows and talk shows, which lends credence to a perception of religious authorities as increasingly susceptible to commercial gains and therefore as untrustworthy.

Moreover, even within the format of religious shows that have a more instructional focus, religious scholars are held accountable for their (in)ability to respond appropriately to viewers' religious queries. To illustrate how this happens, I revert to my meeting with Asma, a young government college student in her early twenties. I came across Asma while attending a discussion that I had organized with the government college students. During the discussion, Asma did not hesitate to openly articulate her unfavorable impression of traditional scholars, explaining that she considered them as less erudite versions of their self-taught counterparts. While justifying her lack of regard for the former, Asma narrated to me her recent viewing experience of a religious talk show. In the talk show, a Christian priest had been present in the capacity of a studio audience member. The priest had asked the religious panel presiding over the show a question on *Shab e Mi'rāj* (the night of the Prophet Muhammad's [PBUH] ascension to the heavens on a celestial horse). The priest had inquired as to why, if it were indeed true that the Prophet Muhammad (PBUH) had ascended to the heavens on his horse, there was no gap left behind in the sky as proof of the Prophet's (PBUH) ascension. Asma recounted that none of the religious scholars present on the show had been able to offer a logical response to the priest's query. Instead, the issue had been resolved by one of the lay audience members, who had supplied the only logical explanation for the dilemma. After witnessing a nonscholarly audience member respond more effectively to the priest's challenge, Asma felt justified discounting the interpretative abilities and religious erudition of all traditional religious scholars. Instead, she believed that self-taught scholars, and even lay educated Muslims, by virtue of their secular education, were better equipped to interpret Islamic texts than those who claimed traditional expertise in this task.

What is interesting about Asma's case is that she lacked faith in traditional scholars despite the fact that she herself owed her religious education to a neighborhood *kuttāb*, which she had attended during her childhood. Asma recalled how, unlike the self-taught scholars featured on contemporary religious shows, her *kuttāb* teacher had never attempted to enlighten her on the underlying meaning of various Qur'ānic verses. He had mainly schooled her in the correct form of Qur'ānic diction. Her personal childhood experience of studying religion with a traditional scholar, coupled with what she had recently witnessed on the religious show, had convinced Asma that understanding the Qur'ān was more important than learning how to recite it correctly, or even memorizing it. However, based on her personal experience, Asma felt certain that the former mode of religious learning could not be accessed at most traditional Islamic institutions such as the seminaries, *kuttābs*, and mosques, which in her opinion were only capable of providing a rudimentary understanding of Islamic scriptures. Asma's narration is useful for understanding the limitations of religious television for the authoritative influence of traditional scholars. These limitations are jointly imposed by the forms of scrutiny religious shows expose traditional scholars to and by the comparisons these shows provoke between traditional scholars and their self-styled counterparts, on the basis of both authorities' capacity to respond adequately to the religious queries raised.

For those of my scholarly interlocutors who frequently appeared on television, the prospect of their rulings being increasingly scrutinized by the viewing public also gave way to an extreme fear of being caught unawares in relation to a religious query. Religious scholars most prominently voiced this concern in relation to their live presentations on religious talk shows, when unforeseen questions and events intensified the likelihood of the scholars not being adequately prepared for the task at hand. In fact, some scholars were so fearful of appearing ignorant and eliciting negative appraisals from their audiences that they were even prepared to dissimulate erudition and offer their opinions when unsure of the correct response to a particular query. Professor Rahman admitted this while detailing some of the compromises that religious shows elicited from their presenters. With a view to avoid such problematic instances, Professor Rahman also insisted that it was important for religious show producers to apprise the religious scholars of the discussion topics well in advance of the episode, so as to give the scholars ample preparation time for tending properly to their role as religious specialists. Professor Rahman felt that this initiative by the shows' producers would mitigate the likelihood of a scholar being embarrassed on the show. I would like to extend these scholarly concerns over "impression management" (see Goffman 1959) to also invite a consideration of how the scholars' presence on religious shows can confer more authority on the viewers.[5] The resulting relocation of religious authority from religious scholars to religious show viewers is mediated jointly by the omnipresence of the television screen and the scholars' awareness regarding their increased scrutiny on television. Both developments put televised scholars under a great deal of pressure to perform adequately.

THE NEED TO BALANCE DOCTRINAL ORIENTATION WITH POPULAR APPEAL

For many scholars, the fear of being negatively appraised and the corresponding compulsion to perform appropriately did not arise merely in relation to their live appearances on religious programs. These scholars additionally felt that the confrontational nature of some doctrinal debates on television, as enabled by the pluralistic environment of religious shows, would affect people's engagement with Islam, as people would come to regard the religion as non-definitive and therefore as adaptable to the practitioners' varied concerns. In addition, some scholars also felt that their participation in the polemical format of some religious shows would tarnish their image and perceived credibility by reinforcing a notion of them as divided along sectarian lines. Alternatively, for religious show viewers, the televised representations of multiple and competing perspectives on Islam meant that they no longer knew who to turn to for religious advice and guidance. While the broader implications of these developments for religious authority and practice are discussed in detail in chapters 6 and 7, suffice it to say here that these adverse appraisals of scholarly polemics on television also extended to religious scholars who did not present on religious talk shows. One scholarly narration that helps illustrate this point is that of a Deobandi *qarī* who presided over a small *madrasa* in the neighborhood of Shireen Jinnah Colony. The *qarī* was strongly of the view that religious shows were indirectly responsible for encouraging viewers to disrespect religious scholars. To buttress his proposition, he gave me the example of a religious show where the participating scholars had taken up an entire episode fighting over the correct form of a religious practice. The *qarī* recalled with shame that rather than elaborating on the different forms of Islamic verification relevant to the issue, the scholars had ended up impressing on the audiences the differences between the various schools of Islamic thought. "Sometimes the discussions on such shows turn into loud altercations between the *'ulamā*. I even heard someone saying once, look at these *'ulamā*, they are barking like dogs. Our enemies use these shows to portray the *'ulamā* as misleading 'lay' Muslims. Therefore, these shows give those who are opposed to the religion, such as the Shi'as, Jews and Qadianis [a derogatory term used for Ahmadis] a chance to condemn all the *'ulamā*."

Given the potentially adverse implications of such debates for the scholars' image, the *qarī* insisted that such instances of doctrinal interaction, as mediated by religious shows, were pointless unless they culminated in some sort of scholarly consensus. The *qarī*'s narration raises an important point regarding the modes of religious authority privileged by religious shows. His remarks suggest that, at least within the pluralized format of contemporary religious shows, religious authority is increasingly contingent on the scholars' ability to rise above their doctrinal affiliations. It was on account of these differing engagements with religious authority that some of my scholarly interlocutors also expressed their hesitation to deal with viewer queries on doctrinally sensitive and contested Islamic practices and issues of faith. During my third meeting with *Mawlānā* Ahmed, the Barelwi television scholar identified four such practice- and faith-related issues that he felt should not be broached on television: "The Ahl-i Hadīth and Deobandi disagree with us [Barelwi] on what *imān* (faith) is and what it involves. They don't revere the Prophet (PBUH) like we do. So we should avoid debates on issues of *imān* altogether. Also, the Ahl-i Hadīth disagree with us on the conditions of *talāq* and the procedure for *halālā* [conditions for remarrying your ex-spouse]. They also say their prayers differently from us."

Likewise, a concern for appearing more neutral also prompted Dr. Fateh, a Deobandi television scholar and professor at the Karachi University, to confess to me his extreme fear when dealing with sectarian and doctrinally oriented topics on television. He recounted to me how a recent query by an audience member regarding the Islamic standing of the Shiʿa custom of *taʿziyas* in *Muharram* had triggered his unease. Dr. Fateh described how he had deliberately avoided proffering the Deobandi position on the custom, which deemed it forbidden. Instead he had confined himself to explaining the etymology and literal meaning of the word *taʿziya*. Dr. Fateh highlighted another useful strategy for dealing with such provocative questions: to provide viewers with the different doctrinal perspectives on the practice under consideration and suggest that they opt for the perspective that suited them best, on the basis of either their doctrinal affiliation or their individual sensibilities. Dr. Fateh's admission regarding the need to appear neutral on television illustrates the ways in which religious television can compel important transformations in religious authority. Within the pluralistic format of religious shows, religious authority does not so much derive from scholars' affiliation with an established Islamic seminary or a particular doctrinal group as it does from scholars' ability to rise above their respective doctrinal orientations. This in turn implies that even the merest hint of religious difference on television could potentially have adverse implications for the religious authority of traditional scholars. My following conversation with *Mawlānā* Ahmed on the scholar's personal experience of presenting on an episode of *Aalim Online* adequately illustrates this point.

During the recording of the stated episode, an audience member had asked a general question of all the scholars present about the prescribed Islamic method for calculating *zakāt* (obligatory Muslim tax). While *Mawlānā* Ahmed had responded with a brief answer, the Shiʿa scholar had responded in much greater detail. The audience member had given his feedback on the two answers by simply stating, "*Sau sunar ki, ek lohar ki,*" which literally translates into "a hundred from the goldsmith is equal to one from the ironmonger." The idiomatic translation, however, implies that the few words of an intelligent man are equivalent to the many words uttered by an idiot. *Mawlānā* Ahmed felt that such a controversial statement should have been ignored by the host. However, Husain had deliberately tried to stir controversy by asking the viewer to identify which of the two scholars was the goldsmith and which the iron monger. *Mawlānā* Ahmed felt that in doing so Husain had implicitly encouraged the audience member to insult the Shiʿa scholar. Drawing on this experience, and taking into consideration the contested nature of certain Islamic practices and principles, *Mawlānā* Ahmed now maintained that scholarly debate on television should be confined to the domain of *akhlāqiyyāt* (social conduct), on which there was general consensus between different Islamic schools. For the resolution of everyday practice and faith-related issues, the *Mawlānā* advocated that people should refer to the *mustanid ʿulamā* (established scholars) in their neighborhood mosques and seminaries.

Mawlānā Ahmed's suggestion is very useful for exploring the impact of religious talk shows on both religious debate and religious authority. His remarks clarify the significance of televised Islamic pluralism in enabling the reconceptualization of religious debate as essentially devoid of discussion on the finer details of Islamic practice. The religious debate reconfigured on these lines effectively nullifies the benefits of television in allowing featured religious authorities to shape "modern [political] subjectivities" (Abu-Lughod 1998; Rajagopal 2001), through the institution of standardized Islamic practices and expressions of morality (see Hirschkind 2001, 2006; Mahmood 2005; Ismail 2007). Within these newly reconfigured boundaries of religious public debate, not only do religious scholars have little say on how Muslims practice Islam, especially in its public ritual form (see Soares 2004b: 217–18), but they also have little control over the Islamic "institutions of collective life" (Hirschkind 2001, 5). From this perspective, the scholarly attempts to circumscribe the boundaries of religious public debate and render it free from discussion on Islamic practices can also be viewed as a scholarly relinquishment of the advantages of television in extending the scope of influence of traditional religious authorities.

THE DRAWBACKS OF APPEARING FREQUENTLY ON TELEVISION

In drawing attention to religious television shows as both enabling the influence of traditional scholars and posing multiple challenges to their authority, I underscore the complexity of the relationship between televisual media and religious authority. One can assess the impact of religious shows by viewing them as helpful in extending the scale and scope of the scholars' influence. This extension is a function of the ubiquitous nature of television, which gives scholars access to a broader viewership that would otherwise be impossible to penetrate. Within this framework, traditional scholarly authority is also mediated through the *fatwā* orientation of religious shows, which allows the ʿ*ulamā* to both standardize Islamic practice and insinuate themselves into the everyday lives of lay viewers. However, television scholars pay a heavy price for their enhanced celebrity status and popularity, as enabled by their presence on these shows. Within the format of religious shows, scholars are subjected to greater viewer scrutiny and critiqued for their failure to rise above Muslim politics. They are further relegated to their self-styled counterparts for their failure to logically explain or defend their propositions (see chap. 5 also), and they are compelled to adapt their messages to viewer preferences and religious sensibilities.

Therefore, to acknowledge television's role in extending traditional religious authority without accounting for the ways in which it undermines it is in effect to present a skewed analysis of the implications of religious shows for general perceptions of traditional religious authority. Moreover, by employing television to educate lay Pakistanis on the correct mode of Islamic practice, religious scholars also inadvertently contribute to the relocation of religious authority from the *madrasa* to television, and by extension to lay viewers. This development is not only a function of how religious shows invite viewers to turn to television as opposed to the *madrasa* for the resolution of their everyday Islamic issues but also a product of how these shows implicitly encourage viewers to choose between multiple authoritative claims and draw on the ones that best correspond with their individual sensibilities. These contradictory influences on religious authority correspond with Nyamnjoh's (2015, ix) observation that the "appropriation of modern media by individuals, lay persons, and religious activists is as empowering (enabling) as it is threatening (subversive and disabling)."

Also relevant to a discussion on the consequences of religious television for religious authority is the entertainment format of religious game shows, which is controversial, although show producers consider it necessary for eliciting a broader interest in religious programming. The game shows thus conceived are aimed at thwarting the attraction of secular entertainment programming and at evoking religious fervor in less pious viewers. Religious scholars presenting on these shows may need to negotiate between representing "authentic" Islamic values and appealing to a larger audience. Wise (2005) makes a similar observation in the context of "ethical" reality TV on the Egyptian Al Risala satellite channel. For Wise, the entertainment focus of these shows "reflects a larger political and cultural negotiation taking place between socially conservative Islamists and more liberal secular elements in the Arab world." Both, according to Wise, "are struggling to define the norms people live by in society or, to put it more precisely in this case, to define whose version of 'reality' is more authentically 'real.'" In Pakistan, the traditional scholars' willingness to participate in game shows, their efforts to acquire secular education, their enhanced focus on contemporary applications of divine texts, and their desire to present themselves as "moderate" and above Muslim politics all necessitate a consideration of religious shows as not merely representative of the struggle between conservative and liberal elements in Pakistan society but also as more supportive of the latter's understanding of Islam.

NOTES

1. Starrett (1998, 8–9) defines *objectification* as "the growing consciousness on the part of Muslims that Islam is a coherent system of practices and beliefs."
2. Moll makes this claim in the context of religious programming in Egypt.
3. According to Zeghal (1999), in Egypt the popular appeal of the Al Azhar scholar al Qaradawi is a function of his willingness to tailor his preaching style and content to popular demand. Similarly, in relation to Pakistan, Zaman (2009, 229) notes how the 'ulamā's attempts at acquiring "modern" education reflects a concern for "showing how they, unlike many others among their fellow 'ulamā, embody the qualities their modern-educated audiences prize most."
4. "Break with the past" is a phrase Meyer (1998) has taken directly from the Pentecostals in Ghana.
5. The salience of the audiences in determining the success of presenters is implicit in Goffman's (1959) emphasis on "impression management" and "self-presentation" in performance.

FIVE

SELF-STYLED SCHOLARS AND RELIGIOUS SHOW HOSTS
Emerging Sources of Religious Authority

IN ADDITION TO CREATING UNPARALLELED opportunities for more moderate articulations of Islam on television, the relative easing of governmental control over televised religious content and the competitive media environment have also enabled the emergence of two novel sources of religious authority: self-styled celebrity preachers and religious show hosts. This chapter engages with the growing prominence of both forms of religious authority, whose relevance in Islamic public debate owes exclusively to their appearances on religious talk shows. Since both religious authorities often also lack the requisite religious credentials subscribed to by traditional Islamists, their inclusion on religious shows represents a marked shift in the conventional view of *ijtihād* and Islamic debate as the sole prerogatives of traditional scholars. The resulting significance of both sources of religious authority in people's minds poses a direct threat to the historical standing of the *madrasa* and by extension traditional religious scholars as the key arbiters of religious knowledge in the country. Religious shows are exclusively responsible for constructing and enabling the authoritative status and prominence of both forms of religious authority, which underscores their relevance in mediating regnant conceptions of Islam and religious authority in Pakistan.

The authority of religious show hosts is a function of the role they perform as moderators of religious talk shows. In this capacity, the show hosts mediate not only between the religious scholars appearing on a particular episode but also between the scholars and their audiences. For many religious show hosts, the promotion of more moderate ways of Islamic thinking in Pakistan guides their performance of both roles. While a similar aim also informs the inclusion of self-styled scholars on expert panels, these religious authorities' significance in shaping contemporary Islamic thought and practice owes in large part to their critically oriented pedagogical style and their willingness to provoke a reconsideration of certain traditionally endorsed and historically established Islamic concepts. Javed Ahmed Ghamidi, who gained public recognition as a religious scholar and exegete on account of his regular presence on religious talk shows, many of which focused on "the person of Ghamidi," constitutes the most prominent example of this mode of authoritative representation in Pakistan (Sadaf Aziz 2011, 599).

In what follows, I consider the detailed implications of the emergence of both religious authorities for the authoritative religious standing of the *madrasa* and of those who have graduated from it. Especially in relation to the religious authority of self-styled scholars, I discuss two distinct types of religious shows: those that favor the parallel presence of self-styled scholars alongside traditional scholars, such as *Aalim Online* and its adaptation *Alif* (also featured on Geo Television), and those that invite self-styled scholars to present exclusively, such as *Ghamidi Kay Saath* (Together with Ghamidi). Both approaches to religious programming are useful for considering the role of religious shows in popularizing novel modes of interpretation and Islamic thinking in Pakistan.

THE SELF-STYLED SCHOLAR, JAVED AHMED GHAMIDI

Javed Ahmed Ghamidi's prominence as a religious scholar emerged in tandem with the "official elaboration" of President Musharraf's "'Enlightened Moderation' agenda," subsequent to the liberalization of Pakistani media, in 2002 (Sadaf Aziz 2011, 598). Handpicked by Musharraf in 2006 for the Council of Islamic Ideology (CII), a constitutional religious body that consults for Pakistani legislature, Ghamidi began his journey as a student of religion under Abul A'la Maududi (1970), the leader of the religiopolitical movement Jamā'at-i-Islamī. Later, on account of the movement's greater focus on "active political contest" as opposed to "working to inculcate personal pietism and virtue," Ghamidi withdrew from the Jamā'at and deepened his association with Amin Ahsan Islahi, a theologian and also a former member of the Jamā'at (Sadaf Aziz 2011, 612–13). In 1991, Ghamidi cofounded the Al Mawrid institute for religious edification and research. According to Aziz (613), Al Mawrid is "neither a *Madrassah* nor modeled on the revivalist or *dawa* movements which primarily engage their adherents more exclusively in projects of personal reform." Rather, in Aziz's (613) opinion, Al Mawrid is "a think-tank and one that is particularly savvy and adept in its use of various media for disseminating its findings."

Ghamidi's religious commentary has been touted by Pakistani and international media as challenging "vestiges of a conservative social order attributed to particularly stringent interpretations of Islamic prohibitions" (Sadaf Aziz 2011, 599). This is primarily on account of Ghamidi's interpretations of Islamic law and certain Islamic practices, which often stray from mainstream understandings of Islam as propounded by traditional Islamists. Ghamidi has openly called out Pakistan's traditional scholars for their endorsement of certain problematic Islamic laws, such as the blasphemy law. The celebrity preacher has strongly advocated that these laws have "no justification in Islam" and fearlessly labeled the traditional Islamists as liars for stating otherwise (Walsh 2011). His daring has been noted by Walsh, who maintains that "Ghamidi . . . is the only religious scholar to publicly oppose the blasphemy laws since the assassination of the Punjab governor, Salmaan Taseer." This explains why the Pakistani liberals view Ghamidi as the sole "voice of reason in a babble of noises seemingly dedicated to irrationality" (Ayaz Amir, quoted in Walsh 2011). However, despite his growing influence in popular media and his appeal among Pakistani liberals, Ghamidi's distinct views on Islam also make him a hugely controversial figure who is "adored, hated, popular, and notorious all at once" (Sadaf Aziz 2011, 599). While death threats from the Taliban compelled Ghamidi to flee from Pakistan, his subsequent immigration to Malaysia, in 2009, has done little to mitigate his appearances on Pakistani television. Not only does Ghamidi continue to play an active role in Pakistani religious debate, but he also employs the internet as a platform from which he disseminates his religious message to a global audience.

According to Mufti (2007), Ghamidi's popular appeal among the urban-based middle- and upper-class Pakistani Muslims draws heavily on the scholar's stance against the traditionalist Islamic viewpoint. By offering the viewers more lenient Islamic interpretations that are in stark contrast to the rigid modes of Islamic understanding espoused by traditional Islamists, Ghamidi encourages a perception of the Islamists as unduly strict and normative. Ghamidi's popularity, which is simultaneously a function of his distinct interpretative style and his regular appearances on religious talk shows, also implicates these shows in encouraging comparisons between traditional and self-styled religious authorities that are often to the detriment of the former. By enabling such comparisons, religious talk shows implicitly privilege the authority of self-styled scholars over traditional scholars, who are by contrast depicted as mired in literalist and regressive perspectives of Islam. Moreover, such comparisons are also elicited by the self-styled scholars themselves, whose claims to religious authority are often premised upon proliferating a perception of traditional scholars as possessing an inferior understanding of Islam. Particularly in Ghamidi's case, this has also involved openly designating all *maulvīs* (an honorific title exclusively reserved for traditional scholars) as low-ranking clerics. In the context of the Nigerian cleric Sheikh Abu Bakar Gumi, Larkin (2015, 65) explains how such negative portrayals of traditional sources of religious authority serve the more contemporary movements that seek to stigmatize their opponents as backward.

A similar consideration of Ghamidi's role in undermining traditional forms of religious authority also dominated the majority of my discussions with traditional scholars, who perceived his growing popularity with Pakistanis as attenuating the scholars' authoritative standing in religious debate. During my fieldwork, I often came across traditional scholars who would underscore Ghamidi's example when articulating their disapproval of televised Islamic pluralism. In this context, the remarks of a Deobandi *muftī* adequately reflect the wider scholarly community's concern over the role of religious shows in promoting Ghamidi's authoritative influence: "The TV has become the *qibla* [the direction of prayers] for the *awam* [the people] and these people [self-styled scholars] the messengers of God. Then where should the *ʿālim* go?" However, if traditional scholars worried about the sorts of comparisons elicited by religious talk shows, they themselves implicitly reinforced these distinctions while seeking to uphold their institution's discursive authority. In the following section, I elaborate on the form of these distinctions and their potential benefit for upholding traditional claims to religious authority.

THE DISTINCTION BETWEEN A *MUSTANID* *ʿĀLIM* AND A SELF-STYLED SCHOLAR

I first became familiar with the term *mustanid ʿālim* (authentic religious scholar) while visiting the prestigious Deobandi *madrasa Dār al-ʿUlūm*, Korangi. The *ʿālim* I met with invoked the term to distinguish himself (and his fellow scholars, who like him also owed their religious credentials to the institution of the *madrasa*) from his self-styled counterparts who had pursued their religious study independently or at secular institutions. I discovered later that the term *mustanid* essentially derives from the Arabic term *sanad* (pl. *isnād*) and literally means chain or link. It denotes the authoritative standing of a *ḥadīth*, whose authenticity rests on it being sourced through a chain of reliable narrators back to the Prophet Muhammad (PBUH).[1] When used to designate a religious scholar, the term denotes the scholar's "legitimate" authority to interpret Islamic texts and impart scholarly advice. It does so by rendering the scholar as part of a chain of reliable and established authorities on account of the scholar's tutelage under the *madrasa* (see Robinson 2013).[2]

When I met with the Deobandi scholar *Mawlānā* Kamaluddin, he employed the term *mustanid* to impress upon me the importance of *madrasa* education for conferring interpretative expertise on a religious practitioner. According to the scholar, without the benefit of *madrasa*-based education, a religious practitioner was much more likely to make interpretative errors, as the requisite skills for discerning the hidden meanings underlying divine texts could only be acquired through the scholar's enrollment in a long-term religious study program at an established *madrasa*. This belief also informed *Mawlānā* Kamaluddin's engagement with the self-styled preacher Ghamidi. The *Mawlānā* felt that since the self-styled scholar had ventured on the religious path on his own accord, he was less likely to be familiar with the basic tenets and rules of interpretation mandated under Islamic code. While validating his propositions, *Mawlānā* Kamaluddin invoked the example of an equivocally worded Qur'ānic verse that in his opinion required greater sagacity on the part of the exegete for correct interpretation: "There are two words in the verse whose literal meaning is black thread and white thread. However, an interpreter solely relying on the literal meaning will lose the significance of the entire verse. Only one who has been properly trained at a *madrasa* will be able to discern the true meaning of the two words, as denoting nighttime and daytime respectively."

Mawlānā Kamaluddin's insistence on the indispensable nature of *madrasa* education can be attributed directly to the pluralism of religious talk shows, which implicitly pit traditional Islamists against self-styled scholars. As alternative interpreters of Islam, self-styled scholars undercut the *madrasa*'s exclusive monopoly over the terms of Islamic debate. Their presence on religious shows, together with their willingness to reconsider the contemporary relevance of certain religious concepts characterized by prior scholarly consensus, serves to perpetuate a notion of religious debate as no longer limited to asserting the meaningfulness of past practice. Nor are authoritative claims regarding Islamic practice any longer exclusively premised on references to divine texts or recognizable authorities. Instead, self-styled scholars accustom religious show viewers to the possibility of undertaking a more critical engagement with divine texts and established concepts, wherein traditional perspectives on Islam are deliberated upon rather than taken for granted. The resulting discursive space bears a striking resemblance to Habermas's (1991) public sphere. Within this space, not only is religion forced to "work for the market" (40), as opposed to select members of the orthodoxy, but self-styled scholars also enjoy interpretative equality with traditional religious scholars, as the status of the latter is increasingly subordinated to the authority of the "better argument" (54). Moreover, the discussions originating within this discursive space also presuppose the problematization of certain areas that had until very recently eluded questioning or reconsideration.

These transformations in the way religion is publicly discussed and debated are not just enabled by religious shows that favor pluralistic representations of Islam, as even shows that exclusively invite self-styled scholars to present encourage such transformations by offering alternative perspectives on Islam. In doing so, they also provoke a more critically inspired viewer engagement with established Islamic concepts and ideas. Moreover, the fact that the opportunities for exclusive presentation are generally only extended to self-styled scholars serves to sustain a pervasive understanding of *madrasa* education as inferior to the knowledge possessed by self-taught scholars. This makes it even more pressing for traditional scholars to assert the importance of the *madrasa* as the only reliable source of religious knowledge. While elaborating on the implications of "small media" on religious public debate in Mali, Schulz (2006a, 145) points out that "small media, rather than unequivocally broadening access to public debate, exacerbate conflicts over participation and often feed into already existing strategies of exclusion."[3] To make her point, Schulz highlights the tendency of scholars to depict alternative authoritative claims as "doctrinal deviation." Drawing on her observations of the Malian preacher Haidara, Schulz (145) argues that "Haidara's sermons illustrate that Muslim activists currently engage in public debate to assert and contest identities based on claims to moral superiority." Schulz's suggestions on "small media" are consistent with how some of my traditional scholarly interlocutors, such as *Mawlānā* Kamaluddin, asserted the interpretative fallibility of Ghamidi. Their remarks in this context constitute both a strategy of exclusion and a strategy for sustaining their institution's ascendancy in religious public debate, as necessitated by the emergence of alternative forms religious authority. However, we can also view Ghamidi's condescending references to traditional scholars as indicative of the self-styled scholar's own insecurities regarding his tentative position in Pakistani religious public debate.

THE SUBVERSIVE INTERPRETATIONS OF SELF-STYLED SCHOLARS

A pertinent consideration in relation to the incorporation of self-styled scholars in religious programming is how their regular appearances on religious talk shows alter the form of "public religious discourse" (Salvatore and Eickelman

2004, xxi). As mentioned earlier, in Ghamidi's case, his popularity is not merely a function of his perceived expertise in Qur'ānic Arabic and his comprehensive and in-depth knowledge of Islamic texts (see Schulz 2006b); it is equally, if not more so, sustained by his willingness to openly challenge codes of Islamic conduct endorsed by traditional scholars and his ability to subvert scholars' interpretations of canonical Islamic texts.[4] Not only do Ghamidi's televised sermons display a complete disregard for traditionally mandated norms of Islamic appearance and dress, but his interpretations of Islamic texts have often stood him in direct opposition to his traditional counterparts, whose views on *Sharī'a* he has openly challenged on numerous occasions. Deserving particular mention here is Ghamidi's condemnation of certain Islamic laws, such as the *Hudood* Ordinances, as un-Islamic. His controversial endorsement of interest-based banking and his unwillingness to deem veiling as an essential aspect of a woman's piety have also aroused the concern of some Islamists. Ghamidi's ability to challenge established scholarly claims while employing the language of Islam has endeared him to many urban middle- and upper-class Pakistanis but has rendered him problematic for traditional scholars, who have found it difficult to counter his subversive propositions on many occasions.

Mufti (2007) endorses this point when he notes that Ghamidi's arguments are essentially rooted in his command over the Arabic language and his proficiency with divine texts. According to Mufti, unlike the critique proffered by "'moderate' secular Muslims," Ghamidi's "purely fundamentalist approach" "offers a more forceful and profound deconstruction" of traditional rulings on "*jihād*, on the penal code of rape and adultery, on the curricula in the religious schools, or madrassas." This makes Ghamidi an especially effective bulwark against traditionally mandated Islamic norms and principles, and by extension against the Islamists' control over religious knowledge. In this context, Ghamidi's regular appearances clarify a role for religious shows that is not limited to enabling new representatives of Islam but that also extends to encouraging new representations of Islam (see Eickelman and Anderson 2003, which makes this claim in relation to "new" media). This is particularly true of religious talk shows that invite Ghamidi to participate alongside traditional scholars, so that his parallel presence with these scholars implicitly encourages a perception of scholarly rulings as "perspectival rather than 'absolute' and 'literal'" (see Kazi 2018). The result is a more agentive and idiosyncratic viewer engagement with Islam, and a corresponding notion of the religion as a "series of options the believer chooses between" (Larkin 2015, 75). While to an extent these developments are also mediated by religious talk shows that exclusively invite traditional scholars of varying persuasions, they are even more so enabled by shows that additionally include self-styled scholars on their expert panels. By encouraging the inclusion of self-styled scholars in religious debate, religious shows pose a direct challenge to traditional religious authority, which is a function of such scholars' growing appeal within a section of the Pakistani elite that is increasingly disillusioned by the traditional denominationally driven, normative discourses on Islam. Eickelman and Piscatori (2004, 13) make a similar observation when they note that on account of religious media, contemporary Muslim politics is marked by an absence of the 'ulamā's monopoly over sacred authority and by the inclusion of "'new' religious intellectuals," thereby giving rise to the fragmentation of and contestation over religious authority.

I would like to clarify here that the presence of self-styled scholars on religious shows is not a new phenomenon. Scholars such as Israr Ahmed, Tahirul Qadri, and Ghulam Murtaza Malik have been familiar faces on religious television shows since the days of PTV's monopoly of broadcast religious content. However, despite the ostensible similarities between these scholars and Ghamidi, all of whom lack the credentials of a conventional *madrasa* education, there is a marked difference in the preaching styles adopted by those appearing earlier and Ghamidi. The self-styled scholars appearing earlier on PTV were more willing to conform to the traditional norms and conventions of Islamic debate, whereas Ghamidi has displayed no such inclination. It is perhaps for this reason that the traditional scholarly antipathy toward Ghamidi was particularly marked. In fact, throughout the course of my fieldwork, I did not come across a single traditional scholar or cleric who spoke favorably of Ghamidi.

TAFSĪR BI-L-RAI

The 'ulamā's greatest fear in relation to Ghamidi's growing popularity was that his controversial interpretations of divine texts would be appropriated by ordinary Muslims to serve as a rallying point against the *madrasa*'s normative control over understandings of Islam in Pakistan. This fear also provoked the Ahl-i Hadīth televangelist *Shaykh* Salafi to claim that Ghamidi's intentions toward Islam were insincere. I met with *Shaykh* Muhammad Salafi on the advice of *Mawlānā* Safdar Usman, a religious scholar who presided over a prestigious Ahl-i Hadīth *madrasa* in the affluent neighborhood of DHA, Karachi. *Shaykh* Salafi, a graduate of the Saudi-based Medina University, was a regular participant on multiple religious television shows. On my first visit to his *madrasa*, we discussed the general benefits and drawbacks of religious television shows. However, during our second meeting, which was also attended by his students, our discussion veered toward a more focused consideration of self-styled scholars. When Ghamidi's name came up, *Shaykh* Salafi made the following observation: "There is no doubt that Allah has blessed him with the gift of the gab comparable to none, and he also has comprehensive knowledge of Islamic texts and expertise in Arabic, but all these gifts are meaningless if you are not sincere to the Islamic cause. This is Ghamidi's problem."

Shaykh Salafi's condescending references to Ghamidi's sincerity, which he makes despite his grudging admission of Ghamidi's religious acumen, express the wider scholarly community's misgivings regarding the self-styled scholar's recourse to opinioned reasoning in Qur'ānic interpretation. *Shaykh* Salafi's mode of reasserting religious authority draws on a long-standing Islamic debate between Muslim scholars on the role of *'aql* (intellect/reason) and *naql* (mimicry) in Qur'ānic exegesis and interpretation. Mohsin, an adherent of the Tablīghī Jamā'at, was the first to draw my attention to the importance of *taqlīd* and *naql* for Barelwi and Deobandi traditional religious authority. Mohsin was profoundly influenced by *Mawlānā* Tariq Jameel and his school of thought. Prior to joining the *Jamā'at*, Mohsin had worked as a model in the fashion industry. However, after meeting with *Mawlānā* Jameel, he had decided to abandon this "sinful" career path and to instead devote his life to the higher Islamic cause. Like many other traditionalists that I encountered in the field, Mohsin fervently opposed the idea of employing personal opinion and *'aql* in Qur'ānic interpretation. He viewed this mode of interpretation as evidence of a scholar's tendency to privilege his own opinion over what was divinely ordained. For Mohsin, the concept of Islam as a *dīn* (code of life) necessarily entailed mimicking what the Prophet (PBUH) had revealed through the Qur'ān, enjoined on his companions, or shown by example. Mohsin firmly maintained that it was not a practitioner's job to understand why something had been ordained. We simply had to follow! Mohsin's statement is useful for noting that, while Ghamidi's subversive interpretations may appeal to Pakistani liberals, his authority does not sit comfortably with the more conservatively inclined Pakistanis.

For scholars subscribing to the more traditionalist view espoused by Mohsin, any exegetical commentary that draws on a scholar's personal opinion is impermissible under Islamic law and falls within the scope of *tafsīr bi-l-rai* (exegetical commentary based on personal opinion). This view particularly applies to scholarly rulings that seek to challenge Islamic laws and practices on which there is prior scholarly consensus with regard to their Islamic standing. It is important to highlight here that *tafsīr bi-l-rai* does not necessarily imply a literalist translation of divine texts. This point is also implicit in *Mawlānā* Kamaluddin's remarks above in relation to a *mustanid 'ālim*'s ability to discern the underlying meaning of divine texts. As clarified by *Mawlānā* Kamaluddin, if a literalist interpretation were the primary goal of Qurʾānic exegesis, then there would have been no discord between the Prophet's (PBUH) successors on the intended meaning of divine texts, as everyone would have discerned the same meaning. However, for the *tafsīr* to qualify as legitimate, it cannot be overshadowed by a scholar's self-interests, including the scholar's desire to gain victory over an opponent or receive praise from the general public. In his book *Taleef-e-Usmani*, the historically renowned religious scholar *Allama* Shabbir Ahmed Usmani (n.d.) reinforces this point while clarifying why a recourse to critical deliberation and opinioned reasoning within Islamic doctrine is reserved exclusively for spiritually enlightened scholars. Usmani argues that only these scholars can remove their personal interests from any exegetical or deliberative undertaking. Usmani does not hold the same to be true for less spiritually evolved Muslims (in other words, those who have not undergone the rigors of a *madrasa* education), who are thus encouraged either to conform unquestioningly to literalist Qurʾānic interpretations or to follow what has been mandated by Islamic jurisprudence (*taqlīd*) and established religious authorities (*mustanid ʿulamā*). Drawing on the religious scholarship of his predecessors, Usmani maintains that ultimately the divine texts cannot be made subject to lay interpretation, as the lay intellect (*ʿaql*) is less than "pure" and is subjective, personal, and therefore misguiding.

This belief is best expressed in the following comment from a Deobandi *imām* justifying his misgivings on the pluralistic nature of televised religious discourse: "What is opinion? We have to give the truth! There is only one truth, not the myriad opinions that are presented as truth on television." The *imām*'s comments reveal that even though a recourse to *ijtihād* is permissible under Islam law, its application in the contemporary context has been made subject to certain regulations by traditional Islamists. These Islamists maintain that the allowance for partaking in *ijtihād* should be strictly reserved for *mustanid* scholars and primarily for cases where a recourse to *taqlīd* (or literalist interpretations in the case of the Ahl-i Hadīth *maslak*), *qiyās* (precedent), and *ijmā* (scholarly consensus) does not constitute a viable option.

The strict regulations governing the exercise of *ijtihad* also gave way to a corresponding traditional scholarly concern regarding its employment by lay Muslims. Many of the scholars who owed their religious erudition to the institution of the *madrasa* believed that the alternative interpretations of key Islamic texts expounded by self-styled scholars would implicitly pave the way for an understanding of *ijtihād* as an exercise that any Muslim could undertake. While my scholarly interlocutors also voiced this concern in relation to the distinctions in traditional scholarly viewpoints, it was especially pronounced in relation to the dominant or exclusive presence of self-styled scholars on religious shows. A noteworthy consideration here is that the prominence of self-styled scholars and their innovative rulings in televised religious debate necessarily draws on a popular view of traditional scholarly knowledge as limited. Moreover, in provoking lay doubts about the mandatory nature of certain historically established Islamic concepts, self-styled scholars implicitly undermine the right of traditional scholars to mandate these concepts as obligatory. While I discuss the detailed implications of these developments from a lay viewer perspective in chapter 7, for now I limit myself to suggesting that because these self-styled preachers' presentations on television are intended to expose the limitations of traditional scholarly interpretations on key Islamic provisions, they provoke traditional scholars to renew their efforts to control and circumscribe the role of personal opinion in religious public debate.

Since Ghamidi has largely focused on countering Islamic concepts and provisions otherwise mandated by the ʿulamā, I was not surprised when numerous madrasa-based scholars came to designate his rulings as consistent with tafsīr bi-l-rai. The ʿulamā would generally make these claims as regards Ghamidi's proposition on female veiling, his rulings on music and financial interest as both permissible under Islamic law, and his opposition to jihād as no longer applicable in the contemporary context. I would like to point out here that because the employment of ʿaql in Islamic interpretation is generally associated with self-styled scholars, in contrast to naql and taqlīd, which are deemed more essential to traditional authority, religious shows that invite self-styled scholars (whether exclusively or alongside traditional scholars) exacerbate the tension between these two distinct modes of interpretation. For this reason, religious authority comes to be increasingly claimed on the basis of one interpretative mode or the other, depending on the proclivities of the religious specialists. It was while asserting the limitations of the ʿaql in Qur'ānic interpretation that the religious scholar Mawlānā Kamaluddin also drew my attention to the flaws inherent in Ghamidi's ruling on veiling as a redundant Islamic practice, essentially superfluous to female piety: "Ghamidi has declared on television that those days are gone when a woman would wear burqa [veil] and stay at home. According to Ghamidi this is no longer possible as the woman has entered every field. By arguing that there is no need for veiling, Ghamidi is choosing to ignore the ḥadīth for fame and popularity. He deals with Islamic issues based on his own whims."

In Mawlānā Kamaluddin's opinion, Ghamidi's recourse to opinioned reasoning for an already established Islamic practice constituted a grave violation of the terms of Islamic debate. It revealed that the self-styled scholar had strayed from the "truth" and succumbed to his own personal and illicit whims and desires. In this context, *Mawlānā* Kamaluddin also argued that the self-styled scholar was displeasing Allah by privileging his own commercial interests over Allah's commands. *Mawlānā* Kamaluddin's portrayal of Ghamidi as driven by commercial interests and as acting on caprice, in defiance of Islamic injunctions, is consistent with Salvatore's (1998, 96) view regarding the featuring of religion on popular media as encouraging preachers to privilege media popularity and "regimes of consumption" over Islamic tradition. Alternatively, I would like to draw attention to the strategic relevance of such portrayals in allowing traditional scholars to simultaneously reclaim the *madrasa*'s religious authority and circumscribe the boundaries of religious debate. While examining the popularity of Al Huda, the center for Qur'ānic learning, among Pakistani middle- and upper-class women, Ahmad (2010, 324) makes a similar claim in relation to the *'ulamā*'s misgivings about Al Huda, which as she notes are despite the center's conventional, interpretative, and pedagogical orientation. Drawing on this observation, Ahmad locates the traditional scholarly rhetoric against Al Huda in the concern for religious authority rather than in a regard for proper religious guidance.

Bayat (2007, 456) inadvertently clarifies the reasons for this scholarly concern while stressing the relevance of the "shared paradigm" in sustaining conventional perceptions of religious authority. According to Bayat (456), any aspect of Muslim belief that does not fall within the purview of the "shared paradigm" offers Muslims a way out of complying with traditional scholarly influence, thus rendering the latter "powerless." Bayat's clarification is particularly useful for making sense of the traditional scholarly objections to Ghamidi's exegetical method, which as Sadaf Aziz (2011) points out is, in fact, not very different from the method adopted by traditional scholars. In this context, Aziz (614) also effectively debunks the traditional scholarly claim that Ghamidi's interpretative methods follow a rationalist episteme, "one wherein the spirit and not the letter of the Quran needs to be abided." According to Aziz (615), in spite of popular belief, Ghamidi continues to give centrality of place to the words of the Qur'ān, although his exegetical method differs from traditionalist methods in that it involves "finding consistent and verifiable meaning from within the Quranic text." In line with this view, Aziz maintains that the misperceptions regarding Ghamidi's interpretative style owe mainly to the differences between his interpretations and traditionalist scholarly interpretations. By drawing attention to the tenuous grounding of the *'ulamā*'s claims against Ghamidi, Aziz also clarifies an understanding of *Mawlānā* Kamaluddin's attempts at undermining the self-styled scholar, as similarly provoked by an overwhelming concern for sustaining his institution's religious authority in a religiopolitical landscape where the *madrasa's* ascendancy in religious public debate is increasingly uncertain and fragile. Within this framework, it is not so much that personal opinion has no place in Islam; it is more so a question of who should be allowed recourse to it, in which contexts, and to what extent. As detailed above, my conversations with traditional scholars reveal that, at least from a "traditionalist" perspective, the employment of opinioned reasoning is the sole province of *madrasa*-educated scholars, is to be reserved exclusively for issues on which there is no prior scholarly consensus, and is permissible only in so far as it does not provoke the rethinking or reconstitution of historically established Islamic practices. From this lens, we can also view the scholarly discourse on *ijtihād* and the regulations pertaining to it as constituting a useful discursive strategy by means of which traditional scholars can highlight the interpretative limitations of self-styled scholars and reassert their monopoly over popular forms of religious understanding. All such portrayals of self-styled scholars draw on literalist and monolithic understandings of Islam, which correspondingly seek to denote all alternative religious viewpoints as a digression from Islam.

ROSHAN KHYALI AND INDIVIDUAL FREEDOM

The traditional scholarly discourse targeting Ghamidi also included derogatory references to the self-styled scholar's proclivity toward *roshan khyali* (enlightened thinking). Despite its literal translation as implying something positive, the term, as it was employed by traditional scholars, alluded to the self-styled scholars' Westernization and their subsequent desire to cater to the liberal viewer majority who had strayed from the religious path and who desired emancipation from Islamic directives. My *madrasa*-based interlocutors often employed this term in conjunction with *azad khyali* (free thinking) to allude to Ghamidi's transgression of the normative boundaries imposed by Islamic moral and ethical codes. Similarly, while justifying his opposition to Ghamidi's rulings, Aslam, one of *Shaykh* Salafi's students, explained to me that within Islam there was no allowance for liberty and autonomy: "We are like bonded slaves with no free time away from religion. Even a slave gets time off, but we are bound to obey God at all times."

While explaining the difference between Islamic and Judeo-Christian discourse, Asad (1993) highlights a concept of Muslim being similar to the one proposed by Aslam. Drawing on an oration of the well-known lecturer and *khaṭīb* Āl Za'ayr, Asad (219) notes that under Islam the virtuous Muslim is "seen not as an autonomous individual who assents to a set of universalizable maxims but as an individual inhabiting the moral space shared by all who are together bound to God (the *umma*)."[5] In this world the central idea binding the *umma* is "obedience to God's commands and the exemplary practice (*Sunna*) of the Prophet," a conception of a Muslim as *Muta'abbid*, which implies that a Muslim is ineluctably "bound to God" as God's "'*abd*" (221–22). Asad uses the term *'abd* to denote both a "slave" and a "worshipper." Asad (221) argues that a relationship thus conceived between God and his *'abd* is at odds with the Judeo-Christian discourse, which roots the relationship with God in the "figure of kinship (God as Father) and the figure of contract (the Covenant with God)." Thus, Asad (221–22) argues, what is required from a Muslim is "unconditional obedience." Alternatively, in Aslam's case, I would like to suggest that we consider his emphasis on "unconditional obedience" as a strategy of exclusion, by means of which traditional Islamists can bracket off any recourse to *ijtihād* by self-styled celebrity preachers as evidence of the latter's *roshan khyali*. Such claims also assist traditional scholars in circumventing the diffusion of moderate, "modern," Western, and liberal understandings of Islam. By including self-styled scholars in their panels, religious shows play an important role in provoking such claims to religious authority.

RELIGIOUS SHOW ANCHORS

In addition to the presence of self-styled scholars, many of my scholarly interlocutors also expressed their reservations about the increased presence of show hosts as moderators on religious talk shows. In relation to this concern, my scholarly interlocutors highlighted the figure of Aamir Liaquat Husain. As they lamented, Husain rose to prominence despite his lack of formal religious education. I have already highlighted that Husain's career as a religious show anchor was launched by his presence on the religious talk show *Aalim Online* in November 2002. Husain, who had earned his MBBS at Liaquat Medical College in Hyderabad and later embarked on a career in journalism, initiated his religious career in tandem with the launch of Geo Television Network in 2002. Subsequent to his rise to fame as the host of one of the most popular religious programs, Husain joined the Muttahida Qaumi Movement (MQM), a political party under the Mohajir (immigrant) leadership of Altaf Hussain. On account of his affiliation with the MQM, Husain was nominated the minister of religious affairs. However, he resigned from the post after a falling-out with MQM over his "hard line" stance against blasphemy (DAWN 2007a) and the Ahmadi community. He is currently serving as a minister of the National Assembly, as an affiliate of Imran Khan's political party, Pakistan Tehreek-i-Insaf.

Despite his vast popularity with the general Pakistani public, Husain has garnered mixed reactions from Pakistani religious show viewers in relation to his sincerity to the religious cause and his ostensible preference for the Barelwi viewpoint. Controversies associated with Husain include the inciting of hatred against the Ahmadis on *Aalim Online*, the release of a controversial behind-the-scenes video of Husain "using vulgar language and speaking crassly with his [scholarly] companions," the giving away of babies in his *Ramaḍān* game show, and his inability to authenticate a degree in Islamic studies from an institute of dubious repute in Spain (DAWN 2013). Moreover, the scholarly status ascribed to Husain by some of his fans has contributed to the general scholarly reservations regarding him. In this context, my scholarly interlocutors expressed a concern regarding Husain's televised projection as a religious scholar in his own right. Many scholars felt that this projection would have the effect of rendering the ʿ*ulamā*'s expertise over religious knowledge effectively meaningless. The Ahl-i Hadīth scholar *Shaykh* Salafi similarly objected that Husain was ill-equipped to handle viewers' queries by himself, as while he was a good debater, he was not trained to be a religious scholar or exegete. For *Shaykh* Salafi, the religious show host's lack of formal religious training further implied that he was incapable of measuring up to the ʿ*ulamā* in matters of Islamic etiquette and conduct. In this context, the *Shaykh* also feared that the religious anchor's inappropriate conduct on television would reflect poorly on the entire scholarly community and adversely affect the community's authoritative standing. Schleifer (2004) highlights a similar debate in the context of objections from *Shaykh* Al Qaradawi (the popular Al Jazeera preacher and Al-Azhar university graduate) to Al Jazeera's featuring of the popular Egyptian lay preacher Amr Khaled. Schleifer (2004) notes that Al Qaradawi's misgivings in this context are mainly on account of Amr Khaled's lack of formal scholarly credentials.

THE ANCHOR'S CONDUCT

The scholarly concerns regarding Husain's conduct were most prominent in relation to his featured presence as the moderator of a religious game show. Given Husain's personal allegiance to the Barelwi tradition, his conduct became an even greater source of concern for the adherents of this tradition, who feared that Husain's notoriety, as mediated by his presence on the religious game show, would reflect particularly poorly on the Barelwi school. I had been in Karachi for a few months when I met up with the students of the Barelwi Islamic Mission School for women. I had spotted the *madrasa* earlier, while driving up to an Ahl-i Hadīth *madrasa* located in the same vicinity. I was intrigued by the *madrasa's* presence in an older part of the city, given its focus on women. Religious institutes catering exclusively to women tend to be a rare site in Pakistan, where greater emphasis generally tends to be placed on the religious education of Muslim males. Thus, even though most of the seminaries I visited during my fieldwork boasted a *banāt* (female section) for imparting religious education to women, these generally offered only a basic level of religious education that extended to, at most, a period of four years. This was in stark contrast to the seven- or eight-year period of dedicated religious study prescribed for males striving to attain a more comprehensive status in religious erudition. On returning home from my visit to the Ahl-i Hadīth *madrasa*, I called the Barelwi school's principal to request her permission to conduct a group discussion with the school's students. On my subsequent visit, the principal invited six of her students to join our discussion.

The female students, although generally dismissive of all contemporary religious talk shows, were especially critical of Husain's role in undermining the religious authority of the Barelwi school. These students were primarily concerned about Husain's attempt to edify viewers on the "proper" rules of Islamic conduct on his talk show and his blatant disregard for the same rules when hosting his game show. On the game show, Husain encouraged the free mingling of men and women, poked fun at various members of the live studio audience, and featured background music. More recently, he had even gone so far as to offer a female audience member a prize for having the longest hair in the audience. The students felt that this conduct was in bad taste and went against the norms of Islamic comportment. Throughout the meeting I noted that the girls were less troubled by Husain's deviation from Islamic norms and values and more concerned about how the host's failure to conduct himself properly would reflect poorly on the Barelwi school. As one girl remarked, "On the surface he represents us and is one of us, but in reality, he has made us, the Ahle Sunna [Barelwi], very controversial along with himself."

When I questioned Husain about his controversial conduct on the religious game show, he explained that it was part of a deliberate production plan to promote more tolerant and moderate representations of Islam on television. On the same basis, Husain also justified the more inclusive format of his game show, with its mix of free-thinking and conservative audience members, which, he explained was intended to encourage tolerant interactions between people espousing different religious sensibilities and different degrees of religiosity. According to Husain, his game show's diversity reflected his vision of an "ideal" Pakistani society where, for instance, women with and without *hijab* and men with and without beards could inhabit the same environment without passing judgment or imposing their views on one another. While conducting my research with religious show viewers, I found people very much divided on the matter of the continued telecast of religious game shows. Whereas some people tended to oppose these shows on account of the Islamic inconsistencies characterizing them, others appreciated Husain's role in spreading tolerance and promoting unity between Muslims. For the latter group, Husain's game show also marked a positive transition from the *'ulamā*'s normative control over religion. In this context, my interlocutors also expressed their appreciation of the child adoption segment on Husain's game show. They lauded the game show host's ability to garner the *'ulamā*'s support for the practice of child adoption in Pakistan. They appreciated the segment despite their acknowledgment of its controversial nature. A pertinent consideration here is how the controversy surrounding the segment draws more on the inappropriateness of the venue than it does on the Islamic transgressions involved in the practice itself. Therefore, it needs to be acknowledged that Husain has been able to promote a practice of dubious Islamic standing on public television in spite of the *'ulamā*'s reservations regarding it. At the very least, Husain's endorsement of child adoption on his game show has succeeded in drawing the government's attention to the gaps in Pakistani legislation for ensuring the transparency of the practice and the safety of adopted children (see BBC News 2013). This development indicates that, just as self-styled scholars subvert the *'ulamā*'s prescribed boundaries of religious debate, so too do religious show hosts play a crucial role in constantly challenging extant Islamic values.

ANCHOR AS INTERMEDIARY

An important aspect of the presence of anchors on religious shows is their position as intermediaries between the invited religious scholars and the show audiences. *Shaykh* Salafi justified his resentment of this development by emphasizing the anchors' lack of Islamic erudition for adequately performing this role. For *Shaykh* Salafi, the anchor's presence further implied that the true spirit of the scholarly message was lost by the time it reached the audience. Moreover, it was not merely the absence of requisite Islamic knowledge but also the intent of the anchor that formed the basis of *Shaykh* Salafi's critique. He felt that some religious anchors deliberately attempted to trap the *'ulamā*, so as to generate more sensational content for their shows. *Shaykh* Salafi maintained that it would be better if religious scholars were permitted to answer the questions comprehensively without any interruptions from anchors. As he argued, "Challenging an ʿālim's ruling is akin to disrespecting him and encourages other Muslims to do the same." While Galal (2009, 155) makes a similar observation on the role of the anchor in the Al Jazeera–featured Islamic show *Sharīʿa waʾl Ḥayāt* (Sharīʿa and life), he views the anchor as also underscoring the agency of the audiences on whose behalf the anchor intercedes and asks difficult questions of the religious scholar. However, there are some important distinctions between the role played by anchors such as Ahmed Mansur in the Al Jazeera show *Sharīʿa waʾl Ḥayāt* and the role played by Husain and Bilal Qutab on Pakistani religious shows. Even though, as Galal (2009) notes, the former may sometimes adopt a confronting and polemical style to ask controversial questions of scholars such as Qaradawi, the delineation of religious authority is nonetheless clear and rests exclusively with the scholar present on the show. In Pakistan, this is not necessarily the case, as the distinction between the authority of religious scholars and that of the anchors is frequently blurred by the anchors themselves, who in many instances assume the role of religious authorities by imparting religious advice to viewers without referring the questions to the scholars.

Mawlānā Ahmed drew my attention to this point while recounting his experience with Husain on an episode of *Aalim Online*. He noted that Husain would often take over the whole show, thus not allowing the scholars ample time to respond to viewers' queries. "We the *ʿulamā* were invited, but Husain would take it upon himself to answer most of the queries raised by the audiences. The *ʿulamā* would just be sitting there." *Mawlānā* Ahmed viewed such behavior as damaging to the sanctity of the scholar's institution and, by extension, Islam. "He gives too much valence to his own opinion. You cannot put your own opinion over that of the *ʿulamā*'s or attempt to explain what they have said, as the meaning is lost in translation." While many of the scholars I met with in the field rooted their contentions in this context, in the loss of "true" religious meaning and the lay incapacity to grapple with profound Islamic texts, I had a feeling that their contentions were, at least partly, also prompted by the scholars' fear of losing their influence in religious public debate. This fear also inspired some scholars, such as the principal of the Islamic Mission School, to advocate for the removal of religious show hosts from the show format. The principal believed that the anchors' presence would implicitly encourage lay Muslims to consider themselves religious experts. "They [the laity] mimic him [Husain] and follow him and start to issue their own religious rulings. They have also recently taken to challenging the *ʿulamā* as they have seen the anchor do." While justifying her proposition, the principal gave me the example of a talk show recently viewed by one of her students. On the show, a reporter had gone around asking nonscholarly Muslims about their views on the Islamic standing of music. The principal noted that the presenter had declared music permissible on the basis of the responses received from the lay majority. Complaining about the growing propensity of this trend, the principal protested, "How can these people without any prior knowledge of Islamic texts be regarded as authorities on the Islamic status of music?"

When I put forth the ʿulamāʾs complaints to Husain, he laughed knowingly and shrugged them off. He explained that part of his job as the religious anchor of a religious show was to undertake in-depth Islamic research on the topics marked for discussion. While defending his position to me, Husain also insinuated that his knowledge of Islam, which had been accumulated over an extensive period of fourteen years, was far more comprehensive and superior to that of a *muftī* whose religious erudition had been acquired over a mere period of seven to eight years. Husain also bragged, "I can give you ready answers to more than eight thousand Islamic queries, whereas the *muftī* can probably only manage three thousand without referring to the texts." From Husain's words, we get a sense that, at least within the format of religious talk shows, religious anchors inhabit multiple roles and yet limit themselves to neither category. They represent the viewers on whose behalf they ask questions of the scholars; they act as moderators, thus dictating the topical direction of each episode; and they assume the role of religious authorities in some instances, by dealing with the viewers' queries by themselves, without any recourse to the religious scholars present. These multiple spaces that religious anchors occupy also allow them to pose more provocative questions to featured scholars. Within this framework, there is an alternative way to analyze the religious authority of show hosts such as Aamir Liaquat Husain who lack the customary scholarly credentials generally deemed necessary for claiming religious authority. As Larkin (2015, 64) notes in the context of the Nigerian preacher Sheikh Abu Bakar Gumi, the preacher's religious authority, rather than accruing from his religious credentials, derives more so from his representation of himself as an "ordinary Muslim." Larkin (64) argues that by representing himself in this manner, Gumi seems to suggest that "ordinary Muslims, by corollary, can ascend to the position he occupies." Larkin's observation can also be applied to understand Husain's religious authority as emerging from a popular and widespread regard of him as more in tune with an ordinary Muslim subjectivity. However, it is also true that Husain's dual self-representation as a lay Muslim and a religious scholar, together with his lack of formal religious training, also contributes to his dubious authoritative standing, more so among religious scholars but also among some members of the Pakistani laity.

On religious anchors' proclivity to deliberately interrogate or ask provocative questions of the featured scholars, the Barelwi ʿālim Mawlānā Ahmed clarified how this tendency put great pressure on the ʿulamā to prove their authoritative standing to the general public. While exploring the implications of media for religion, some academics have argued that because religious authorities on television are expected to rationally support their views, the audience can see themselves on a par with these authorities, thus encouraging wider participation in religious debate.[6] Alternatively, in the context of the Egyptian religious show Sharīʿa wa'l Ḥayāt, Galal (2009, 155–56) argues for a consideration of the media context as privileging the audience's viewpoint in religious public debate. According to Galal (159), this is because the "Islamic public" that the show is promoting "is in competition with other kinds of Islamic programmes." In Galal's opinion, the viewers' ability to choose between different options accords them a privileged place and at the same time explains the willingness of religious authorities such as Al Qaradawi to deal with controversial or difficult questions on television. Such authorities know that their failure to do so will benefit their competition. Galal's observation is useful for understanding why traditional scholars on television tend to be more open to defending and rationalizing their propositions than their off-television counterparts. Television scholars are aware that their failure to do so will benefit their competition—self-styled scholars. At the same time, they recognize that their confinement to taqlīd, ijmā, qiyās, and literal Qurʾānic exegesis may resonate only with a limited number of religious viewers. In this context Asad (2003, 185) usefully draws our attention to the role historical forces play in shaping elements of "the public" differently. Asad views this as implying that "particular appeals can be made successfully only to some sections of the public and not to others." Asad's (185) argument is rooted in an assumption that the effectiveness of free speech "depends on the kind of listener who can engage appropriately with what is said, as well as the time and space he or she has to live in." While self-styled scholars and their appeals to "common sense" (see Mufti 2007) are subject to similar laws, traditional scholars' need to defend their claims on television is especially limiting because it implies both forgoing their historical advantage over Qurʾānic exegesis and forsaking their doctrinal perspective on the importance of taqlīd, ijmā, qiyās, or literal translation for undertaking any exegetical pursuit.

ANCHOR AS JUDGE AND CONTROLLER

When accounting for the moderating role of religious anchors on religious talk shows, an important consideration is how this role unfolds within the pluralistic religious programming context. For the Ahl-i Hadīth television scholar *Shaykh* Salafi, asking a religious anchor to moderate on a show with multiple religious scholars present was akin to designating the anchor as final judge over the diverse scholarly claims to religious authority. As *Shaykh* Salafi clarified, only a member of the scholarly community could act as a judge over the rulings of other fellow scholars, as the anchor lacked the requisite knowledge and wisdom necessary for undertaking this task. In terms of a scholarly ruling's evaluation by an anchor, *Shaykh* Salafi also contended that Ghamidi was the only scholar allowed to conduct his own show with minimal interference from religious show anchors. *Shaykh* Salafi's contention on the employment of religious anchors primarily for the purposes of mediating traditional scholarly discourse also inflected the level of control exercised by religious anchors over the format and content of the show: "He [Husain] does not have any religious knowledge. He merely calls ʿulamā from different masālik and asks questions of them that suit him. He manipulates them and enforces his own wishes on them. Our knowledge implies that we are no less, if not better than him. Then why should we get used by him just because he happens to be a better debater?"

Shaykh Salafi's reservations on the relegation of religious erudition to dialectic skills within the format of religious shows has also been noted by Larkin (2015) in the context of the Nigerian televangelist Sheikh Abu Bakar Gumi. According to Larkin (64), the privileged position of debating skills as opposed to hierarchical status on religious media "have an affinity with Habermas's (1994, 36–7) conception of the public sphere 'where the authority of status is reduced to the authority of debating skills.'" Alternatively, as regards Pakistani religious programming, another relevant consideration is how the deliberate placement of anchors on religious shows allows producers to emphasize more moderate and accommodative understandings of Islam on television. While analyzing Egyptian religious shows hosted by "lay" Islamists such as Amr Khaled and Moez Masoud, Moll (2010, 11) notes how such moderate expressions of Islam on religious shows featured on Arabic satellite channels target two distinct audiences, non-Muslims and Muslims. Moll (11) asserts that, whereas for non-Muslims an emphasis on the moderate aspects of Islam seeks to "counter dominant stereotypes of Islam in the West as a violent and irrational religion," for Muslims such conceptions are positioned against more extremist forms of Islamism and Western conceptualizations of the "modern" and secular. Moll's (2010) argument also explains why traditional scholars have limited opportunities to conduct their own religious shows in Pakistan. These observations indicate that one of religious anchors' key tasks is to act as watchdogs over these scholars so as to circumvent any radical articulations of sectarian activism on television. This would explain why Ghamidi, who is generally regarded as more moderate than traditional Islamists, is allowed to conduct his show without any intercession by religious anchors. As already addressed in chapter 2, the allowance given to self-styled scholars in this context is consistent with the Pakistani state's efforts to curb terrorism in the country. However, we need to bear in mind that such privileges, when accorded exclusively to self-styled scholars, also implicitly privilege their authority over that of the ʿulamā. Whereas self-styled scholars are permitted to address audiences directly, religious producers, at least in most cases, do not extend the same allowance to traditional scholars.

THE STRATEGIC POTENTIAL OF SELF-STYLED SCHOLARS AND RELIGIOUS SHOW HOSTS

An important factor contributing to the popularity of self-styled scholars such as Ghamidi is the way that these scholars deliberately position themselves in opposition to traditional Islamists. This tendency allows these scholars to tap into a niche market of viewers who are disillusioned by the ʿulamā's normative emphasis. Pertinent to this discussion is Schulz's (2006a) observation on small media. Schulz (144) argues that the diversification of the "media landscape that was once almost entirely under the control of the state," rather than "simply favoring a greater transparency of and broader inclusion into critical public debate," contributes to the transformation of public debate "into a marketplace of ideas." According to Schulz (144–45), in this marketplace, the "opportunities to advertise competing views of community," as mediated by the commodification of religious television shows, depend on the actors' "access to representatives and resources of the state." From this perspective, we can also view the rising prominence of religious show hosts and self-styled scholars as having as much to do with state patronage (in lieu of the changes in state policy after 9/11, Musharraf's program of "Enlightened Moderation," and the Pakistan military's more recent initiative in Pakistan's tribal belt) as it does with the increased commodification of religious shows and the diversity of viewers these shows aim to cater to.

Particularly in relation to Ghamidi's role in highlighting the failings of traditional scholarly discourses on religion, we need to bear in mind that the self-styled scholar deliberately provoked a widespread disregard for the ʿulamā's involvement in political and power projects. In an interview given to Mufti (2007), Ghamidi admits that part of his mission is to see the ʿulamā restored "to their classical role: as prestigious, independent intellectual theorists of religious text who are above politics and power." It is from this perspective that we also need to view self-styled scholars, and religious shows by extension, as complicit in a political project aimed at minimizing the ʿ*ulamā*'s, and therefore Islam's, role in electoral politics. Both Mufti (2007) and Naqvi (2010) draw attention to Ghamidi's political import by noting that the celebrity preacher was deliberately selected by Musharraf for the Council of Islamic Ideology (CII) and for the state-owned PTV channel, in tandem with a state agenda, to promote more moderate forms of Islamic sociability (see chap. 1).

The political underpinnings guiding the rising prominence of self-styled scholars also apply to the enhanced presence of religious show hosts on religious talk shows. More specifically, the ability of these anchors to exercise control over televised representations of Islam makes them particularly useful for instituting various state and production agendas. Even though Husain has never explicitly claimed this goal for himself, the fact that both his shows support more accommodative ideas of the Muslim community makes him complicit in mitigating the normative influence of traditional scholars in Pakistani society. Thus, what appears to be a more inclusive project of pluralism on religious television shows needs to be reevaluated in terms of its strategic potential in undermining the significance of traditional authorities in religious debate.

Here, I would like to point out that even as religious shows enable the emergence and significance of self-styled scholars and religious show hosts, the place and status of both authorities in Pakistani religious debate remain ambiguous and contested, dependent on their potential to challenge the religious status quo. Despite these limitations, both religious authorities play a significant part in altering the general public's assessments of religious authority and the terms of religious public debate.

NOTES

1. See Fischer and Abedi (1990) and Bowen (1993) for a further understanding of this concept.

2. Robinson (2013, 3) denotes *isnād* (list of authoritative transmitters) as a traditional mode of authenticating religious authority, which involves "going back to the original author of the book, and indicating how this piece of knowledge was deeply-rooted in the Islamic past."

3. For Schulz (2006a, 144), "small media include decentralized, aural and visual media such as audiotapes, radio broadcasts, and videotapes.

4. Schulz (2006a) makes this claim in relation to the Islamic televangelist Chérif Haidara in Mali, whose claims to religious erudition are bolstered by his fluency in religious texts and his firm command of canonical debates.

5. This oration is available on a tape recording entitled *ad-dīnu an-nasīhatu*, which is easily accessible in Saudi Arabia (Asad 1993, 214).

6. See Hoover (2002, 2), who notes that "individuals and communities" are seen as equally relevant in the "construction of meaning," and Babb (1998, 2), who similarly emphasizes the participative role of religious specialists and the audience in the propagation and construction of symbolic meaning. Eickelman and Anderson (2003, 2) similarly argue that on account of religion's proliferation on media, the religious message and its production are no longer "confined to formal [religious] institutions."

SIX

CHANGING VIEWER ASSESSMENTS OF RELIGIOUS AUTHORITY

WHEN I INITIATED MY RESEARCH in Karachi, it was the holy month of *Ramaḍān*, a time of intense religious fervor imbued with more than the customary glimpses of religiosity seen during the rest of the year. *Ramaḍān* in Pakistan is a time when people put their corporeal pursuits on hold and immerse themselves in a world replete with spirituality and acts of religious devotion and worship. This momentary transformation and heightened religious fervor, as witnessed throughout the month, also expresses itself through people's television viewing practices. Reduced working hours and more time to kill in the run-up to *iftār* tempt even viewers who are generally less riveted by televised religious content to partake in the pleasures of pious modes of television viewing. The initial period of my research was thus indebted to *Ramaḍān* and the animated living-room discussions that accompanied people's enhanced interest in religious television. It was during this period that I first began to get a sense of the diversity that characterized people's engagement with religious television. People either loved the entertainment format of *Ramaḍān* game shows, such as *Amaan Ramazan*, or lamented the incorporation of religious television into a competitive and primarily commercial world of satellite media. Similarly, if for some of my informants the pluralism (doctrinally inspired and rooted in educational differences) of religious talk shows represented a favorable change from the more unified focus of earlier religious programming, for others it implied a more troubled relationship with televised forms of religiosity.

A similar equivocation also marked people's thoughts about religious scholars on television. People would either revere them for their knowledge or condemn them for their participation in the commercial world of religious programming; place their trust in them or look to them with suspicion on account of their perceived contribution to sectarian politics. My informants' varied relationships with religious shows and those who featured on them constantly made me aware of the "multifarious subjectivities" (Mankekar 1999, 17) that emerge from the complex relationship between televised discourses, the viewers' preconceived notions of Islam and religious authority, and their lived experience of religion. The varying perceptions of religious shows also indicated to me that the decision to participate in the pluralistically driven world of religious television was not without its complications for religious scholars, whose regular appearances on religious shows could just as easily work against them by putting their religious authority at risk.

How does the confusion generated by the diverse and conflicting representations of Islam and religious authority on television affect the viewers' perceptions of religious authority? In asking this question, I draw on McLuhan's (1964, 31) emphasis on the formal qualities of communication technologies and the resulting circulation of "too much information" in rendering a world once "experienced as knowable" as unknowable. McLuhan's work has since been critiqued for its technological determinism (see Williams 1974, 1980), on account of its tendency to elide the historical, social, and cultural contexts that also determine the way people employ technology. Taking Williams's criticism into account, I consider not only how the featuring of religion on satellite television affects people's engagement with religious authority but also how people employ religious shows in varying contexts to resist and challenge, or preserve, the religious status quo.

Rather than simply investigating the role of religious television in the fragmentation of religious authority, I explore the nature of this fragmentation. A key issue that I highlight in this context is the role of religious talk shows in prompting viewers to employ novel criteria when discerning between multiple and competing claims to religious authority. In particular, I explore how the diversity of Islamic content on television shifts the viewers' attention from the scholars' requisite mastery over classical texts to other modes of assessing religious authority. This part of my analysis is also inspired by Robinson's (1993) claim about the changing contexts of knowledge transmission (from oral to print in Robinson's study). According to Robinson, one of the main consequences of print Islam was that it raised doubt regarding the trustworthiness of circulated knowledge. What Robinson posits for print Islam is also useful for exploring the impact of the changing production context in relation to religious shows.

My investigation into television's role in transforming the means of assessing religious authority is primarily rooted in my fieldwork interactions with viewers, but it is also inspired by anthropological scholarship that posits the growing prominence of attributes other than the scholars' mastery of religious knowledge in conferring religious authority (Mahmood 2005; Larkin 2008; Moll 2010). Therefore, while some academics continue to postulate a perceived mastery of religious texts as central to the performance of religious authority (Schulz 2003, 2006b), others have compellingly highlighted the need to look beyond religious erudition when analyzing religious authority (Larkin 2008; Moll 2010).[1] For instance, discussing the religious authority of Egyptian televangelist Amr Khaled, whose popularity persists despite his lack of command over Islamic texts, Moll (2010) explains that Khaled's authority is primarily a function of his affinity with the viewers, who view him as one of them. Similarly, Larkin (2008, 103–6) points out that the popularity of South African Islamic preacher Ahmed Deedat partly derives from his ability to appropriate "the forms of the secular public sphere" and has more to do with his "mastery of Christian rather than Muslim texts and his skill at English rather than Arabic." Likewise, in the context of the women's religious movement in Egypt, Mahmood (2005) argues that the ultimate form of scholarly arguments is not always grounded in elite religious scholarship but is to an extent contextually determined.

Mahmood's emphasis on the significance of the context, while invoked to clarify the shifting nature of scholarly arguments, is also relevant for understanding my interlocutors' varied engagements with religious authorities on television. For my interlocutors, their investment in a particular mode of living (pious or less pious), their religious affiliations, and their understanding of intra-Muslim politics also framed their assessments of religious authority and the relevance they assigned to Islamic tradition. In this, they were aided by the pluralism of televised Islamic discourses. In this context, I examine how the diverse and often conflicting interpretations and applications of Islamic texts on religious television influence broader evaluations of religious authority that have historically been vested in the religious scholars' mastery over the Qurʾān and ḥadīth.[2] As already indicated in earlier chapters (4 and 5), prior to the liberalization of media, religious expertise was traditionally claimed and performed by religious scholars on the state-owned PTV channel in two ways. The first was by demonstrating sufficient proficiency over classical Islamic texts. The second was through a more embodied enactment of this proficiency, in which a scholar had to be seen as a living manifestation of the Qurʾān and Prophetic tradition, paying special attention to the physical and sartorial aspects of appearance, such as the proper length of beard, wearing the *shalwar* (trouser) above the ankle, and donning a cap or turban. These modes of Islamic dressing were upheld even by self-styled scholars such as Dr. Israr Ahmed and Ghulam Murtaza Malik, who appeared frequently on PTV. However, these traditional ways of performing and claiming religious authority are not upheld by religious show hosts and celebrity preachers (such as Husain and Ghamidi, respectively), whose neatly trimmed beards and modern Pakistani attire, together with their tendency to stray from conventional modes of claiming religious authority, position them as purveyors of a modern Islamic sensibility. The religious authority of these personalities is not so much a function of their scholarly credentials as it is a product of their charismatic personalities or their ability to rise above their doctrinal affiliations.

When analyzing the viewers' engagement with issues of religious authority, I aim to transcend the notion of a reified and passive viewing public by focusing on the diversity of views related to the relevance and influence of religious television. Morgan (2008, 6–7, 17) endorses this approach by warning us of the dangers of perceiving religious television shows as "fixed" and as therefore discrete from "consumption" practices and the "process of engagement that includes struggle, resistance, and an ensuing transformation of consciousness." Like Abu-Lughod (2005, 21), I am more interested in understanding how television interacts with "localizable and tangible" contexts, which in the case of Pakistan includes both the viewers' individual religious orientation (liberal, moderate, or conservative; denomination oriented or sans denominations) and the manner in which they experience Islam and doctrinal diversity on a day-to-day basis. Especially important in the latter context are the growing incidence of sectarian violence in Karachi and the extent to which Pakistanis increasingly link doctrinal activism with the dissipating unity among Muslims.

As noted in the introduction, I initially conceived my research on religious television viewers while keeping in mind the sociological categories of class, gender, age, and education. This manner of conceptualizing viewer-based research is not new to media scholarship (Morley 1980; Mankekar 1999; Abu-Lughod 2005), wherein the viewing contexts, along with a consideration of the audience reception and media as texts, form an essential part of the analysis. To access the diversity of Pakistani viewers, I visited schools and colleges, including those managed by the government, that cater to working-class students and provide instruction primarily in Urdu. I also visited those schools and colleges that are privately owned, which cater to the more affluent Karachiites and whose medium of instruction is English. In addition, I met with housewives, working and retired men, students educated at Western universities, journalists, and writers to undertake a more contextually rooted analysis of religious show viewers.

My initial research involved viewing religious shows with some of my lay interlocutors. However, I soon abandoned this form of research in favor of discussions outside the viewing contexts. This was primarily due to the difficulties associated with this mode of research. People in Karachi do not have fixed schedules when it comes to their viewing of religious shows. They view them erratically and at their own convenience. Some housewives with whom I viewed Husain's morning show would often miss substantial portions of the telecasts to finish their domestic chores, such as cooking, seeing to their children, and so forth. Alternatively, those of my interlocutors who worked would mainly access repeat telecasts of some religious show episodes aired too late at night to make it possible for me to join them. Some Karachiites also displayed a mercurial interest in religious shows, turning to them intermittently rather than regularly. Yet others mainly expressed their interest in the more sensational content floating on social media websites. The broadcast schedules of religious shows also contributed to my interlocutors' irregular viewing habits. Some programs were aired seasonally, while others, such as Husain's talk shows, frequently switched broadcasting times, thus making it impossible for my interlocutors to keep abreast of the changes in transmission time. Regular access to religious shows was thus only possible in the case of dedicated religious channels, of which the most popular was QTV. As already noted in the introduction, my analysis in this chapter and the next one mainly focuses on the commentaries of my female interlocutors. Given that the previous chapters in this book elaborate on issues of religious authority and consequently focus on the opinions of male religious scholars and religious show hosts and presenters, the privileging of female voices in these two chapters should be seen as an attempt to balance out an otherwise male-centric ethnography. I have organized the ethnographic portraits that follow in terms of their ability to clarify television's role in engendering new ways of perceiving, evaluating, or identifying with claims to religious authority.

DOCTRINAL MEDIATIONS OF RELIGIOUS AUTHORITY

It was during *Ramaḍān* that I first came across Fatima, a young devout girl in her late teens who studied at the Government Girls Degree College. The college, which was located in the affluent Clifton neighborhood of Karachi, catered primarily to the daughters of rural immigrants who had relocated to Karachi in the hope of gaining access to better economic prospects. The principal of the college allowed me to conduct multiple discussions with her students. Fatima, who participated actively in one of these discussions, referred to herself as an avid viewer of religious talk shows. She admitted to watching them regularly with her mother and sisters. However, she confessed that her favorable opinion of the talk show *Aalim Online* did not extend to its host, Husain, whom she viewed as duplicitous and untrustworthy. Throughout the discussion, Fatima firmly maintained that Husain merely dissimulated piety on the show. "He is not really religious. He merely puts on a show for the viewers." When I pressed her for a clarification, she responded with the following explanation: "In *Ramaḍān*, he [Husain] is a neutral Muslim, in *Muḥarram* he becomes Shi'a, and on *'Īd Mīlād-un Nabī* [Prophet Muhammad's (PBUH) birth anniversary] he transforms into a Barelwi. How can he belong to all the *masālik*? When his *nohas* [songs to mourn the martyrdom of Ḥazrat Ali (RA) and his family] come on television he performs *mātam* [self-beating or flagellation]."

To Fatima, the varied doctrinal personas that Husain donned on television came to reflect his lack of sincerity toward Islam. They implied to Fatima that Husain had become too commercial. For Fatima, Husain thus represented part of a larger problem—the commercialization of religious television shows. Fatima felt that the scholars' hesitation to claim their doctrinal proclivities on television demonstrated their susceptibility to commercial appeal. She came to see the more overt displays of doctrinal affiliation as one of the markers of a scholar's sincerity. Drawing on this attribute, Fatima could thus make sense of the "confusion" on television. This was despite the fact that Fatima did not subscribe to any specific doctrinal ideology. As she explained to me, the ideological and practical differences between different religious groups held little import for her and her family. Instead, the scholars' manifest association with a particular doctrinal ideology implied to Fatima their refusal to be swayed by commercial interests.

Fatima's example is useful for analyzing the viewers' shifting engagement with Islam and religious authority. In this context, it is important to note how the pluralism of religious talk shows and television's propensity to draw attention to the more visible aspects of piety implicitly encourage the association of public religion with doctrinal activism. Television, as an audiovisual medium, emphasizes exteriority. This in turn implies that the television scholar has to fit a visible ideological mold not only to accommodate viewers' diverse affiliations but also to assure viewers of his sincerity. The latter is increasingly difficult to achieve given the widespread perception of religious television as essentially commercial and the propensity of religious shows to accommodate competing claims to religious authority. As Salman, a media teacher at SZABIST, explained to me, "People do not deal well with confusion. They want to know what they are listening to. They want clear concepts in order to easily determine their religious preferences."

Fatima's comments are also pertinent for evaluating what happens to religious authority when Islam is represented as multiple religious viewpoints on television. Viewers who were earlier only exposed to one mainstream Islamic perspective are thus compelled to choose from multiple and competing claims made by different religious authorities, all of which claim to be rooted in classical Islamic texts. The pluralistic focus of religious talk shows implicitly motivates viewers to shift their attention from the scholar's claimed expertise to other variables, in order to discern the scholar's piety. Fatima's emphasis on a scholar's manifest affiliation with a religious group was only one such means by which television scholars could gain favor with the viewers. Many of my lay interlocutors confessed to employing alternative means when determining their viewing preferences. Their criteria were as varied, as they were influenced by my interlocutors' religious sensibilities and the dynamics of religious public life in Pakistan.

TOLERANCE AS A MARKER OF RELIGIOUS AUTHORITY

One of the most controversial and talked about features of religious talk shows is their propensity to feature religious polemics between traditional scholars of varied doctrinal persuasions. While the debates between these scholars contribute significantly to the educational and entertainment value of religious shows, they simultaneously instigate Pakistani concerns regarding the peaceful coexistence of various doctrinal groups. Amber's distaste for most religious talk shows was prompted by such a concern. I made Amber's acquaintance on my visit to a prestigious nursery school in Karachi. Amber, who was in her midthirties and came from an affluent background, was very candid throughout our discussion. She confessed to me that whereas earlier she had watched some religious talk shows, she now avoided most of them. This she mainly blamed on the conduct of religious scholars who presented on television and the debates and altercations that she frequently witnessed while viewing religious shows. Amber could not reconcile her notion of proper scholarly conduct with the hostile scholarly images on television. Instead, she lamented that most of the scholars who appeared on television displayed little restraint when dealing with competing doctrinal and Islamic perspectives. Their tendency to get embroiled in arguments about the correct forms of Islamic practice signaled to Amber their inability to rise above petty sectarian politics. Amber was thus ambivalent about the religiosity of most television scholars, whose actions she felt belied their words. Amber's remarks express the growing Pakistani wariness of the more contentious modes of religious activism and assertions of religious authority, which have tended to characterize religious discourse in Pakistan in recent years. According to the 2013 Pakistan Security Report issued by the Pakistan Institute for Peace Studies, there has been a marked rise in the incidence of sectarian violence in Pakistan, with 208 acts of sectarian violence reported in 2013 alone (DAWN 2014). However, while the wariness that Amber alludes to can be viewed as a function of the confrontational nature of doctrinal politics in Pakistan, it is also engendered by the pluralism of religious talk shows. For a Muslim population whose unity is already under threat, the hostile exchanges between scholars on television often manifest as a further blow to intra-Muslim harmony.

Moreover, religious talk shows that feature debates between scholars of varied persuasions also compel viewers to engage more closely with Muslim conflict. The conflict viewed on television screens is no longer perceived as instigated by unknown forces and factors, with little impact on one's own religious practice. Instead it pervades the setting of the living room, where viewers are compelled to both engage with and participate in the conflict more intimately. The polemical format of religious shows implicitly encourages the viewers to take sides and identify more closely with a particular Islamic perspective. However, the sense of immediacy as mediated through television also enables a closer engagement with the conflict. Meyer (2011, 26) speaks of this in the context of the "divine" when she argues that "practices of religious mediation appear particularly able to invoke a sense of the immediate presence of the divine," whereby the "media become so much entangled with what they contribute to mediate that they are not visible as such, at least not for those who are partaking in mediation." What Meyer says of the divine can just as easily be applied to denote viewers' experience of religious conflict on their television screens. A major consequence of this development is a changed assessment of religious authority, which comes to be increasingly vested in the scholars' ability to exercise restraint and accommodate alternative perspectives into religious public debate. Amber's disregard for the more vitriolic displays of religious authority represents this shift in perspective. Further, even religious shows that seek to avoid a more competitive format play an important role in tilting viewer preferences toward more accommodative assertions of religious authority. When I spoke to Amber regarding the hostile interactions between scholars on religious talk shows, she offered me Husain's game show *Amaan Ramazan* as a more favorable alternative to doctrinally oriented interactions.

Amber's positive regard for religious game shows was in large part attributable to their propensity to promote mutual respect and tolerance between different religious groups. She explained, "His [Husain's] game show is helping change this [violent] perception of Islam. It shows Pakistani Muslims that even Islam promotes *aman* (peace). The *Amaan Ramazan* show is like a small town where everyone participates in religious discourse peacefully and harmoniously."

From Amber's words, it is apparent that religious shows that feature more peaceful interactions between scholars position themselves in contrast to the more confrontational assertions of religious authority. In so doing, they also encourage viewers to compare different sources of religious authority, not on the basis of a scholar's religious erudition and perceived mastery over religious texts, which all television scholars are expected to demonstrate, but on the basis of the scholar's exclusionary or accommodative proclivities. However, of equal import in eliciting such modes of comparison is the role played by self-styled scholars and religious show hosts. Amber was aware of the off-television dynamics of Muslim politics in Pakistan. In contrast, shows such as *Amaan Ramazan* demonstrated to her the positive role that traditional scholars could play in defusing intra-Muslim tension in Pakistan. However, she lamented that most traditional scholars were currently not performing this role adequately. In this context, Amber's misgivings regarding traditional scholars and their apparent disinterest in defusing doctrinal conflict also drew on her view of these scholars as more invested in doctrinal politics, on account of their visible association with select doctrinal ideologies. By contrast, self-styled scholars and religious show hosts who presented themselves as above these differences appeared more tolerant to Amber. Self-styled scholars were not necessarily devoid of such sensibilities or even more accommodative of alternative Islamic perspectives. In fact, these scholars' refusal to ostensibly align themselves with a particular doctrinal affiliation contributed to such perceptions of them. Within this framework, religious shows do not simply provoke alternative ways of evaluating religious authority but also reduce the influence of traditional scholars, whose manifest association with doctrinal Islam delineates them as the key arbiters of intra-Muslim conflict.

The types of comparisons religious talk shows elicit also extend to scholars who do not have a presence on television. To elaborate on this proposition, I revisit one of my discussions with Nadia, a middle-class female in her midforties who was also a close friend of mine. Nadia lived in Nazimabad, in the north of Karachi. While once home to Karachi's elite, Nazimabad currently primarily houses Karachi's middle classes. In the last twenty years, its affluent residents have relocated to the more prestigious DHA locality. Since it took a good hour for me to travel to Nazimabad, I would usually confine myself to visiting Nadia during the weekend. Nadia had been raised by a Sunni mother who did not hold a positive view of Shiʻa faith and practices. Because of her strict Sunni upbringing, Nadia had always been curious about the Shiʻa perspective on Islam. When I asked Nadia about her views on religious talk shows, she confessed that her interest had primarily been instigated by the access they facilitated to multiple Islamic perspectives. Whereas Nadia had been predisposed to view the Shiʻa with some suspicion, she explained that viewing religious talk shows such as *Aalim Online* had helped allay some of her concerns regarding the Shiʻa adherents' Islamic conformance. As a result, Nadia now believed that the differences between the Sunnis and the Shiʻas were not as profound as traditional Sunni scholars had made them out to be. Traditional Sunni scholars, Nadia complained, had a tendency to depict Shiʻa adherents as non-Muslims. Nadia felt that such portrayals of Shiʻa Muslims implicitly justified violence against them by overly zealous Sunni adherents. Acknowledging Husain's role in allowing Shiʻa scholars to defend their group's point of view on *Aalim Online*, Nadia argued that religious shows that privileged the representation of multiple doctrinal perspectives also played a key role in alleviating the tensions between different religious groups. They did so by rendering viewers' immune to alternative conceptualizations of Islam and Islamic practice.

Nadia's comments raise an important point about the role of religious talk shows in spreading awareness about the beliefs of competing religious groups. In this way, religious talk shows also implicitly encourage the significance of tolerance as an indispensable scholarly attribute. This development simultaneously mitigates the influence of traditional scholarly discourses that seek to marginalize select groups in religious public debate. Eickelman and Piscatori (2004, xi) make a similar point when they note that "open communications" have enabled the "increased scrutiny of received ideas as Muslims realize the diversity of the Muslim world and the multiple Islamic ways of doing things." In Nadia's case, especially, her more accommodative approach toward alternative Islamic traditions has important political ramifications for the religious authority of traditional religious scholars, which effectively draws on overplaying the differences between those scholars and other religious groups. As Zaman (2002, 111, 135) and Nasr (2010, 336) note, sectarianism is inextricably linked to, and partly the reason for, the *ʻulamā*'s continued relevance in Pakistan. Its importance, in Zaman's (1998, 714) opinion, accrues from its potential to aid the revival and extension of the *ʻulamā*'s influence. Especially in the Deobandi context, both Zaman (1998) and Nasr (2010) argue that sectarian activism allowed the Deobandi *ʻulamā* to maintain their ascendancy and mobilize top-down

Islamic reform. Alternatively, Nadia's remarks demonstrate that her increased awareness of the Shi'a perspective, as mediated by religious shows, compromised her faith in the Sunni 'ulamā, whom she now perceived as spreading unsubstantiated rumors and prejudice against the other sect.

El Fadl (2002, 15, 30) argues that even though interpretations of Islamic texts are dominated by jurists who discourage their reinterpretation and "use them to preserve the intellectual and political status quo," Qur'ānic discourses can just as easily be employed to "support an ethic of diversity and tolerance." According to Eickelman and Piscatori (2004, xi), the tendency to "challenge local religious ideas and practices" is encouraged by the "intensity of open communications, combined with higher levels of education." However, talk shows did not just allow lay Muslims such as Nadia to challenge doctrinally inspired claims to religious authority. For many self-proclaimed moderate Muslims, the value of religious talk shows also lies in their potential to serve as a rallying point for justifying their opposition to the 'ulamā. An important point to be made on the representation of Islamic diversity on television is its varying relationship with religious authority and its contradictory relationship with doctrinal Islam. Even though Amber favored a more generic framing of religious authority, Fatima, as noted above, was conversely more drawn to a scholar's willingness to visibly associate himself with a particular religious group on television. Therefore, rather than viewing my interlocutors' remarks as signaling a straightforward relationship between the 'ulamā's manifest association with a doctrinal group and their declining religious authority, we need to focus on the complexity of this relation. In fact, Fatima's and Amber's conflicting views on doctrinally inspired claims to religious authority illustrate that in most cases the viewers' preconceived and contextually determined notions of Islam also play a key role in influencing their engagement with religious authorities. A valid consideration here is also how televised forms of pluralism contain within them the potential to instigate viewers' religious anxieties in relation to their existing belief systems.

LAY ANXIETIES ABOUT PLURALISM

Even though Amber and Nadia appreciated religious shows that highlighted the positive aspects of Muslim diversity, the majority of my interlocutors did not reflect a similar regard for televised Islamic pluralism, irrespective of the form it took on television. The anxieties that accompanied this trend were most often associated with the way in which pluralism instigated doubts regarding certain aspects of their faith and the ambivalence it generated in relation to which Islamic discourse to follow. This was irrespective of my interlocutors' "conservative" or "moderate" religious proclivities. For instance, Hufsa, a young Sunni middle-class girl in her early twenties and a self-declared "liberal Muslim," viewed the pluralism of religious talk shows as synonymous with the imposition of a more conservative strain of Islam. Hufsa had studied at the prestigious Grammar School, a legacy of Karachi's colonial past, patronized predominantly by the city's elite. Although Hufsa came from a strict religious background, she herself held very different views on religion. Hufsa tended to mostly view religious shows with her mother, whose views on religion were very different from Hufsa's. I once witnessed them arguing about the importance of animal sacrifice, while watching a religious show's debate about the relevance of this practice. Hufsa, who loved animals and was a confirmed vegan, could not condone the practice. She was, therefore, more inclined to agree with the scholar who viewed the practice as superfluous to Islam. The fact that her mother insisted on supporting the other scholar, who described the practice as an essential tenet of Islamic belief, annoyed Hufsa. It was thus that she insisted to me that "the more discrepancies there are in scholarly interpretations, the more likely it is that people will accept the more 'fundamentalist' interpretation as the correct one. You see, we all know in our hearts that religion is primarily a restrictive and controlling force. Therefore, the more rigid and controlling the interpretation, the more likely are people to view it as credible. What we ideally need is, therefore, one uniform, liberal interpretation that all Pakistanis can follow."

Hufsa's propensity to view pluralism as enabling more restrictive and rigid ways of thinking about Islam was intimately tied to her perception of Muslim diversity. She saw such diversity as implying the resonance of both liberal and conservative discourses on Islam, as mediated by religious talk shows that invite traditional and self-styled scholars. However, as discussed earlier, this is not the only aspect of religious diversity highlighted on television. In fact, on most religious shows the shift toward pluralism involves representing the doctrinal diversity that characterizes mainstream Islamic discourse in Pakistan. My interlocutors' anxieties over the latter aspect of televised pluralism most often found expression in their designation of themselves as "just Muslims." In the case of Momin, an undergraduate business student in his early twenties, this mode of self-designation also reflected a broader desire to contain the excesses of Muslim politics and hence a refusal to participate in any doctrinally rooted form of Muslim conflict. Thus, if a recourse to tolerance toward other doctrinal groups allowed Amber to cope with the vagaries of Muslim politics, for Momin, the denial of Muslim diversity served a similar purpose. Alternatively, Momin's refusal to align himself with a particular religious group can also be viewed as an attempt to assert the superiority of his own Islamic perspective as the only legitimate perspective. When I asked Momin about his views on televised pluralism, he responded with the following statement: "I don't like these *masālik* on television. I am just Muslim. Even the Qurʾān claims that only one group of believers is truly Muslim. For me it is more important that I strictly follow the Qurʾān, as this is what I have been asked to do as a Muslim."

Even though Momin's self-designation as "just Muslim" is ostensibly rooted in a negation of the concept of Islamic pluralism, his remarks nonetheless betray a preference for a distinct understanding of Islam that is closely aligned with the Ahl-i Hadīth school's emphasis on the Qurʾān and *ḥadīth*. As already highlighted in chapter 3, this understanding involves considering all other Muslim practices and ways of thinking to be idolatry and religious innovation. Momin inadvertently clarified this preference to me while disclosing that his assessments of religious authorities on television involved a consideration of their propensity to favor a unified understanding of Islam that did not diverge in any way from what was contained in the Qurʾān and *ḥadīth*. Momin also used these terms to justify his preference for the Indian Ahl-i Hadīth scholar Zakir Naik. In Momin's words, he preferred Naik over other scholars on television because "he [Naik] only gives us examples from the Qurʾān, which he translates and thus makes easy for us to comprehend. I am mainly influenced by the Qurʾān. Whoever confines himself to the Qurʾān and *ḥadīth*, I mainly follow him."

Momin's emphasis on exclusively following the Qurʾān and *ḥadīth* and his consequent effacement of sectarian and denominational distinctions are not very different from Zappa's (2015) observations about print Islam in Mali. Zappa (2015, 53) compellingly argues that "it is precisely the act of presenting one's systematized reading of Islam as anti-sectarian that is conducive to excluding the possibility of any alternative reading." According to Zappa (53), at the root of anti-sectarian articulations of Islam is also an attempt to attract "the largest possible following," which is prompted by the "transformation of the public arena of debate into a market of ideas and by the parallel transformation of access to religious knowledge into a market of religious printed and media items." However, in addition to viewing Momin's remarks as reflecting his preference for a particular Islamic perspective, we can view them as also clarifying the general wariness that increasingly characterizes the Karachiites' engagement with televised Islamic pluralism. As Amber's comments above reveal, some viewers worry that the airing of doctrinal debates on television will serve to reinforce sectarian and doctrinal identities in the country. In this context, Nelson (2009, 591) has usefully revealed that the Pakistani majority eschews sectarian diversity and views Islamic pluralism as inimical to the concept of a "democratic nation." Alternatively, I would like to propose that it is not merely a concern for Pakistani nationalism but also the ambivalence associated with the veracity of Islamic content on television that inspires a more cautious viewer engagement with televised pluralism. In addition, pluralism contains within it the potential to subvert certain basic assumptions regarding Muslim faith. Viewers who now have access to conflicting authoritative discourses are compelled to either reconsider the notion of "pure" Islam or obliged to come to terms with the possibility that their understanding of Islam may not be in accordance with the "pure" Islam that they aspire to. Since both eventualities contain within them the potential to shake the tenacity of individual faith, the need to either cull out the "truth" from the many "falsehoods" or to reassert the correctness of one's beliefs becomes ever more pressing for religious practitioners. Whereas the former mode of dealing with the uncertainties of pluralism appears in Fatima's, Amber's, and Nadia's recourse to alternative criteria (displaying one's doctrinal affiliation and exercising tolerance toward other Islamic perspectives, respectively) for assessing religious authority, Momin's denunciation of Muslim difference epitomizes the latter. However, for some viewers the desire to avert the uncertainties of pluralism implied an even narrower focus that confined their viewing activities to a particular authoritative source or religious personality.

CELEBRITY STATUS AND RELIGIOUS AUTHORITY

I came across Khalid, a young student of the English language, while discussing religious shows with the students of the Pakistan American Cultural Centre (PACC). The center primarily caters to working-class students who have not had access to English-medium instruction at the primary or secondary educational levels. In recent years the center has suffered economically because of reduced student enrollment. This can be attributed in part to the growing anti-American sentiment that has characterized Karachi's population since 9/11 but also to the increased attraction of information technology (IT) institutes for Karachi's youth, who view such institutes as more beneficial for their employment prospects. While Khalid, who came from a working-class background, shared the Pakistani concern regarding religious talk shows as enabling confusion, he, unlike my other interlocutors above, did not enlist the aid of preestablished criteria to deal with the confusion. Instead he proposed a very different course of action: "There are many people who say one thing is right and others, who say that is wrong [sic]. Like Ghamidi says one thing, and Dr. Israr another. This is very confusing for us. We need a particular leader that we can follow, so we do not get confused."

Khalid's comments are very useful for understanding how some Karachiites make sense of the "confusion" on television. They focus on particular personalities and place their trust in them. Bina, a teacher at a government-managed girl's primary school, most effectively epitomized this category of viewers. I met Bina during a group discussion that I conducted with the teachers in the school's staff room. Bina stood out to me during this discussion, on account of her high regard for Husain. She confessed that she watched most of Husain's shows. She maintained an unwavering adulation of Husain in spite of the serious nature of media allegations against him, in relation to the leakage of his controversial outtakes from an episode of *Aalim Online* and his very public denigration of the Ahmadīyā community. While defending Husain against what she believed to be manufactured evidence against him, Bina insisted that she would continue to follow him as long as he appeared on television:

> I watch Husain's *Ramaḍān* program. I love him. He tells us about orphan children and also displays his charitable nature by giving away gifts to people. I am very taken in with his personality and very inspired by him. When he speaks of religion, in that moment I feel that the material world is an illusion and completely unimportant. Then, when I watch his behind-the-scenes videos, it upsets me greatly that someone would malign him in this manner. How can a person who speaks so sincerely of *dīn* [religion] also sway to Indian movie songs? If he were really what the internet and newspapers portray him to be, then why would Geo Television Network let him continue on the network's religious show? Why would he come in such a pure month and help those in need and speak so purely and sincerely?

While Bina acknowledged the video, her refusal to attribute much credence to it is a testament to the resilience of celebrity power, even in matters of religion. During this conversation, Bina looked askance at me while tentatively turning toward me to question my sentiments regarding the video and the celebrity anchor. She asked, "What do you think? Could this possibly be true?" Unable to bring myself to give her a definitive reply, I responded with a noncommittal shrug. I did not want to be the one to divest Bina of her faith in Husain. Bina's favorable impression of Husain can be viewed as part of the process by which television creates heroes, who are so perceived on account of their fame and popularity rather than on the basis of any "real accomplishment" (Rothenbuhler 2005, 95).

Husain's celebrity appeal can also be used to evaluate Nadia's and Amber's perceptions of Husain as more tolerant than his *madrasa*-educated counterparts. They maintain a favorable impression of Husain despite his past record of Ahmadīyā persecution. While Husain's inflammatory statements against Ahmadis have provoked widespread debate in Pakistan and elicited criticism from some sections of Pakistani society, Nadia's, Amber's, and Bina's remarks indicate that they have done little to undermine the religious anchor's popular appeal. As indicated in the introduction, Husain has also been hailed by the *New York Times* (Walsh 2012) as a "broadcasting sensation in Pakistan." Similarly, on three consecutive occasions, the Jordan-based Royal Islamic Strategic Studies Centre has included Husain in its internationally derived list of the five hundred most influential Muslims (*Express Tribune* 2015). The fact that Husain's appeal persists despite his opposition to the Ahmadis merits the consideration that perhaps for many Karachiites the insistence on tolerance and accommodation is selectively motivated. Therefore, when it came to the Ahmadīyā community, who inspire widespread hostility from the majority of Sunni Muslims, some Muslims may have deliberately chosen to look the other way. From this perspective, it is also possible that Husain's anti-Ahmadi rhetoric may have served to earn him a larger following.

In defense of Husain's continued credibility, Bina raised an important point in relation to his continued appearances on Geo Television. When I asked Hufsa about the general viewing habits of her family, she informed me that they primarily watched shows that were broadcast on Geo Television Network. Hufsa's comments and Bina's attempts to defend Husain in terms of his continued patronage by Geo Television illustrate the channels' significance in guiding viewers' religious preferences and conferring religious authority. This feature also renders the channels themselves a key authoritative religious source. It is perhaps for this reason that Mir Shakilur Rahman, the owner of Geo Television Network, is also included in the Royal Islamic Strategic Studies Centre list of the five hundred most influential Muslims (*News* 2013).

AFFINITY AS A MEDIATOR OF RELIGIOUS AUTHORITY

The manner in which Husain presents himself on the television screen contributes to his celebrity appeal and distinguishes him from other religious scholars. Amber hinted at two distinct aspects of Husain's self-presentation on television while describing her greater regard for the religious show host: Husain's demeanor and his appearance. She said, "Husain is very modern and suave. He really appeals to women whose husbands do not have the same gentle and soft demeanor that he portrays on television. They are also attracted to him because of the way he looks. He has a neat beard and is very well dressed." Amber's description of Husain as "gentle" and "modern" is reminiscent of how television renders the same attributes that are generally associated with the popularity of entertainment celebrities as also pertinent to conferring religious authority. Abelman and Neuendorf (1987, 53, quoted in Wuthnow 1990, 102), in the context of Christian televangelism, emphasize the importance of certain attributes, such as a "dynamic personality, telegenic good looks, and an educated eye for the camera," as increasingly relevant for televangelists who hope to "attract and maintain" their viewers. These attributes are generally more reminiscent of Christian tradition pioneered in the 1950s by preachers like Billy Graham (see *Economist* 2011) as opposed to Islam, within which assessments of religious authority are usually grounded in the scholar's depth of religious knowledge and conformity to Islamic norms (e.g., Soares 2004a).[3] However, by eluding the bearded *maulvī* stereotype, religious show hosts and preachers like Husain and Ghamidi, respectively, not unlike their "modern," "moderate," and "sharp-suited" Egyptian counterparts Moez Masoud and Amr Khaled (*Economist* 2011), also create a heightened regard for these attributes within Pakistani Muslim viewers.

Amber's remark on Husain's "modern" appearance is useful for exploring an additional element of religious authority. Anthropological scholarship that does broach the role of appearance (Soares 2004b; Marsden 2008) in establishing scholars' authority does not provide us with any definitive understanding of the extent to which visible appearances of piety, such as mode of dress and physical appearance, can facilitate claims to religious erudition. In a study of piety and its "public" manifestations in Mali, Soares (2004b, 206) notes the salience of the *seere* (a black mark on the forehead that provides evidence of regular praying, referred to as *mehrab* in Urdu) in enabling favorable perceptions of a person's piety. However, in contrast, Marsden (2008, 409) observes that Chitral's *mullahs* have popular appeal despite their ostensibly "playful" and "modern" styles of dress. While both Soares and Marsden focus on the significance of appearance in mediating claims to religious erudition, I propose a slightly different approach to appearance, one that focuses less on its association with religious erudition than it does on its role in making a scholar appear more relatable to viewers. To clarify my proposition, I recall my conversation with Salman, a media teacher at the privately owned prestigious business school Shaheed Zulfiqar Ali Bhutto Institute of Science and Technology (SZABIST). While speaking of Husain's popularity, Salman made the following observation: "Husain is popular as he is the man of the people. I don't know why, but sometimes I feel that he is actually a sex symbol. The way he does his beard, it's all very metrosexual. I think it all ties into the fact that he is trying to tell the people that he is one of them [the people] and very 'modern.' He is just a 'regular guy.' Some women actually call into his show because he is Husain, and he looks a certain way."

Salman's reference to Husain as a "regular guy" also underscores the symbolic relevance of appearance in making a scholar seem more relatable. When I spoke with another of my colleagues at SZABIST, Mansoora, a middle-class female administrator at the college, she admitted to me that she much preferred viewing "progressive" women on television, as opposed to those who observed the *niqāb* and spoke in a harsh voice. "It appears that to listen to them and to follow them, one has to be like them, and this puts me off." In this case Mansoora referred to the formidable and rigid female preacher Farhat Hashmi (see chap. 3), who is the leader of the popular female piety movement Al Huda in Pakistan (see Ahmad 2010). For Mansoora, the main issue with female scholars like Hashmi, who tended to adhere to very rigid understandings of the Islamic rules of *'awrah*, was that they epitomized a perception of Islam as overly harsh and repressive, out of sync with Mansoora's own reality. As clarified through Mansoora's comments, a determination of religious authority is not so much about the tendency of self-taught scholars to don the "modern" attire but more so about how their attire delineates them as more relatable to the viewer majority.

When I met Husain, he admitted to using his appearance to appeal to the masses. Husain explained that it was far more important for him to appear approachable and relatable to the viewers than to conform to the traditionally mandated codes of Islamic dress. The importance of relatability is also implicit in the Barelwi television scholar *Allama* Noorani's observation that television was responsible for altering the appearance of traditional scholars, who were increasingly discarding their caps and turbans to appear more fashionable and contemporary to their viewers. While *Allama* Noorani phrased this observation as a lament, I propose that the desire to appeal to a wider section of Muslims, including the more "liberal" ones, is in effect a realization of what Eickelman and Piscatori (2004, xv), drawing on Browers and Kurzman (2004) predicted, would be the enhanced ability of liberal Muslims to assert their voice "among the vast majority of Muslims who aspire to better lives and more open societies." These observations clarify the ambiguity of Marsden's (2008) claims regarding the appeal of Chitral *mullahs*, which I suggest are popular perhaps not despite their "playful" and "modern" attire but because of it.

Furthermore, my interlocutors' preference for contemporary attire should not necessarily be seen as a disregard for the norms of appearance as mandated under Islam. Instead, we should consider how the diverse manifestations of religious authority on television enable the agency of lay practitioners. The appearance of self-taught celebrity preachers, which is in stark contrast to modes of comportment adopted by traditional scholars, acts as a symbolic marker for insinuating alternative modes of living Islam that are more in sync with viewers' everyday realities. In this context, the significance of appearance is not confined to instigating alternative assessments of religious authority but is equally apparent in facilitating alternative representations of Islam. Thus, appearance acts at two levels—by enabling alternative assessments of religious authority and by engendering distinct representations of Islam—to undermine the influence of traditional scholars, whose authority is closely linked to the institutionalization of certain norms and Islamic practices, of which appearance is an integral component.

RELIGIOUS TELEVISION SHOWS AS REPRESENTING CONTINUITY

The commentaries I have thus far analyzed suggest a role for religious talk shows in enabling a changed relationship with Islam and religious authority. However, there were also instances when televised pluralism reinforced a continued association with one's religious group and therefore also bolstered the persistence of certain Islamic concepts and ideas about religious authority. On my first visit to the Government Degree College for women, I came across Sadia, a student at the college. Sadia, who came from a working-class background, considered herself a devout and practicing Muslim. An important aspect of her identity as a devout Muslim was her doctrinal affiliation. Sadia's family aligned itself with the Barelwi tradition. Customs such as celebrating Prophet Muhammad's (PBUH) birthday were thus of profound importance to them. Sadia could not imagine her Muslimness as distinct from her Barelwi orientation. This also affected her engagement with the multiple religious authorities on television. Sadia confessed that she did not follow self-styled or traditional scholars on television unless they were Barelwi. Even if she were open to following other scholars, she admitted that her father, a devout Barelwi practitioner, would not have allowed it. For Sadia, then, listening to scholars of other doctrinal orientations constituted a form of religious betrayal, as did learning from those who presented themselves as above these denominations.

Sadia was not the only person to subscribe to this philosophy. For some of my other interlocutors, the idea of "being" Muslim was essentially linked to a definitive doctrinal affiliation. According to the International Crisis Group's

(2005, 6) report, "being a Muslim in Pakistan is no longer the sole religious identity" but instead increasingly involves a "denominational prefix." Religious shows play an essential role in enabling doctrinally inspired identities by providing viewers easy access to scholars from their respective schools. As such, for viewers who conform to a particular Islamic tradition, the doctrinal orientation of scholars, rather than their depth of religious knowledge, acts as a key marker of religious authority. Following Sadia, we get a sense that for some Karachiites, religious television does not represent change but rather a continued understanding of Islam as essentially a monolith and of religious authority as necessarily linked to ideas of "truth" and "purity."

However, I suggest here that what appears to be a practitioner's continued focus on doctrinally inspired Islamic perspectives also needs to be analyzed in the context of religious transformation. Muslims sometimes navigate the troublesome frontiers of televised Islamic pluralism by confining their viewing to authoritative sources affiliated with a particular doctrinal denomination. Thus, it can be claimed that the ambivalence generated by the multivocality of Islamic discourses on television makes some Muslims, like Sadia, even more protective of their doctrinal identities. This is best illustrated by Sadia's following observation: "How can we all be Muslims? Look at what is happening in Iran and Iraq. If all these people had the same religion, then why are they killing one another? Only one doctrinal group is truly Muslim, and all others are the enemies of Islam."

By highlighting the varying individual contexts in which people encounter and consume religious television, this chapter sheds light on how the scholars' participation in the pluralistic world of religious shows shifts viewers' attention from the scholars' mastery over classical texts to other forms of gauging religious authority. I indicated earlier that to evaluate religious authority, my interlocutors have employed some important criteria—including the scholars' demonstration of tolerance, my interlocutors' sense of shared affinity with television scholars, and the scholars' celebrity status—that owe their rising significance to religious talk shows. None of these factors is commonly associated with religious authority, and all of them place traditional scholars at a disadvantage to self-styled scholars. Thus, if preexisting religious sensibilities sustain the diversity of Islamic thought on television, so too does the diversity of religious content on television transform the way in which people designate religious authority. Moreover, a central point emerges from a comparison between Sadia's preference for Barelwi-inspired Islamic teachings and Momin's effacement of doctrinal difference: how the traditional scholars' participation in the plural world of television puts their religious authority at risk. On the one hand, these scholars' continued association with specific schools of Islamic thought proliferates a widespread notion of them as purveyors of sectarian violence and dissent within the Muslim community. The nation's problematic religiopolitical history and the growing incidence of sectarian violence in the country further contribute to such unfavorable perceptions of these scholars. Conversely, even presenting themselves as neutral on television has adverse ramifications for traditional scholars, as followers may view their efforts to accommodate alternative Islamic perspectives as akin to betrayal—or at the very least as evidence of hypocrisy.

Another key point emerging from my interlocutors' alternative assessments of religious authorities is that televised pluralism allows viewers to privilege individually preferred aspects of religious authority. In this context, the choices of ordinary Muslims are a direct function of their enhanced agency, as mediated by religious shows that invite a range of scholars who offer multiple Islamic perspectives, all of them rooted in claims to Islamic "authenticity." However, it needs to be highlighted here that this more agentive engagement with Islam is perceived varyingly by different Karachiites. As pointed out earlier, an enhanced sense of individual agency may also instigate viewer anxieties regarding the legitimacy of their existing beliefs, thus placing the burden on viewers to figure out the "truth" for themselves. Although this way of engaging with Islam led to more confusion for some Karachiites, in the next chapter I show how it implied a more expedient relationship with Islam for others. When the latter happens, it has lasting consequences for the terms of Islamic debate; for the authority of traditional scholars, which is ineluctably linked to their monopoly over religious public debate; and for Islamic knowledge, which comes to be increasingly vested in an individualized sense of morality.

NOTES

1. In the context of electronic media, Schulz (2006b) emphasizes that Malian preacher Chérif Haidara's religious authority is buttressed by his perceived proficiency with canonical Islamic texts.

2. Mandaville (2007, 11) and Zaman (2002) have noted that "traditional" religious authority is vested in the ʿulamā and their recourse to traditional Islamic texts and sources of religious knowledge.

3. Soares (2004a, 922) claims that the authority of the African preacher Tierno Mansour in France primarily derives from his ability to project himself as a "moral exemplar, who embodies certain positive values—exceptional piety and a particularly strong commitment to Islam."

SEVEN

REDEFINING THE BOUNDARIES FOR CRITICAL DELIBERATION IN ISLAMIC PUBLIC DEBATE

ANY ATTEMPT TO UNDERSTAND THE scale of religious transformation mediated by religious shows in Pakistan must also entail a consideration of these shows in terms of their impact on existing structures of religious knowledge. In this chapter, I focus on the role of religious shows in creating unprecedented opportunities for more individualized, deliberative, and agentive engagements with divine texts. I explore the implications of these individualized modes of religious engagement for the controlling influence of traditional institutions (the *madrasa*, the mosque, and the *'ulamā*) over "legitimate" forms of religious knowledge. However, rather than focus on religious television exclusively in terms of its role in instigating the fragmentation of religious authority, I also consider what this fragmentation implies for established forms of religious knowledge and for the rules and boundaries of Islamic interpretation and debate as mandated under Islamic *Sharī'a*. The instructional and pluralistic emphases in religious programming instigate modes of reflexive thinking that threaten to subvert historically established hierarchies of reasoning and knowledge within Islam. This is a consequence of the ways in which religious shows implicitly privilege the authority of lay Muslim practitioners in matters of everyday religious belief and practice, by allowing them to choose between competing religious viewpoints. In this context, the forms of reflexive thinking that I explore are not confined to religious practitioners discerning the "authentic" nature of certain practices. Nor do I limit myself to outlining modes of critical deliberation that reflect my interlocutors' overwhelming concern for piety. Instead, I also outline instances when my interlocutors' critical evaluations of televised religious discourse involved a privileged consideration of the discourse's commensurability with their everyday lives and secular values.

When writing about the scope of critical deliberation within Islam, academics within the disciplines of anthropology and religious studies have taken issue with the naivete of Western discourses that portray Muslims as "passive" and "non-reflexive" (Marsden 2010, xvi; Hirschkind 2001) recipients of the Islamic ideology in contrast to the followers of Judeo-Christian discourse (see Asad 2003, 10–11; Mahmood 2005; Hirschkind 2006; Zaman 2002, 2009, 2010). Arguing for a recognition of Islam as a religion that makes allowances for and encourages reflexive and critical modes of thinking, these academics have explained that the bases of rational argument within Islamic tradition are very different from the form that reasoning takes in secular debate, as "the practice of reason occurs within a social context and thus presupposes commitment to the principles sustaining that context" (Hirschkind 1996).[1] In line with this understanding, Hirschkind (2001) identifies certain principles and virtues that any form of critical thinking must subscribe to in order to be deemed legitimate within Islamic moral doctrine. The foremost of these, as noted by Hirschkind, is an acknowledgment by all those partaking in *ijtihād* or religious debate of the immutability of divine texts. According to Hirschkind, this acknowledgment does not circumvent rational debate but rather constitutes the discursive foundation around which Islamic debate revolves.

In addition to an unwavering belief in the fixedness of divine texts, Hirschkind (21) also stresses the importance of cultivating certain virtues of *da'wā*, such as *ikhlās* (sincerity), *khushu* (humility), and *taqwā* or *khauf* (both terms imply a fear of God), prior to engaging in any deliberative or interpretative pursuit. Hirschkind's (1996) emphasis on upholding and cultivating these beliefs and virtues prior to partaking in critical deliberation draws on his observations regarding the religious debate about Cairo University professor Nasir Hamid Abu Zayd, who was denied tenure. The university refused tenure on charges of apostasy on account of the professor's refusal to acknowledge the divinity of the Qur'ān. Analyzing the reasons for Abu Zayd's dismissal, Hirschkind explains that Abu Zayd's arguments against the divinity of the Qur'ān, while displaying considerable knowledge of the text, had essentially transgressed the boundaries of reasoning deemed permissible within Islamic moral doctrine. On the basis of the works of Fahmi Howaydi (1993, quoted in Hirschkind 1996), Hirschkind proposes that "for any critical engagement (*ijtihad*) with the religious texts to be acceptable and legitimate, it must begin with a commitment to the text. . . . Every critical activity which seeks to undermine and destroy the *shari'a* texts, is not protected under the notion of intellectual freedom, but rather falls within the range of that which society must prohibit and prevent, especially where the constitution identifies Islam as the religion of state and the *shariʿa* as the primary source of law."

The importance of subscribing to these principles and virtues within the context of televised religious debate is also sustained by the traditional scholarly discourse targeting Ghamidi, which denotes the self-styled scholar's interpretative style as devoid of the requisite humility, sincerity, and regard for the rules of reasoning mandated under Islamic law. In chapter 5, I drew on this traditional scholarly discourse to argue for the political relevance of these beliefs and virtues in permitting traditional scholars to delineate any alternative rulings on religious practices and norms as falling outside the prescribed scope of Islamic reasoning. I revealed that the essentialization of these principles allowed traditional scholars to make a case for restricting the practice of *ijtihād* to their own institution. Through such assertions, traditional scholars could also work toward sustaining their controlling influence over popular forms of religious thinking. I implicated religious talk shows, particularly those that include celebrity preachers on their expert panels, in necessitating such claims to religious authority.

Alternatively, in this chapter I want to revisit the essential nature of the virtues and elements of beliefs outlined above, by drawing attention to aspects of my interlocutors' engagements with religious shows that refuse to be circumscribed to these principles. Through this analysis, I hope to invite a more nuanced assessment of Islamic media movements that accounts for both the complexity of Muslim lives and the uncertain and contradictory outcomes of Islamic media movements. In this context, I demonstrate that even though scholarly debates on television do not per se violate the boundaries of ethical and moral reasoning prescribed by Islamic *Sharīʿa*, they can nonetheless pave the way for such violations by ordinary Muslims. The ethnographic portraits that follow highlight some of the ways in which religious shows do so, by focusing on their role in inspiring reconsiderations of the fundamental nature of Islamic tradition and established Islamic practices. Of particular relevance to this consideration is the formal transformation characterizing religious shows, particularly their pluralistic and instructional emphases. Whereas the former programming development calls into question the mandatory status of scholarly rulings, thus prompting a greater lay recourse to personal opinion in matters of faith, the latter emphasis works to draw viewers' attention to the difficulties of reconciling certain elements of Islam with their lived experiences, the pressures of everyday life, and their existing worldviews. In promoting these forms of Islamic engagement, both programming developments also extend the application of critical deliberation to Islamic concepts that had until recently managed to elude critical evaluation. The forms of lay critical evaluation that I am suggesting here are not confined to the interpretative differences between Muslims (cf. Asad 1993, 2009a, 2009b; Hirschkind 2001, 2006). Rather, I shed light on elements of Muslim contestation where religious show viewers—on the one hand overwhelmed by their growing knowledge of Islam and the prospect of incorporating certain Islamic concepts into their lives, and on the other, emboldened by the diversity of Islamic representation on television—are also rendered more open to contesting the privileged place of Islamic values in defining their lives and ideas of personhood. In this context, I also highlight forms of Muslim religiosity that involve a continuous negotiation on extant understandings of piety and on the importance of the Islamic foundational texts in mediating the everyday lives of practitioners.

On the basis of these observations, I propose that, rather than analyzing religious media only in terms of their prominence in enabling greater Islamic conformance, we should also explore their relevance in inspiring religious show viewers to engage more strategically with, or oppose the application of, certain Islamic concepts in their lives. This approach allows us to acknowledge forms of Muslim religious engagement wherein the "existential significance" of "practical [religious] knowledge," "rather than its ideological justifications," constitutes the key basis for "living a [Muslim] life" (Schielke and Debevec 2012, 10; see also Jackson 1996, 34). Also pertinent to this consideration are the "pragmatic considerations" of everyday life (Schielke 2010, 12) and the moral contradictions (Simon 2009) characterizing people's interactions with religious shows—and by extension Islam and religious authority. Drawing on this analytical framework, I shed light on aspects of Muslim engagement with the Islamic tradition that reflect how people "think through and manage" the "broader subjective tensions" of everyday life (Simon 2014, 3). Within this mode of religious engagement, people's considerations of their everyday lives also mediate their engagement with the pluralistic religious discourse on television, so that they are likely to privilege forms of morality that correspond more closely with their existential concerns and extant worldviews. At the same time, I also consider how people's immersion in particular social contexts can shape their understanding of and regard for different aspects of the Islamic tradition. I therefore approach the following discussion not only in terms of the conceptual order that may "underlie or precede" my interlocutors' varied engagement with religious television shows but also from the point of view of "what is accomplished" through a more critical engagement with religious shows (Schielke and Debevec 2012, 10).

As in the previous chapter, the discussion in this chapter mostly revolves around the viewing experiences of Pakistani women. While some elements of this discussion, especially those that relate to female religious practices, lend themselves to a gender-based evaluation, I also want to urge a consideration of other factors, such as my interlocutors' individual, religious, social, and moral proclivities, in terms of their prominence in shaping my interlocutors' reflections on religious programming content. At the same time, I also want to underscore the relevance of the commentaries below in illuminating aspects of my male interlocutors' religiosity. A noteworthy consideration here is how some of my male interlocutors also took issue with the scholarly emphasis on female veiling on religious shows, as they, much like the women I encountered, also considered the practice an important mediator of the 'ulamā's power and worried about its role in radicalizing Pakistani society.

THE NEED TO VERIFY: A PRECURSOR TO CRITICAL DELIBERATION

It was not unusual for Karachiites to discuss their religious viewing experiences outside the immediate contexts of viewing. People often exchanged views, disputed, and conferred with their friends and families on the legitimacy of televised Islamic content. These discussions were at least partly influenced by the contradictory nature of televised Islamic discourse, which generated uncertainty regarding which scholarly viewpoint to believe and whom to follow. On one occasion, I was approached by Mariam, a middle-class housewife in her midforties, to confirm the proper form of the Islamic practice of *sutra*, which involves the correct etiquette for passing in front of a praying person. Mariam was aware that the nature of my research involved frequently meeting with religious scholars, some of whom commanded great respect within their respective communities. Her curiosity regarding the practice had been aroused while she was watching a religious show on the Sunni Barelwi religious channel *Madani*, where the traditional scholar presiding over the show had demonstrated an elaborate procedure for the practice. Since Mariam's interest in Islam had only recently been inspired by her participation in a private Qur'ān study group, which she now attended every Wednesday, she was still unsure of how to integrate her growing awareness of Islamic rules and regulations into her everyday life. For that reason, she decided to seek scholarly consensus on the practice, and she forwarded me a video clip of the religious show so that I could watch the demonstration for myself and confirm the procedure with my scholarly informants.

At first glance, Mariam's concern for knowing the correct procedure appears to express the role religious talk shows play in institutionalizing religion and expanding the influence of religious specialists who present on them. By focusing viewers' attention on the minor aspects of Islamic practice, television scholars can thus sustain their relevance in shaping viewers' everyday relationship with Islam. However, the fact that Mariam was driven to verify the correct form of the practice also gives us a sense that the relationship between religious talk shows and religious authority is highly complex, one that we need to unpack. In this particular instance, Mariam's hesitation to unquestioningly follow the scholar's direction was intimately tied to the competing scholarly rulings regarding the practice on television. By inviting scholars to present their distinct viewpoints on the correct implementation of Islamic principles, religious talk shows generate uncertainty regarding the authenticity of competing scholarly rulings, all of which claim to be grounded in classical Islamic texts and references to established religious authorities. This development, in turn, undermines the efficacy of scholarly rulings in enabling collective enforcements of morality. The emerging Muslim disposition, as mediated by religious talk shows, thus involves a more informed and cautious engagement with scholarly rulings, as viewers learn to rely on their own prior knowledge and understanding of Islam when determining the contemporary relevance and application of Islamic concepts. In Mariam's case, because she did not align herself with a particular religious group, she could not rely on a particular doctrinal perspective. Her case is useful for illustrating the growing viewer perplexity engendered by televised pluralism, one of the consequences of which is a diminished faith in all religious authorities.

For some of my other informants, who were similarly no longer content to simply accept the scholarly testimonies regarding a practice, it became increasingly important to verify the "authenticity" of scholarly propositions for themselves. The motivation to do so was the strongest when my informants could not reconcile certain scholarly claims with their prior understanding of Islam. In these instances, they tended to confer with their friends and families to gauge the legitimacy of competing scholarly propositions. Shaista, a government college student, betrayed this proclivity when she recounted to me how an emotional presentation by a Shi'a scholar on the tenth night of *Muḥarram* had triggered her unease regarding the "authenticity" of a narrated tradition:

> On the 10th of *Muḥarram*, a scholar came to present *Sham e Ghariba* [Night of mourning during *Muharram*] on ARY Digital. He told the viewers that when Prophet Muhammad's (PBUH) grandson *Imām* Hussayn's (RA) body was

lying on the battle field of *Karbalā*, his daughter Sakina (*RA*) had recognized the body, despite its severed head, and come running to embrace it. Her aunt, *Bibi* Zaynab (*RA*), had later questioned Sakina (*RA*) on how she had come to recognize the body. Sakina (*RA*) had revealed to her aunt that, when Sakina (*RA*) had come out on the field of *Karbalā*, her father's body had called out to her: "Oh, Sakina, I am your father. Come and embrace me."

Shaista confessed that after viewing the program she had attempted to verify the scholarly narration by referring to her religious books. On finding nothing to corroborate it, she had turned to her parents and, subsequently, to her friends at college. All had unanimously confirmed her suspicions regarding the dubious credibility of the narration. Shaista now attributed the wrongful narration to the scholar's Shiʿa orientation and his consequent interest in promoting his own doctrinal school's religious ideology. This experience had taught Shaista to reconfirm everything she heard on religious shows. She declared to me that she would never believe a scholar until she had verified for herself the "legitimacy" of his claim. Shaista's example offers us an important glimpse into how religious shows implicitly encourage viewers to engage more cautiously with scholarly propositions. For Shaista, thus, "being" Muslim increasingly became about a reduced reliance on scholars and a greater reliance on her own understanding of Islam, although she still took into account the opinions of her family and friends. In Shaista's case, these shifting perceptions of religious authority were mediated jointly by televised pluralism and by the scholars' enhanced presence on television. Her example indicates that viewers who are implicitly encouraged by the transformed religious show format to engage more cautiously with varying scholarly propositions are also rendered more sensitive to the possibility of the scholars' investment in doctrinal politics or their complicity in promoting certain political and commercial agendas. It is from this perspective that we can also understand the growing popularity of Islamic teaching institutes, such as Al Huda and Quest in Pakistan, that claim to teach Qurʾānic Arabic to their students. Their popularity is a testament to ordinary Muslim practitioners' increased desire to acquire religious knowledge for themselves, given their diminishing trust in religious authorities. As more people are driven to turn to themselves when gauging the authenticity of scholarly arguments on television, their engagement with Islam is also affected.

INCREASED SELF-RELIANCE

The growing significance of the self in assessments of religious authority was repeatedly driven home to me during my interactions with Karachiites, who frequently expressed a desire to discern for themselves the rationale underlying various scholarly claims on television. Although Sadia, a young, working-class woman, did not really question most aspects of Islamic practice, she confessed that she had nonetheless become more appreciative of the explanations offered by religious scholars in relation to the practical relevance of certain Islamic concepts. In these terms, Sadia also explained her preference for the self-styled scholar Zakir Naik:

> I love Zakir Naik's show. He proves everything scientifically, e.g., my son once asked me why Muslims have to eat *ḥalāl* even when traveling to non-Muslim countries where *ḥalāl* food is not easily available. I had no logical explanation to offer him, until I watched Naik's show where he explained the scientific significance of *ḥalāl* slaughter. Rendering the meat *ḥalāl* involves first reading the *kalima* [Qur'ānic verse] over the sacrificial animal and then slaughtering the animal by running a knife across its throat. According to Naik, the recitation of the Qur'ānic verses together with the process of slaughter allows for the draining of all blood from the animal's body, thus purging the meat of all its impurities. I finally had the scientific justification for why *ḥalāl* slaughter is mandated under Islam, and so I could employ this to convince my son.

It was not that Sadia did not believe in, or adhere to, the concept of eating *ḥalāl*, or even that she felt that Qur'ānic reasoning should be made subject to scientific rationality. Knowing the scientific reasons behind the need for *ḥalāl* meat, however, allowed Sadia to justify her conformance to the practice to her son and simultaneously appeal to him to follow her example. At the same time, and perhaps even more importantly, it allowed her to justify her conformance to herself. Naik both reaffirmed and strengthened her faith in the practice. Sadia's example is useful for noting how self-styled scholars, such as Ghamidi and Naik, introduce novel forms of argumentation in Islamic debate that are not limited to invocations of divine texts, *taqlīd*, or established scholarly opinion. For Sadia in particular, Naik's ability to explain the scientific rationale underlying Islamic provisions came to reflect his superior knowledge and intellectual ability. Sadia subsequently began to view this ability as an important marker of a scholar's erudition. In the case of the popular South African Islamic televangelist Ahmed Deedat, Larkin (2008, 102) observes that the televangelist's tendency to present lectures in public spaces (such as town halls) and in stage debates with famous Christian preachers resembles "the rationalist, secular modes of the public sphere." A similar claim can also be made for self-styled scholars, whose authority derives less from their command over canonical texts and more from their willingness to explain to their viewers the rationale underlying various Islamic provisions.

I do not intend to imply that the divine texts are not supported by their own underlying reason, but to instead point to the ways in which televised Islamic pluralism can create an appetite for more reason-based modes of sermonizing, thus transforming the terms of Islamic public debate. Pertinent to this discussion is the perceived difference between scholars who advocate a "literalist" interpretation of divine texts and those who favor "a metaphoric interpretation" of Qur'ānic verses (Hirschkind 2001, 24). Hirschkind denotes the latter style of interpretation as a willingness to acknowledge that certain "sections of the Quran . . . may have been applicable at the time of their revelation but no longer carry a mandatory status." Even though Ghamidi's interpretative method does not, per se, involve denying the fixity of textual meaning, his tendency to diverge greatly from established interpretations of divine texts is often perceived as such by his audience (see Sadaf Aziz 2011). As clarified in chapter 5, Sadaf Aziz (2011, 615) attributes this (mis)perception to Ghamidi's exegetical method, which involves a greater focus on unearthing "intentions and generalizable laws from within the text." This focus also explains why Ghamidi's rulings on the *hijāb* and *purdah* differ greatly from those issued by traditional Islamists. However, in Ghamidi's case, one must consider his tendency to ground his interpretations of divine texts in the contemporary context, whereby viewers are not only made aware of the contemporary application of certain Islamic provisions but also implicitly encouraged to gauge the contemporary (im)practicability of regnant Islamic concepts.

Because self-styled religious scholars like Ghamidi generally lack the educational credentials that allow traditional scholars to naturally assume religious authority, they are under greater pressure to establish their authority and assure their viewers of their religious expertise. What they lack in *madrasa* training, they compensate for in their novel approach to sermonizing, which involves more than a traditional reference to "published sources" and invocations of "recognizable authorities" (Eickelman and Piscatori 2004, 38), although these also constitute an important part of their presentations. By focusing on the "intended" rather than the "literal" Qur'ānic message, these scholars also create an enhanced regard for this form of engagement with Islam, regardless of their followers' conservative, moderate, or liberal proclivities. These transformations can be viewed as clarifying the scholarly attempt to integrate Islam into viewers' contemporary realities so that the emerging Muslim subjectivity is essentially also a self-regulating one. Hirschkind (2001) offers an important insight into this proposition by opposing the simple dichotomization of the

Islamic "public arena" into a deliberative or normative space. While speaking about the production and consumption of audio cassette sermons in Cairo, Hirschkind (2001, 4, 25) argues that the public arena in Egypt "is both normative and deliberative, a domain for both subjection to authority and the exercise of individual reasoning," in which "public deliberation" is one of the modalities of "the disciplining power of ethical speech."

Hirschkind's (2001) emphasis on the public arena as both deliberative and normative can be usefully applied to understand Sadia's recourse to Naik as a way of strengthening her faith and as a form of self-regulation. From this perspective the modes of critical deliberation enabled by self-styled scholars such as Ghamidi and Naik also constitute a "modality of power" for extending these scholars' normative influence in Pakistan. Sadaf Ahmad (2009) illustrates this point when speaking about Al Huda's attempts at creating a unitary religious consciousness, which according to Ahmad (2010, 310) includes a contemporary emphasis on the processes of "self-reflection" and "objectification." Ahmad explains that these processes are central to Al Huda's efforts toward the formation of an ethical subject. Alternatively, in *Politics of Piety*, Mahmood (2005) offers an additional insight into Sadia's predicament, one that posits Sadia's attempts at self-regulation as an exercise of agency. Mahmood makes this proposition in the context of the female adherents of the piety movement in Egypt, whose critical reflections on Islamic tenets corresponded closely with their desire to lead more pious lives. Drawing on these pious aspirations, Mahmood (15, 22) argues that, rather than viewing agency as entailed only in those acts that resist and subvert social norms, we should also perceive it as inherent in the multiple ways that norms are "performed, inhabited and experienced." In this context, Mahmood also contests the limitations of the secular-liberal emphasis on autonomized agency and the poststructuralist feminist tendency to locate agency in the subversion of and resistance to norms (cf. Butler 1997).[2] Instead, she argues for a conceptualization of agency that locates its exercise within the structure of Islamic norms and values. Central to Mahmood's propositions on agency (2005, 54–55, 122) are the roles of "bodily practices" and "self-reflexivity" in enabling the realization of the religious subject.[3] Mahmood (2005, 26) is critical of Kantian ethics and its focus on rationality and of Bourdieu's (1977) emphasis on the relevance of practice in symbolizing the "much deeper and more fundamental reality of social structures and cultural logics." Mahmood (2005, 166) argues that for the adherents of the Egyptian Daʿwā movement, the body did not function as a sign but rather constituted the means for ethical formation. However, while Mahmood's argument may work well to elucidate the pious impetus underlying Sadia's preference for scientifically geared scholarly explanations, it does little to clarify those crucial moments when religious shows instigate forms of self-reflexivity that are more strategically and expediently motivated, as opposed to piously driven. In the following sections, I tease out some of these modes of reflexive thinking. I analyze two elements of this strategic engagement below: this form of engagement's implications for the rules and boundaries of ethical reasoning and Islamic public debate (see Hirschkind 1996, 2001) and the engagement's effects on Islamic thought and the structure of religious knowledge.

NOT ALL MUSLIMS ARE PIOUS MUSLIMS

For Mariam, Shaista, and Sadia, the pluralistic format of religious shows instigated the need to verify the authenticity of scholarly propositions or created an appreciation for more rationale-driven modes of authoritative representation. However, for others the uncertainty generated by scholarly polemics on television enabled a more expediently motivated approach to Islam, one that involved a consideration of the consistency of Islamic principles with individual circumstances and value systems. This happened with Ayra, an affluent woman in her midforties, after she watched a televised debate between religious scholars on the female Islamic practices of *hijāb* (head covering) and *niqāb* (veiling). Ayra, who taught at a prestigious nursery school in Karachi, considered herself a devout and practicing Muslim. As she stressed to me, she prayed regularly and kept all her fasts during *Ramaḍān*. While her appreciation for accumulating Islamic knowledge made her an avid fan of religious talk shows, she confessed that these shows simultaneously made her question her past assumptions about Islam. Giving me the example of a recent episode she had viewed that incorporated the controversial self-taught scholar Javed Ahmed Ghamidi, Ayra recounted that Ghamidi had declared the *hijāb* and *niqāb* to be superfluous to female piety. Ayra believed that the self-styled preacher had correctly attributed these practices to cultural rather than religious imperatives. Following Ghamidi's proposition, Ayra now argued that even if it were as the *ʿulamā* claimed and these modes of Islamic comportment were obligatory under Islam, they should be granted less importance than other aspects of piety. Ayra felt that it was more important for Muslim women to pay attention to their internal, moral, and spiritual transformation than to focus on the more "superficial" elements of piety. The *hijāb* and *niqāb*, in Ayra's opinion, fell into the latter category and therefore constituted less meaningful aspects of her pious transition. Ayra believed that if it were meant to happen, she would adopt these practices naturally.

Despite Ayra's claims regarding the superficial status of these modes of female Islamic comportment, I was aware that the perceived difficulty of accommodating the *hijāb* and *niqāb* in her upper-class lifestyle inspired her arbitrary placement of them as practices meant to follow her inner transformation. Ayra's lesser regard for these practices is primarily due to the myriad images and discourses that women from Ayra's socioeconomic background are exposed to throughout their lives, some of which are not in keeping with the hegemonic discourses on female piety propounded by local male clerics and religious authorities in Pakistan. For many of these women, "ordinary" life includes viewing American and British movies and television series; reading books written by American and British authors; pursuing their higher education at Western universities; traveling to European and American cities for their summer vacations; aspiring to ideals of feminism, fashion, and public comportment popularized by Western celebrities; and organizing and attending local events inspired by Western culture, such as Thanksgiving dinners, Halloween parties, and Christmas balls. Thus, even as the recent proliferation of Salafi-inspired Islamic learning centers and private Qur'ān study groups has made the *hijāb* and *niqāb* more popular among middle-class and affluent Pakistani women, the majority of women from these backgrounds continue to associate these modes of Islamic comportment with a more conservative or radicalized Arab-Islamic sociability. Moreover, even the adoption of these forms of dress by Pakistani working-class women is more a function of the cultural imperatives associated with them, including the protection they offer women from unwelcome male advances and neighborhood gossip, than of their perceived obligatory status under Islam. In Pakistan, women from less affluent backgrounds are generally subjected to stricter culturally and religiously inspired controls regarding their sartorial choices, their presence in public places, and their interactions with the opposite gender.

From this perspective, Ayra's refusal to follow the prescribed modes of Islamic female conduct can also be viewed as an assertion of her class position, because of which she could exercise more control over how Islam should come to bear on her body in a religio-cultural landscape where women are generally excluded from determining how Islam should affect their lives. By outlining an understanding of female piety that is both rooted in the rejection of certain established ritual practices prescribed by male scholars and closely tied to her upper-class, Western, and liberal goals and aspirations, Ayra exposes the limitations of anthropological literature that has tended to analyze Muslim lives from the point of view of "paradigmatic models of piety" (e.g., Mahmood 2005) or in terms of the West/Islam dichotomy. In *Muslim Cool*, Khabeer (2016, 75, 165) makes a similar proposition with regard to the importance of race in prompting Black American Muslims to adopt certain distinct sartorial styles that were considered too Western and Black to be deemed Islamically "legitimate" by Arab and South Asian Muslims. Khabeer (75, 165) argues that, rather than analyzing these sartorial interventions through the lens of "paradigmatic models of piety," which would presume a necessary opposition between these styles and Islam, we should view them as clarifying ways of "being" Muslim that are forged in opposition to the "authoritative aesthetics of Arab and South Asian American hegemonies that continually bracket off Blackness as outside 'the Tradition.'" Khabeer's argument, much like Ayra's comments, highlights the diversity of Muslim lives and demonstrates how "being" Muslim can mean different things to different people.

For Ayra, terming her spiritual transformation a journey meant that she could accommodate her Western goals and aspirations without relinquishing her pious subjectivity. She found the justification to do so in Ghamidi's lenient ruling on these practices. The benefits of following Ghamidi for Ayra were thus manifold, and they involved more than a simple discernment of authenticity. Ghamidi allowed Ayra to shift the burden of her failure to conform to the traditional scholars and their propensity to place undue restrictions on Muslims. Because of Ghamidi's ability to state his propositions in strictly Islamic terms, Ayra could appease her Muslim conscience while simultaneously avoiding what she perceived as the more restrictive and problematic aspects of Islam. She could consider herself a devout and practicing Muslim without making the requisite sacrifices that she would otherwise have been required make under the 'ulamā's authoritative influence. Gibbins (1989, 5–7), drawing on philosophers such as Wittgenstein and Oakeshott, offers us a similar view of politics, considering it to be a public's negotiation of the rules and discourse that morally bind the community together. Controversial and hugely debated Islamic practices such as veiling generally constitute the focal point of such negotiations.

In addition, Ayra's critical thoughts on the discourse of *hijāb* and *niqāb* serve to illuminate a dimension of aspirational piety that is markedly distinct from the modes of piety reflected by the commentaries above: her comments suggest the importance of social and cultural values in determining a practitioner's religious subjectivity. In illuminating this form of Muslim religiosity, Ayra clarifies a notion of agency that cannot be explained in terms of an overwhelming concern for piety (e.g., Mahmood 2005) or as a straightforward desire to subvert or resist religious norms (e.g., Butler 1993, 1997). Rather, the form of agency expressed by Ayra locates its exercise at the disjuncture between Islamic tradition and Muslims' everyday existential realities. The resulting internal conflict compels a hierarchization of Islamic values, which in Ayra's case involved a preference for internal transformation and goodness over the exteriority of embodied practices such as the *hijāb* and *niqāb*, which she discarded as secondary or superfluous to piety. Alternatively, Schielke and Debevec (2012, 11) offer us a useful insight into the internal conflict characterizing Ayra's engagement with these practices by proposing a reconsideration of the agentive aspect of Islamic practice. Because, as Debevec (2012) notes, religion can both offer solace to its practitioners and simultaneously place a burden on them, there needs to be space for different interpretations and practices at different times (see also Simon 2014).[4] In Debevec's (44) account, the Muslims in Burkina Faso struggled "with the constraints of a complex life," which were "not made any easier by the very strict and detailed prescriptions of a proper life as a Muslim." Delaying certain obligatory Islamic practices allowed these Muslims to privilege their everyday concerns and accommodate "different pressures, urges and aims without having to openly challenge" widely accepted notions of piety (Schielke and Debevec 2012, 12). While noting Muslims' justifications for delaying piety, both Schielke and Debevec distance themselves from a view of these as simply excuses or exercises of choice. Instead, drawing on Jackson's (1996, 34) argument for focusing on what people accomplish through concepts rather than what concepts explain about the world, Schielke and Debevec (2012, 11) propose a reconsideration of the "openness, indeterminacy and ambiguity of religious practice" as "choice in a liberal sense." In their opinion, in most instances, people "have little choice—on the contrary they cope with circumstances over which they have little or no power" (12). Schielke and Debevec's argument also applies to Ayra, for whom delaying the adoption of the *hijāb* and *niqāb* allowed a sustained relationship with Islam. The context in which Ayra followed Ghamidi to delay her adherence to certain religious practices alludes to the importance of looking beyond activism-inspired engagements with Islam when evaluating Muslim lives (cf. Hirschkind 2006; Mahmood 2005).

SELECTIVE PIETY

While following a select scholar constituted the preferred mode of Islamic engagement for Ayra, for other Muslims, the pluralism of religious talk shows implied an even more selective engagement with Islamic concepts and practices. This became apparent to me when I met Zainab, a woman in her midthirties and a domestic worker in the elite Defence Housing locality in Karachi. When we met, Zainab had recently gotten divorced. A mother of three, she worked hard all day to sustain her family and to offer her children the education that she had been deprived of in her youth. Having been married to a drug addict, Zainab had been obliged to work throughout her married life. As she confessed to me, her husband would often abuse her when she refused to feed his drug addiction. During these difficult times, Zainab frequently supplicated to God to grant her emancipation from her abusive spouse. While Zainab's adverse marital experience had increased her religious observance, she confessed that she rarely turned to religious shows for guidance. This she attributed to her adverse viewing experience of a past episode of *Aalim Online*. On the episode, two male scholars had justified the practice of Muslim males beating their wives as permissible within Islamic guidelines. As a victim of domestic abuse, Zainab refused to accept that Islam would condone such a practice. Instead, she relied on the general lack of consensus between televised scholars to argue against the ruling, despite the scholarly consensus characterizing it on that particular occasion. On the basis of her negative viewing experience, Zainab now maintained that these shows had little to offer her in terms of Islamic guidance.

From Zainab's account we get the sense that religious talk shows can preclude a clear designation of religious authority as rooted in any particular religious group or specialist's understanding of Islam. By giving viewers access to competing scholarly rulings, religious talk shows also provide viewers the ability to move in and out of different understandings and subjectivities and to thus determine their own religious preferences. As Zainab's example indicates, viewers who engage more critically with scholarly discourses are also freed from the burden of conforming to a particular normative order, one that they cannot reconcile with their lived experience. Within this framework, a scholar's relevance persists only insofar as his understanding of Islam resonates with the viewers' existential concerns and notions of piety. However, as in Ayra's situation, this approach allowed Zainab to sustain her relationship with her faith. She could challenge the authority of male scholars and the unequal and excessive constraints their interpretations placed on Muslim women rather than question or defy her faith (see Debevec 2012; Schielke and Debevec 2012).

Whereas religious talk shows (including the doubts they raise regarding scholarly propositions) allowed Ayra and Zainab to accommodate their existential concerns without challenging their faith, there is an alternative way to analyze these shows, considering them as also enabling choice in the "liberal sense" (c.f. Schielke and Debevec 2012, 11). In Sabiha's case, a scholarly ruling on television, which caused her pious subjectivity to come into conflict with her liberal ideals of female empowerment and gender equality, prompted her to make such as choice by provoking her to reevaluate her relationship with Islam.

Sabiha, a female in her midthirties, came from a background similar to Ayra's. Like Ayra, she also considered herself an observant Muslim; she paid her *zakāt* (obligatory alms), prayed regularly, and kept all her fasts during *Ramaḍān*. However, for Sabiha, unlike Ayra, the commensurability of Islamic injunctions with her existing values constituted an essential precondition for her continued relationship with Islam. This became apparent to me during Sabiha's narration of what had transpired on a religious show that she had recently viewed with her mother-in-law. On the show, the participating religious scholar had described the concept of female subordination as Islamically ordained. Sabiha, who usually viewed these shows with her mother-in-law, explained how, in that rare instance, she had not agreed with her mother-in-law's endorsement of the scholarly ruling. Sabiha, a keen proponent of women's rights and empowerment, could not accept that a "truly" divine power would accord women a lower status than men. Narrating her subsequent argument with her mother-in-law, Sabiha said,

> We are reasoning creatures, and God has given us reasoning power. Regardless of how many scholars say Islamic injunctions are black and white, there has to be some reasoning underlying them. I recently had an argument with my mother-in-law regarding the status of women, although she is otherwise very liberal. She told me that women were not given the same respect in Islam accorded to men. She told me that if I said otherwise, I would be committing a sin. I told my husband that if I ever found out that the Qur'ān had accorded women a lesser status, I might actually give up my religion because if that were the case, God would have created women without a brain. We need to see the reasoning behind what is said, instead of conforming mindlessly to what we are told.

An important consideration in Sabiha's case is that her rejection of the scholarly ruling was not only about sustaining an unproblematic relationship with Islam but equally about sustaining her self-concept as an intelligent, independent, and empowered woman on par with any male. This was why Sabiha threatened to leave Islam if she ever found out that it ordained otherwise. Sabiha's threat, in this particular instance, outlines a very important role for religious shows: their propensity to draw the viewers' attention to the incommensurability of Islamic values with contemporary life. A pertinent consideration here is the increased emphasis on Islamic rulings on religious talk shows and its role in instigating a more critical Muslim engagement with Islam. By offering Muslims prescriptions on even minor aspects of their everyday lives, religious shows don't simply enable Muslims to lead more Islamically conformant lives; they also prompt them to perceive Islam as an invasive and constraining presence in their lives. This is mainly on account of the Muslim belief that God's commands are absolute and therefore above reconsideration, which, when taken together with the difficulties related to applying Islam to every aspect of contemporary life in Pakistan, promotes a view of Islam as incommensurate with contemporary life and values. In Sabiha's case, this consideration was inspired by the realization that Islam may not confer on her the same status as her husband. Thus, up until Sabiha considered Islam to be congruent with her current mode of existence, she could afford to subscribe to its principles. However, when Sabiha perceived Islam to be interfering with her place in society, she felt compelled to appraise it more critically, even resist it. Sabiha's willingness to critique and contest certain Islamic concepts reflects the ways in which many middle-class and affluent Pakistanis engage with traditional scholarly rulings both within and outside the context of television. Their contentions in these instances are not confined to a critique of the traditional scholarly emphasis on female subordination and modesty but also involve a critical evaluation of Islamic laws and concepts that they deem anachronistic and out of sync with the values of human rights, individual autonomy, and citizen equality. Not only are these values guaranteed under Pakistan's Constitution, but they also provide the basis for organizing urban, middle-class life in Pakistan. Some problematic Islamic concepts that religious shows have highlighted, which have provoked this form of critical appraisal, include the permission within Islam to discriminate against religious minorities, rules about gender segregation, sanctions on blasphemy and apostasy, the conversion of Pakistan into a theocratic state, and the prescribed modes of dress for women.

While it is difficult to predict whether Sabiha would have actually carried out her threat, her refusal to concede to an Islam that subordinated her existence to that of men is in a sense not very different from Ayra's and Zainab's engagement with the pluralism of religious talk shows to avoid certain principles traditionally upheld as Islamic that affected them "negatively and disproportionately" (Eltantawi 2017, 11). All three women outline an understanding of Muslim religiosity that is not limited to a privileged and enduring concern for piety and Islamic tradition but that entails the willingness to reconsider and critique Islamic concepts that seemingly resist being integrated into the practitioners' contemporary lifestyles and value systems. By paying attention to these alternative dimensions of Muslim piety, we can also begin to understand the role that religious shows play in reinscribing the terms of Islamic public debate by calling into question the supremacy of the Islamic tradition for Muslims.

While elaborating on the tendency of young men in the northern Egyptian village of Nazlat al-Rayyis to stray from the moral and ethical norms governing everyday life in the village, Schielke (2009, S32) notes that, for Muslims, "all other moral registers have either to accept or ignore the supremacy of religion, but they cannot openly contest it." Alternatively, by displaying a willingness to concede her faith to her feminist ideals, Sabiha clarifies an understanding of Muslim agentival capacity that locates its exercise at the intersection of conflicting influences that shape notions of Muslim selfhood and personhood. Agency from this perspective does not only reside in the Muslim avoidance of certain Islamic concepts or in the Muslim inclination to downplay the importance of certain Islamic norms and practices; it also inheres in the practitioners' willingness to actively challenge aspects of the Islamic tradition that they consider socially or politically problematic in contemporary times. These ways of resisting or avoiding conformance are inscribed with a reconceptualization of religiosity in which the authority of religious scholars is minimized, as lay Muslims determine for themselves, albeit drawing on scholarly propositions, which Islamic values and practices to privilege and which to discard. The end result of these deliberations is a reconfiguration of Islam on the basis of individual goals and values.

In expressing a form of Muslim religiosity in which the desire to hold on to her ideals of herself as an empowered woman supersedes the concern for Islamic "legitimacy" and "authenticity," Sabiha also clarifies the significance of religious shows in mediating transformations in the nature of religious knowledge. Foucault (1984), drawing simultaneously on Kant's (1983) and Baudelaire's (1964) theses on *Enlightenment* and *Modernity*, respectively, explains such a critical process as a change in attitude that entails work on our limits and involves a critical reflection on ourselves and history, even as we are "historically determined." According to Foucault (1984, 43, 46–50), this form of critical engagement with the present and ourselves is not so much about a quest for "formal structures with universal value" but rather involves "the historical analysis of the limits that are imposed on us and an experiment with the possibility of going beyond them" so that we may constantly invent and produce ourselves. For Foucault (46), the relevance of this critical work we do on ourselves is thus not so much "transcendental" as it is "archaeological." Through this critical self-analysis, Foucault (46–47) argues that "specific transformations" related to "our ways of being and thinking, relations to authority, relations between sexes" come about. In Pakistan, these critical processes can be accessed only by conceptualizing the Muslim community more broadly, not only in terms of its commitment to upholding the principles enjoined by Islamic *Sharī'a* and *fiqh*, but also in relation to its capacity to challenge and oppose the contemporary applicability and relevance of these principles. By considering these alternative perspectives, we can also begin to view the practice of Islam outside its embodied manifestation and duly consider the importance of "thought processes" in shaping the Muslim experience (see also Marsden 2005, 261).[5]

THE LIMITS OF CRITICAL DELIBERATION

If religious talk shows inspired more critical and expedient engagements with religious authorities and Islamic practice, so too did they give rise to debates on the extent to which individual opinion should be allowed to prevail in matters of faith and the form it should take. So, although Salman, the media teacher at SZABIST, was not opposed to *ijtihād*, he firmly believed that its exercise should be subject to some constraints. He clarified this to me while voicing his disapproval of Ghamidi's rationalization of the incident of *Miʿrāj*:

> Ghamidi crossed a line, which is why he had to run away to Malaysia. His views are sometimes too rational, to the point where he says there was no *Miʿrāj* and that it was all a dream. He claims that the Prophet (PBUH) visited the heavens in his dream and that his horse, Buraq, was also part of the dream. This touches on a very core tenet of our belief. We believe that the horse did come, and the Prophet (PBUH) did sit on it and ascend to the heavens, because when Ḥazrat Abū Bakar (the Prophet's companion, RA) looked up toward the sky, he saw it. So Ghamidi crossed a line somewhere, and people did not appreciate that.

Salman's comments are important for noting the limitations of critical deliberation and also of religious talk shows that implicitly privilege this mode of Islamic engagement. Much like my scholarly interlocutors, Salman was of the opinion that Islamic belief could not indiscriminately be made subject to the individual *ʿaql*. Believers sometimes needed to look beyond the rationale underlying an injunction in order to stay firmly grounded in their faith. The incident of *Miʿrāj* for Salman symbolized such an instance. Since Salman felt that Ghamidi's interpretation of the events around *Miʿrāj* had violated the constraints set by Islam, he concluded that Ghamidi had transgressed the boundaries of faith. While it would be tempting to view Salman's concern merely in terms of his regard for piety, my discussion with Sania, a young, Western-educated professional banker in her midtwenties, indicates that in reality the situation is much more complex. When I met Sania during an *iftār* party at a mutual friend's residence, I found her to be a strong advocate of the need to circumscribe the place and form of personal opinion in Islamic debate. Sania's objections to a Muslim's uninhibited recourse to personal opinion mainly drew on her disapproval of Ghamidi's lenient rulings on *hijāb* and *niqāb*. Arguing against these rulings, Sania declared, "Ghamidi is too liberal. He claims that there is no need for *purdah* in this day and age. The reason why I disagree with him is because it is mentioned in the Qur'ān. My view of Islam is more conservative."

It is pertinent to note that Sania's disapproval of Ghamidi was also motivated by her own lived reality in relation to Islam. Since Sania observed the *hijāb* and *niqāb* and believed both practices to be integral to a Muslim woman's piety, it is possible to claim that her objections to Ghamidi's ruling came not merely from a place of religious responsibility but equally from a consideration of her own vested interest in the practices. It could be that Ghamidi's negation of both practices signaled to Sania the meaninglessness of her own religious endeavors, in that it threatened her past association with Islam and effectively nullified the compromises that she had made to sustain this association. Therefore, in Sania's case, her designation of Ghamidi as "too liberal" could have equally if not more so been motivated by her refusal to come to terms with the possibility that her own sacrifices vis-à-vis her faith had been in vain. Sania's allusion to Ghamidi as "too liberal" is not very different from many Pakistanis' ways of speaking about themselves and other Muslims in terms of the binaries of conservative and liberal (see Mamdani 2005; Marsden 2010). In this context, Sania's remarks also clarify a role for religious shows in contributing to the polarization of Islamic thought in Pakistan, which is a direct consequence of their tendency to invite traditional scholars alongside self-styled scholars. In addition, as already indicated, some religious shows display a marked preference for self-styled scholars and the critical modes of Islamic thinking they espouse, in that the shows either invite these scholars to present exclusively or allocate them more time to respond to viewer queries. Both types of religious shows put some of the more conservatively inclined Muslims on the defensive. By paying closer attention to the contexts that shape or reinforce these modes of Islamic thinking, we get a sense that the place of reasoning within Islam is not as straightforward as traditional scholars like Usmani and academics like Hirschkind (2001) would have us believe and is therefore crucial to deconstruct. It is imbricated in people's own existential concerns, the investments they have made in cultivating particular dispositions—conservative or liberal—and in a particular type of Muslim micropolitics, within which not just religious authorities but also ordinary Muslim practitioners have a vested interest in the form religion will take in the Islamic Republic of Pakistan.

RELIGIOUS PROGRAMMING AND RELIGIOUS PUBLIC DEBATE

The commentaries discussed above reinforce the point that religious shows enable diverse and "novel" ways of engaging with Islam and religious authorities, which are also motivated by the practitioners' religious, political, existential, and expedient concerns. Within this framework, the increased prominence of personal opinion and critical deliberation in religious discourse also implies the multivalent significance of religious shows for different people. Thus, if for some viewers religious shows open up the possibility for more critical engagements with scholarly discourse, for others they imply a sustained relationship with religious authorities and established modes of Islamic practice. Viewers' disparate engagements with religious content on television also expose the limitations of media theories that either postulate the media as a source of "mass ideological domination" (Horkheimer and Adorno 2002; Powdermaker 2002) or encourage an understanding of media content as open to appropriation by audiences (Budd, Entman, and Steinman 1990, quoted in Morley 1992, 28).[6] In fact, religious talk shows transform structures of religious authority and bring about religious change, not so much by encouraging particular religious dispositions, conservative or liberal, as by initiating processes in which questions about Islam and religious authority are opened to the public for conscious and critical deliberation, debate, and discussion. While a more critical engagement with Islamic texts and religious authority is by no means a new phenomenon, the modalities of this engagement, as well as the ways in which televised pluralism expands the scope for lay Muslim participation in religious debate, underscore the significance of television in mediating religious transformation.

Notwithstanding the role of self-styled scholars in implicitly privileging more individualized modes of Islamic thinking, I suggest a more nuanced engagement with the Islamic discourses on television, in which varying religious dispositions both sustain and are constructed by the polyvocality of televised Islamic perspectives. Silverstone (1994, ix) makes a similar claim in his book *Television and Everyday Life*, where he acknowledges the power of television and yet cautions us of the danger of analyzing its power without contextualizing it in terms of the "various levels of social reality with which it [television] engages." From the point of view of Karachiites who engaged more critically with religious discourse on television, an important consideration is their historically mediated, troubled relationship with Islam and traditional religious authorities. Hence, what starts out as a pious project on television takes on a profoundly different political and social significance, wherein the role and status of religious authorities and the relevance of Islam to everyday life is constantly challenged and continually reconfigured. Eickelman and Piscatori (2004, 44) offer a similar analysis of print Islam, noting how its introduction offered the possibility of expanding the ʿulamā's religious influence yet ironically led to a reduction in the ʿulamā's authority "in the long run." While Eickelman and Piscatori attribute this long-term consequence to the "increasing number of educated persons and the shift to more accessible vernacular languages," the ways in which religious shows enable more critical and individualized engagements with Islam bring about a similar effect in Pakistan.[7]

My interlocutors perceived Ghamidi as more liberal than his traditional counterparts, not because the self-styled scholar is more liberal per se but because his distinct interpretations can be appropriated by viewers to serve their liberal projects, including those that seek to minimize Islam's, and by extension the ʿulamā's, authoritative influence in the everyday lives of religious practitioners. In this context, Mufti (2007) informs us that Ghamidi categorically rejects a "liberal" title for himself in the same way that he avoids referring to himself as a "conservative." In fact, the scholar chooses to challenge both ways of thinking about Islam. This is also manifest in his clarification that "the liberals in Pakistan are confused by me. The religionists are fuming and have called me everything short of an infidel" (Ghamidi, quoted in Mufti 2007). In the context of the wider Muslim world, Eickelman and Piscatori (2004) similarly acknowledge the issues inherent in designating the ʿulamā and "new" religious intellectuals as necessarily favoring distinct modes of Islamic thinking. Instead, Eickelman and Piscatori (44, 68–69) argue that despite the differences in "type of education, social position and ideology," the ʿulamā and "new" religious intellectuals share a common ground and "compete to gain ascendancy as arbiters of Islamic practice." In the Pakistani context, both sources of religious authority similarly invoke a normative order, albeit conceived of different ideas of what this implies. The relevance of self-styled scholars within this framework arises from their role in initiating "processes by which many aspects of social [religious] and political life become subject to conscious [and critical] reflection, discussion and debate" (Eickelman and Piscatori 2004, 37). In Pakistan, the importance of these processes derives not only from the way in which they enable a more critical "lay" engagement with authoritative religious discourse but also from their capacity to alter the terms of Islamic debate, which in turn transforms the practitioners' engagement with Islam.

NOTES

1. Hirschkind (1996) cites the objections of four Cairo University professors, published in the "Scientific Report on the Views of Nasr Hamid Abu Zayd," to make his argument.

2. Butler's (1997, 13–14) notion of feminists' agency draws on Laclau and Mouffe's (1985) reading of Derrida's (1978) "Structure, Sign, and Play," whereby "a structure gains its status structure, its structurality, only through its repeated reinstatement." Accordingly, Butler argues that "no social formation can endure without becoming reinstated, and that every reinstatement puts the 'structure' in question at risk, suggests that the possibility of its own undoing is at once the condition of possibility of structure itself" (see also Butler 1993 for a similar discussion on drag queens).

3. Mahmood (2005, 139) borrows simultaneously from Foucault's (1988) techniques of forming the self in his work on the history of sexuality; from liberal theory (see Taylor 1989); and from Aristotelian ethics (Aristotle 1941) to argue that "bodily practices do not simply articulate different conceptions of the ethical subject" but also endow "the self with particular capacities through which the subject comes to enact the world."

4. Simon (2014, 181) similarly notes how *shalat* (prayers) for the Minangkabau people in West Sumatra, Indonesia, may either allow for the resolution of people's everyday "moral tensions" or "be a source of anxiety and frustration."

5. According to Marsden (2005, 262–63), "active thought processes play a powerful role in the making of moral valuations and ethical decisions." Since for Marsden these thought processes offer a "distinct window into the ways in which people reflect on and experience authority," any "anthropology of embodiment needs to be complemented by the exploration of thought and thought processes as a marked feature of human experience."

6. See Radway (1996, 244, quoted in Algan 2003, 28), according to whom an emphasis on "reception" merely reinforces the notion of "media use" as a "linear process of reception and response." Also see Carragee's (1990, 84, quoted in Morley 1992, 34) argument against a sole focus on audience agency. According to Carragee, this focus results in a loss of economic and organizational context.

7. Eickelman and Piscatori's (2004) proposition draws on Robinson's (1993, 245) work.

CONCLUSION

A KEY AIM OF THIS book was to explore the ways in which religious shows alter the dynamics of religious authority and Islamic public debate. I approached these issues from multiple perspectives, which involved situating myself in the production studios of *Aalim Online*, with religious scholars, and with members of the viewing public. Locating my research in the production studios gave me access to the differing motivations and contingencies influencing contemporary religious programming. However, only by broadening my research to lay and institutional viewers did I become aware of the far-reaching and unintended consequences of the transformations in religious show format and content. While analyzing television dramas in Egypt, Abu-Lughod (2005, 237) argues that "viewers, as most media studies today confirm, are selective in their readings and appreciation of the messages of television dramas. They can disagree with the politics; they can marvel at and take pleasure in the defiant characters who live as they cannot. In Egypt, they accept the moral stances presented only when these resonate with their worlds." However, to speak of viewers primarily in these terms is to ignore the fact that people don't simply react to media discourses. They also contribute to them, and as I have stressed repeatedly in this book, they factor in production decisions about the form and content of religious programming, even as they oppose religious shows, reject them, appropriate them, and are selectively inspired by them. I have shown how the viewers' varied engagement with televised Islamic content goes far beyond a simple acceptance or rejection of televised Islamic discourses. In fact, only by exposing ourselves to multiple viewing perspectives can we glean closer insights into some of the contradictions that emerge from the transformations in religious show format and content.

A central idea that emerged from my observations in the production studios was that producers and channel owners conceptualize religious shows simultaneously as pious, commercial, and political projects. They are pious projects because the shift from didactic sermonizing toward the issuance of Islamic rulings in response to live, call-in viewer queries is explicitly aimed at facilitating lay Muslims to live their lives in closer conformity with Islamic values. The commercial significance of religious shows is a function of the competitive media environment in which they operate, so that the desire to elicit broader commercial appeal and advertising revenue is reflected in the move toward Islamic pluralism and the enhanced production regard for the wishes and preferences of financial sponsors, respectively. Religious shows are political projects because they are aimed at cultivating more moderate, accommodative, and tolerant religious sensibilities and ways of Islamic thinking, in a highly volatile and conflict-ridden religious landscape. Especially on the nature of their political significance, I have elaborated how state influence in the contemporary liberalized media environment does not generally manifest as direct interference in religious programming content (although at times the state regulatory body, PEMRA, may be employed for this purpose) but rather involves a heightened production consideration of state agendas. These insights into the multiple considerations undergirding religious show production also warrant a broader perspective of religious show audiences as jointly constituted by religious show producers, financial sponsors, the Pakistani state and its institutions, religious authorities, religious television presenters, and lay Muslim viewers.

Through a consideration of the varying and at times conflicting motivations underlying the production of religious shows, we can also begin to unpack and understand the unintended and far-reaching consequences of religious shows, and the paradoxes that emerge from their regular featuring. I have revealed a key paradox in this regard concerning the pluralistic emphasis in religious programming, together with the tendency of religious producers to simultaneously conceptualize religious shows as both politico-commercial and pious projects. As elaborated in this book, the form that Islamic pluralism takes on television can either enable more accommodative and tolerant attitudes toward Islamic difference or, conversely, encourage the hardening of sectarian tendencies. The latter is to do with the way that the diversity of Islamic representation on television stirs viewers' faith-related insecurities by calling into question the "absolute" nature of their beliefs and practices. Thus, even as some key production motivations underlying the introduction of Islamic pluralism on television are to cater to a diverse viewership and promote intra-Muslim harmony, the uncertainty that this development generates can make viewers even more protective of their doctrinal identities.

Moreover, the doctrinally inspired forms of televised pluralism can implicitly encourage viewers, for whom doctrinal categories had little relevance before they viewed these shows, to adopt this mode of engagement with Islam. The representations of doctrinal difference on television implicitly compel viewers to take sides, wherein even directing their questions at a particular scholar implies privileging a particular group's viewpoint over the viewpoints of others. Thus, even as televised pluralism aims to promote tolerance and accommodation as the key characteristics of Muslim personhood, the very fact that religious shows feature staged contests between religious scholars on the correct interpretation and application of the Islamic tradition can work against this aim. Conversely, even a politically motivated emphasis on accommodation ironically threatens to undermine the very premise on which doctrinal claims are staged. To understand my proposition, we need to first comprehend that, even though the presence of different religious groups in Pakistan represents the plurality of Islamic thought, claims of doctrinal legitimacy are made in opposition to Islamic difference. In fact, the legitimacy of doctrinal claims rests on proliferating perceptions of Islam as a monolith constituted of "absolute" truths. Within this perception, each doctrinal group's proponents uphold its perspective as closest to, or most conformant with, Islamic "truth." Thus, any form of religious activism rooted in doctrinal difference is by its very nature premised on denying the legitimacy of competing Islamic perspectives. What is at stake in this battle of "truth" is greater access to, or monopoly over, state institutions and the exclusive right to interfere in matters of the state and legislation. At the basis of all these doctrinal claims is, therefore, the realization of a homogenous Muslim community (see Nelson 2009), an idea that is effectively displaced by the inclusion of alternative Islamic perspectives on religious shows. All these observations make it easier to understand why an ostensible effort by religious show producers to accommodate religious difference either neutralizes the attempt to promote Islamic tolerance or, paradoxically, undermines the very differences religious shows claim to accommodate.

The paradoxes enabled by televised representations of pluralism also extend to perceptions of religious authority. By provoking doubts about the legitimacy and authenticity of existing beliefs, televised forms of pluralism place the burden on viewers to either discover the "truth" for themselves or face the uneasy consequences of losing their faith altogether. Thus, even as the increased focus on Islamic rulings privileges a consideration of religious shows as enabling religious scholars to extend their role and influence over the domain of everyday

Muslim conduct, it also exposes religious scholars to greater viewer evaluation, scrutiny, and criticism. Especially in relation to the pluralistic emphasis in religious programming, I have shown that the propensity of televised pluralism to enable a self-determined engagement with Islam contains within it the potential to undermine the role and significance of religious authorities. It is also in this context that we need to evaluate the anxieties of traditional scholars in relation to this mode of programming, in terms of its role in problematizing claims to religious authority rooted in doctrinal difference. Further, televised pluralism effectively subjects scholarly authority to lay judgments. As a result, traditional scholars find it increasingly difficult to preserve an image of themselves as sole defenders of Islamic "truth." This in turn has adverse implications for the role of these scholars in shaping collective forms of Islamic belief and practice.

The central place of religious programming in undermining, and instigating reevaluations of, religious authority, however, is also on account of the programming shift toward issuing Islamic rulings on various aspects of faith and practice. Within the new *fatwā*-oriented religious show format, the accommodative or argumentative nature of scholarly interactions makes it even more difficult to sustain an idea of Islam as foregrounding "collective interest and the common good" (Schulz 2006b, 222). In this context, I have demonstrated that the combined incorporation of televised pluralism and televised *fatāwā* into the format of contemporary religious programming implicitly undermines a sense of the "imagined" religious community (Anderson 1991; Rajagopal 2001; Lehikoinen 2003; Soares 2004b; Asamoah-Gyadu 2008), which in turn also impedes any scholarly efforts aimed at the collective enforcement of morality (Ismail 2003).[1] Thus, not only do religious shows problematize a straightforward conceptualization of religious authority as rooted in any monolithic conceptualization of Islam, but by drawing attention to the disparity between scholarly propositions, they also inspire more critical and self-determined viewer engagements with scholarly discourses.

Religious shows thus implicitly popularize a notion of piety in which the significance of "individual understanding and responsibility" (Schulz 2006b, 222) implicitly outweighs the value of scholarly propositions. In relation to religious media in Mali, Schulz (223) argues that the increasingly commercialized mass-media culture implies that "new types of religious leaders" are able to "tap into a general trend toward a neo-liberal ideology of choice by presenting different religious positions and practices as a matter of personal conviction and style." According to Schulz (223) these leaders privilege the framing of "religious conviction as a matter of . . . individual consumer choice" so that "many believers come to understand themselves as 'consuming believers,' that is, as believers who choose a religious viewpoint... against contending positions." I have indicated that by enabling viewers to discern for themselves the value of scholarly propositions, religious shows in Pakistan mediate a more critical engagement with religious authorities. For lay viewers, watching multiple religious scholars debating among themselves on the "proper" interpretation of foundational texts implies that they feel less obliged to follow these scholars and prefer to determine for themselves which Islamic norms and rules of conduct merit their greater attention. However, these developments should not be seen as implying a straightforward marginalization of traditional scholars. In fact, traditional scholars, not unlike self-styled scholars, are central to such reevaluations, although their prominence within the format of religious shows is more on account of the diverse opinions they proffer, or the multiple perspectives they elaborate, rather than due to their authoritative capacity for determining the "proper" mode of lived Islam. One consequence of this development is that it is not just the unconventional and oft subversive Islamic representations of self-styled scholars but equally traditional scholarly assertions on religion that are subjected to rigorous lay viewer critique and evaluation. Thus, the nature of religious fragmentation that I have proposed is not just an interpretative one in which lay Muslim viewers are empowered to "determine the meanings of religious symbols" (Hoover 2008, 33; see also Kazi 2018). Instead I have shown that a greater recourse to individual opinion, as enabled by religious shows, renders these talk shows central to provoking a reevaluation of established Islamic concepts and values (cf. Schulz 2006b).[2] This implies that it is not just "modernity" but increasingly also Islamic tradition that is put on an "endless trial," especially those aspects of it that seemingly resist being integrated into viewers' contemporary lifestyles or value systems (Kraidy 2010, 18).

On the significance of viewers' everyday realities and existential concerns, I have pointed out the role of self-styled scholars in foregrounding alternative understandings of Islam that make it easier for lay Muslims to integrate Islam into their everyday lives. I have iterated that the "easy" Islam that self-styled scholars popularize can paradoxically imply either a greater role for Islam in everyday life, or a more expedient and critical lay engagement with Islam. In the latter context, one must consider the forms of critical deliberation self-styled scholars introduce, which can broaden the scope for a more expedient lay engagement with Islam. I have shown that the forms of critical deliberation enabled by religious shows are not confined to gauging the authenticity of scholarly propositions. In fact, ordinary Muslim viewers increasingly also employ their critical faculties to elude what they perceive to be the constraints Islam imposes on them, wherein their existential concerns and attachments to current modes of living play an important role in instigating reevaluations of religious authority and dominant understandings of Islam. In this context, I have also implicated the viewers' increased exposure to Islamic rules and regulations, as mediated by the ʿulamāʾ's normative emphasis, in provoking them to engage more critically with televised Islam, especially when viewers deem the stated rules and regulations to be incompatible with their existing value system and present-day realities.

Drawing on these observations, I would like to urge a more critical and cautious application of the notion of Islam as a "discursive tradition," (Asad 2009b), one that would lead us to view the Muslim evaluations of, and contentions over, religious shows and the religious authorities who feature on them as nonetheless entailing a heightened and uncritical regard for what is enjoined in the foundational texts (see Anjum 2007). Asad (2009b) argues that even though Muslims may debate the legitimacy and value of multiple and competing scholarly propositions, they are bound together into a Muslim community whose central defining feature is its ineluctable relationship with the foundational texts. I would like to invite a reevaluation of this notion of the Muslim community as bound together, however tenuously, through its relationship with Islamic foundational texts. According to Asad, this relationship with the foundational texts remains an overriding concern for all Muslims. While Asad's proposition works well to highlight the nature of scholarly arguments and debates vis-à-vis their distinct doctrinal preferences, it does little to explicate the "lived" aspects of Muslim experience, in which a person's relationship with foundational texts is not the only aspect of Muslim life. In fact, Muslim experience and personhood in contemporary Pakistan are increasingly forged at the intersection of competing narratives, wherein the believers' existential concerns and regard for other values, such as individual autonomy, tolerance, and gender parity, may at times override their concern for religious observance (see Kazi 2018).

Within this framework, I have argued that we need to broaden the scope of anthropological analyses to include Muslims who are "themselves critical of emergent styles of Muslim thought and identity," (Marsden 2005, 250; see Kazi 2018) or for whom cultivating piety is not the single most important aspect of their lives. Marsden (2005, 252) makes a similar argument, noting that "piety, far from being a widely valued religious disposition for Chitral Muslims, a clear and shared standard by which they mark out a transformation towards living a proper Muslim life, is, rather, subject to complex judgment, discussion and criticism, and seen as being needed to be carefully matched with balanced levels of love, affection and humor." For my interlocutors, the social and political context in which claims and exhortations to piety are made in present-day Pakistan prompted them to privilege values and concerns other than, or antithetical to, piety. While explaining his reservations about applying Mahmood's (2001) and Hirschkind's (2001, 2006) analyses to Pakistani Muslims, Marsden (2005, 252) clarifies that both scholars' emphasis on piety largely stems from their study of Muslims whose attempts "to live piously" are framed in opposition to a society dominated by a "secular rationality." In contrast, the 'ulamā and Islamist parties in Pakistan, which have grown immensely in power in the last four decades, have tended to exert "their power in ways that significantly constrain the ability of ordinary Muslims to make decisions about how they want to live a Muslim life" (252). However, in the case of my interlocutors, their disillusionment with sectarianism, and the 'ulamā's perceived role in popularizing this form of Islamic engagement, also contributed to their critical relationship with the religion as a whole. Since a growing number of Pakistani Muslims have begun to affiliate the rise in religious piety with the escalating incidence of sectarianism and the increased power and influence of the 'ulamā, claims to self-determination or individual autonomy in Pakistan are increasingly also staged in opposition to, or as distinct from, piety. My argument is strengthened by Ahmad (2010, 314) and Wickham (2004), both of whom clarify that public and standardized displays of piety can exert a powerful pressure on others to conform, which may be "more effective than overt force" (also see Ismail 2003; Meyer 2006).[3]

The various contradictions that religious shows activate and the transformations in understandings of piety that they enable imply that these shows can both facilitate more autonomously driven and individualized engagements with Islam and make certain viewers more desirous of a uniformly imposed moral and social Islamic order. These dichotomous viewer engagements with religious programming further polarize Pakistani society along religious lines, whereby the country is composed of both those who feel that striving toward faith should be a self-determined pursuit, confined to the private sphere of life, and those who envision a more public, unified, and authoritatively determined role for Islam in Pakistan's society, legislature, and politics. It is from this lens that we also need to view my interlocutors' contentions over the 'ulamā's role in popularizing Islamic practices such as female veiling. I have stressed that we need to look at these practices outside of their role in clarifying gendered enactments of, and engagements with, religion. These practices can also pose a threat to the religious autonomy of lay Muslim males, to the extent that they serve to consolidate the 'ulamā's right to define orthodoxy, thus enabling the sustained influence of the latter over prevalent forms of religious morality and comportment. Thus, the symbolic and real social and political effects of these practices by far exceed the pervasiveness of the patriarchal ethos that is generally associated with them.

An understanding of the general Pakistani apprehension regarding the *ulamā*'s growing power also clarifies why values considered central to Western conceptualizations of "modernity" may resonate more with some Pakistani Muslims than do the values prescribed by the Islamic code. This tends to be especially true for people who fear the *ulamā*'s extended control over their everyday lives. As the *ulamā*'s interference in everyday life, mediated by religious shows, increases, some viewers start to engage more critically and cautiously with Islam and prevalent notions of piety. Therefore, I concur with Marsden's (2005, 252) proposition that "any study of so called revivalist Islam must take into account the visions of power and authority it entails, the constraints on individuality it imposes, the forms of exclusion it develops, and the multiple types of resistance it generates." Just as Islam constitutes a framework for evaluating "modernity," so too does "modernity," and the values it privileges, constitute an important framework for lay Muslim evaluations on the usefulness and correctness of certain Islamic injunctions in the contemporary context. Thus, even if, as Schulz (2006b, 223) argues, religious media may be conducive to promoting Islam as "a privileged reference point within competing community constructions" in Pakistan, we also need to bear in mind that the pluralism of televised religious content and the increased interference of the clergy in social affairs, as enabled by the *fatwā* orientation of religious shows, may equally serve to bolster the case of liberal Muslims. They do so by allowing these Muslims to advocate a secular conceptualization of Pakistan as a country in which the influence of Islam, and by extension religious scholars, in politics and state affairs is minimized.

Do these observations make it possible to claim a role for religious television shows in mediating a decline in the *ulamā*'s religious authority (see Gole 2002; Roy 2004; Schulz 2006b; Hoover 2008)? I argue that it may be both premature and inaccurate to do so, especially if we are to account for the various means by which the *ulamā* sustain their influence in Pakistan. In particular, we need to be aware that the *ulamā*'s authority in Pakistani is not merely discursively staged. It is mobilized in many different ways, through the extensive *madrasa* networks spread throughout the country, the *ulamā*'s participation in electoral politics, state institutions such as the Council of Islamic Ideology, and the various Islamic laws (in particular the Blasphemy Laws) that implicitly privilege and confer power on the *ulamā* and uphold Islam, and the *ulamā*, as integral to Pakistan's conception as an Islamic state. Also underlining my cautionary approach in this context is the Pakistani state's continued employment of ʿulamā for its various political projects.

All these observations attest to the ʿulamā's continued influence over religious public debate. However, despite these assessments, it is possible to foreground religious shows as instigating widespread debate on what role religious authorities—self-styled or traditional—should play in Pakistani society and polity. Can we, in line with these developments, claim a democratizing role for religious television shows? If we were to follow Habermas's (1991) conception of what this democratization implies (cf. Eickelman 2002; Meyer and Moors 2006), then perhaps the answer would be that we cannot, as those who claim expertise in Islamic knowledge continue to occupy a privileged position in televised Islamic debate—and by extension in the determination of an Islamic public legal and moral order.[4] However, if like Kraidy (2010, 199) we were to adopt a broader "definition of democracy as popular contention, deliberation, and performance," then to the extent that televised Islamic pluralism prompted my lay interlocutors to reassess, resist, defy, and denounce certain authoritatively established Islamic values and practices, we can claim a democratizing role for religious television shows.

NOTES

1. See Rajagopal (2001, 283), who argues that everyday religious consumption of the televised Hindu epics Ramayana and Mahabarata led to the emergence of a "Hinduized visual regime," which implicitly facilitated the Bharatiya Janta Party's (BJP) success in electoral politics. See also Soares's (2004b, 217–18) observation of how the media, through the standardization of norms, facilitates perceptions of the imagined community, which in turn shapes the way ordinary Muslims practice Islam, especially in its "public ritual forms." See Asamoah-Gyadu (2008, 59), who asserts the salience of media consumption in shaping religious identity by fostering a sense of belonging and community. According to Ismail (2003, 46), the morality discourses on Egyptian television go a long way to "ritualize" the everyday lives of Muslim believers.

2. Schulz (2006b, 222) proposes that the relevance of Islam to "personal life and public order" is "constituted through commercialization structures and through processes of mass-mediation." According to Schulz, "in this process, the conditions, forms, and contents of intra-Muslim debate are changing without, however, losing their connection to, and inspiration from, local discursive traditions and notions of piety."

3. Ismail (2003, 77) also observes how outward manifestations of piety extend religion's relevance to culture and politics. One particular example of

this is what Ismail refers to as the battle over morality between the liberal, the conservative, and the radical sections of Egyptian society. While the palpable aim of these discourses is limited to the formation of pious subjects, for Ismail, then, it is the "collective enforcement of public morals," facilitated by television, that also renders Islam political. With reference to the link between everyday piety and consumption, Meyer (2006) draws our attention to how "public" displays of piety in Pentecostal Ghana very much inhere in the "public" consumption of religious artifacts, which by privileging public professions of faith over internal belief extends the scope of religion beyond the "private" and religious realm.

4. See Eickelman (2002, 1), who views the emergence of the religious "public sphere" in contrast to the "authoritarian religious world," where articulations of Islam are regarded as imposing "essential constraints on the conduct and thought of those committed to it." Also see Meyer and Moors (2006, 3–6), who propose that the emergence of a "rational" and "autonomous" religious public sphere in "modern" societies is inextricably linked to the "mass" featuring of religion. For a critique of Habermas (1991), see Warner (1992), Fraser (1990), and Salvatore and Eickelman (2004), who propose an understanding of the "modern" "public space" as entailing a certain degree of conformance and as privileging particular interests and groups.

GLOSSARY OF ARABIC TERMS

ʿabāya. A loose gown covering
ʿabd. A slave
adhān. A call to prayer
Ahl-i Hadīth. A subsect within Sunni Islam
Ahmadīyā. A religious sect whose followers believe in the Prophethood of Mirza Ghulam Ahmad of Qadiyan
akhlāqiyyāt. Social conduct
ʿālim (pl. ʿulamā). Religious scholar
Ālim e Dīn. Scholar of religion
Allama. Learned scholar
ʿaql. Intellect
Asalāmualaykum. Islamic greeting
ʿĀshūrāʾ. Commemoration of the martyrdom of Ḥazrat Ali's family
ʿawrah. Covering up
banāt. Women's quarters
Barelwi. A subsect within Sunni Islam
Bayt-i-Rizwān. Vow of Rizwān
bidʿa. Religious innovation
dār al iftāʾ. Center for religious rulings
Dār al-ʿUlūm Islāmīā. Center for learning Islam
dars. Sermon
daʿwā. Invitation to Islam
Daʿwat i Islamī. Subsect of Barelwi persuasion
Deobandi. A subsect within Sunni Islam

dīn. Religion
fatwā. Reasoned opinion
fiqh. Jurisprudence
ḥadīth. Prophetic tradition
Ḥajj. Muslim pilgrimage
ḥalāl. Permissible
ḥarām. Forbidden
Ḥazrat. Honorific title
ḥifz. Memorization
hijāb. Head covering
'Īd al-aḍḥā. A sacrificial celebration to mark the performance of *Ḥajj*
'Īd al-fiṭr. Muslim celebration at the end of the month of fasting
'Īd Mīlād-un Nabī. The Prophet Muhammad's (PBUH) birth anniversary
ifṭār. Time for breaking fast
ijmā. Scholarly consensus
ijtihād. Exercise of individual reasoning and deduction
ikhlāṣ. Sincerity
'ilm. Knowledge
'ilm-i ghayb. Knowledge of the unseen
imām (pl. *a'imma*). Prayer leader
imān. Faith
iṣlāḥ. Guidance
isnād. Chain of learning/narration
Jamāʿat-i-Islamī. Religiopolitical party
Jāmīʿa Islāmīā. Institute for learning Islam
Jazakallāh. As per the will of Allah
jihād. Waging war for Islam
Kaʿba. Holy mosque for pilgrimage
kalām. Speculative theology
kalima. Religious verse
Karbalā. Battle between the Prophet's (PBUH) family members and Yazid
khaṭīb. Person who addresses prayer congregation
khauf. Fear
khushu. Humility
khuṭbā. Address to prayer congregation
kuttābs. Informal centers for *Qurʾānic* memorization and recitation
madrasa. Seminary
maghreb. Evening prayer
maʿrifa. Gnostic knowledge

masjid (pl. *masājid*). Mosque
maslak (pl. *masālik*). Doctrinal school
mātam. Self-flagellation and chest beating
maulvī. Cleric
Mawlānā. Learned scholar
mazār. Shrine
Miʿrāj. The Prophet Muhammad's (PBUH) ascension to the heavens
muʾaddhin (pl. *muʾaddhinūn*). Person who gives the call to prayer
muftī. Interpreter of Islamic law
Muftī e Aʿẓam. Grand *muftī*
muḥaddith. Expert on *ḥadīth*
Muḥarram. Mourning period for the martyrdom of Ḥazrat Ali during the battle of *Karbalā*
mujtahid. Practitioner of *ijtihād*
munāfiq. Hypocrite
murshid. Teacher
mustanid. Established
Mutaʿabbid. Bound to God as his slave
mutakallim. Expert on *kalām*
naʿat. Hymn in praise of the Prophet (PBUH)
naql. Mimic
niqāb. Face veil
nohas. Songs for the martyrdom of the Prophet's (PBUH) family
qarī. Expert in *Qurʾānic* diction
qibla. Direction for prayers
qiyās. Precedent
rahmat. Blessing
Ramaḍān. Month of fasting for Muslims
ribā. Financial interest, usury
ṣalāt. Prayer
sanad. Chain or link
seere. Black mark on the forehead from regular praying
Shab e Miʿrāj. The eve of *Miʿrāj*
sharāb. Alcohol
Sharīʿa. Islamic code
Shaykh. Leader
Shiʿa Ithna Ashari. A Muslim sect
shirk. Idolatry
sufī. Spiritual practitioner

Sulaḥ al Ḥudaybiya. Peace treaty of Ḥudaybiya
sutra. The form of passing in front of a praying person
Tablīghī Jamā'at. A movement for the spread of Islam
tafsīr. Exegetical commentary
tafsīr bi-l-rai. Exegetical commentary based on personal opinion and whim
taqlīd. Following the schools of Islamic jurisprudence
taqwā. Fear of God
taṣawwuf. Islamic mysticism
taṣwīr (pl. *taṣāwīr*). Picture or image
ta'ziyas. Replicas of tombs of the martyrs of Karbalā, taken in procession during the mourning ceremony of Muḥarram
tilāwat. Recitation of the Qur'ān
umma. Community
zakāt. Alms

REFERENCES

Abelman, Robert. 1990. "Who's Watching, for What Reasons?" In *Religious Television: Controversies and Conclusions*, edited by Robert Abelman and Stewart M. Hoover, 99–108. Norwood, NJ: Ablex.

Abelman, Robert, and Kimberly Neuendorf. 1987. "Themes and Topics in Religious Television Programming." *Review of Religious Research* 29 (2): 152–74. https://doi.org/10.2307/3511724.

Abu-Lughod, Lila. 1986. *Veiled Sentiments: Honor and Poetry in a Bedouin Society*. Berkeley: University of California Press.

———. 1990. "The Romance of Resistance: Tracing Transformations of Power through Bedouin Women." *American Ethnologist* 17 (1): 41–55.

———. 1998. "The Marriage of Feminism and Islamism in Egypt: Selective Repudiation as a Dynamic of Postcolonial Cultural Politics." In *Remaking Women: Feminism and Modernity in the Middle East*, edited by Lila Abu-Lughod, 243–69. Princeton, NJ: Princeton University Press.

———. 2005. *Dramas of Nationhood: The Politics of Television in Egypt*. Chicago: University of Chicago Press.

Adorno, Theodor W. 1991. *The Culture Industry: Selected Essays on Mass Culture*. Edited by J. M. Bernstein. London: Routledge.

Ahmad, Sadaf. 2009. *Transforming Faith: The Story of Al-Huda and Islamic Revivalism among Urban Pakistani Women*. Syracuse, NY: Syracuse University Press.

———. 2010. "Al-Huda: Of Allah and the Power Point." In *Islam and Society in Pakistan: Anthropological Perspectives*, edited by Magnus Marsden, 299–326. Karachi, Pakistan: Oxford University Press.

Ahmed, Shahab. 2015. *What Is Islam? The Importance of Being Islamic*. Princeton, NJ: Princeton University Press.

Akhtar, Rai S. 2000. *Media, Religion and Politics in Pakistan*. New York: Oxford University Press.
Algan, Ece. 2003. "The Problem of Textuality in Ethnographic Audience Research: Lessons Learned in Southeast Turkey." In *Global Media Studies: An Ethnographic Perspective*, edited by Marwan Kraidy and Patrick D. Murphy, 23–39. New York: Routledge.
Ali, Babar. 1986. "Pakistan: Pakistan Television Zia-Junejo-Mullah Show." *Economic and Political Weekly* 21 (50). https://www.epw.in/journal/1986/50/our-correspondent-columns/pakistan-pakistan-television-zia-junejo-mullah-show.html.
Anand, Tanya. 2014. *The Game Changer: A Brief History of Television in Pakistan*. Karachi, Pakistan: Ushba International.
Anderson, Benedict. 1991. *Imagined Communities: Reflections on the Origin and Spread of Nationalism*. London: Verso.
Ang, Ien. 1991. *Desperately Seeking the Audience*. London: Routledge.
Anjum, Ovamir. 2007. "Islam as a Discursive Tradition: Talal Asad and His Interlocutors." *Comparative Studies of South Asia, Africa and the Middle East* 27 (3): 656–72.
Aristotle. 1941. *The Basic Works of Aristotle*. Edited by Richard McKeon. New York: Random House.
Armbrust, Walter. 2004. "The Ethnography of Media." *Anthropological Quarterly* 77 (4): 819–25. https://doi.org/10.1353/anq.2004.0049.
Asad, Talal. 1993. *Genealogies of Religion: Discipline and Reasons of Power in Christianity and Islam*. Baltimore, MD: Johns Hopkins University Press.
———. 2003. *Formations of the Secular: Christianity, Islam, Modernity*. Stanford, CA: Stanford University Press.
———. 2009a. "Free Speech, Blasphemy and Secular Criticism." In *Is Critique Secular? Blasphemy, Injury, and Free Speech*, edited by Talal Asad, Wendy Brown, Saba Mahmood, and Judith Butler, 20–63. Townsend Papers in the Humanities, no. 2. Berkeley: Townsend Center for the Humanities, University of California. Distributed by University of California Press.
———. 2009b. "The Idea of an Anthropology of Islam." *Qui Parle* 17 (2): 1–30.
Asamoah-Gyadu, Johnson K. 2008. "Community." In *Key Words in Religion, Media and Culture*, edited by David Morgan, 56–68. New York: Routledge.
Askew, Kelly Michelle. 2002. Introduction to *The Anthropology of Media: A Reader*, edited by Kelly M. Askew and Richard R. Wilk, 1–13. Malden, MA: Blackwell.
Aslam, Imran, and Kamran A. Ali. 2009. "Media Matters in Pakistan: An Interview with Imran Aslam." *Middle East Report* 39 (251): 32–36.
Azhar, Mobeen. 2012. "The Rise of Pakistan's Televangelists." BBC News, July 14, 2012. https://www.bbc.com/news/magazine-18729683.

Aziz, Sadaf. 2011. "Making a Sovereign State: Javed Ghamidi and 'Enlightened Moderation.'" *Modern Asian Studies* 45 (3): 597–629. https://doi.org/10.1017/S0026749X11000163.

Aziz, Shaikh. 2015. "A Leaf from History: Four Journalists Flogged, Two Newspapers Shut." *DAWN*, May 3, 2015. http://www.dawn.com/news/1179170.

Babb, Lawrence A. 1998. Introduction to *Media and the Transformation of Religion in South Asia*, edited by Lawrence A. Babb and Susan S. Wadley, 1–20. Philadelphia: University of Pennsylvania Press.

Bano, Masooda. 2012. *The Rational Believer: Choices and Decisions in the Madrasas of Pakistan*. Ithaca, NY: Cornell University Press.

Baudelaire, Charles. 1964. *The Painter of Modern Life and Other Essays*. Translated by Jonathan Mayne. London: Phaidon.

Bayat, Asef. 2007. "Islamism and the Politics of Fun." *Public Culture* 19 (3): 433–59.

BBC News. 2013. "Abandoned Babies Given Away on Pakistani TV Programme." February 8, 2013. http://www.bbc.co.uk/news/world-asia-23529448.

Benford, Robert D., and David A. Snow. 2000. "Framing Processes and Social Movements: An Overview and Assessment." *Annual Review of Sociology* 26:611–39.

Benjamin, Walter. 2008. *The Work of Art in the Age of Mechanical Reproduction*. London, UK: Penguin UK.

Berik, Günseli. 1996. "Understanding the Gender System in Rural Turkey: Fieldwork Dilemmas of Conformity and Intervention." In *Feminist Dilemmas in Fieldwork*, edited by Diane L. Wolf, 56–71. Oxford: Westview.

Berkey, Jonathan P. 2003. *The Formation of Islam: Religion and Society in the Near East, 600–1800*. Cambridge: Cambridge University Press.

———. 2007. "Madrasas Medieval and Modern: Politics, Education, and the Problem of Muslim Identity." In *Schooling Islam: The Culture and Politics of Modern Muslim Education*, edited by Robert W. Hefner and Muhammad Q. Zaman, 40–60. Princeton, NJ: Princeton University Press.

Bourdieu, Pierre. 1977. *Outline of a Theory of Practice*. Translated by Richard Nice. Cambridge: Cambridge University Press.

Bowen, John R. 1993. "Discursive Monotheisms." *American Ethnologist* 20 (1): 185–90. https://doi.org/10.1525/ae.1993.20.1.02a00100.

Brenner, Suzanne. 2011. "Private Moralities in the Public Sphere: Democratization, Islam, and Gender in Indonesia." *American Anthropologist* 113 (3): 478–90. https://doi.org/10.1111/j.1548-1433.2010.01355.x.

Browers, Michaelle, and Charles Kurzman. 2004. *An Islamic Reformation?* Lanham, MD: Lexington Books.

Brown, Daniel W. 1996. *Rethinking Tradition in Modern Islamic Thought*. Cambridge: Cambridge University Press.

Budd, Mike, Robert M. Entman, and Clay Steinman. 1990. "The Affirmative Character of US Cultural Studies." *Critical Studies in Mass Communication* 7 (2): 169–84.

Bujra, Abdalla S. 1971. *The Politics of Stratification: A Study of Political Change in a South Arabian Town*. Oxford: Clarendon.

Butler, Judith. 1993. *Bodies That Matter: On the Discursive Limits of "Sex."* New York: Routledge.

———. 1997. "Further Reflections on Conversations of Our Time." *Diacritics* 27 (1): 13–15.

Caldwell, John T. 2008. *Production Culture: Industrial Reflexivity and Critical Practice in Film and Television*. Durham, NC: Duke University Press.

Carragee, Kevin M. 1990. "Interpretive Media Study and Interpretive Social-Science." *Critical Studies in Mass Communication* 7 (2): 81–96.

Cohen, Stephen P. 2004. *The Idea of Pakistan*. Washington, DC: Brookings Institution Press.

Curran, James, Michael Gurevitch, and Janet Woollacott. 1982. "The Study of Media: Theoretical Approaches." In *Culture, Society and the Media*, edited by Michael Gurevitch, Tony Bennett, James Curran, and Janet Woollacott, 6–25. London: Routledge.

Davies, Charlotte A. 1998. "'A Oes Heddwch?' Contesting Meanings and Identities in the Welsh National Eisteddfod." In *Ritual, Performance, Media*, edited by Felicia Hughes-Freeland, 141–59. London: Routledge.

Daʿwat i Islamī Organisation. n.d. *TV Aur Movie* [TV and movie]. Pakistan: Shoba Islahi Kutab.

DAWN. 2006. "GEO TV Debate on Hudood Laws." June 11, 2006. http://www.dawn.com/news/196428/Geo-tv-debate-on-hudood-laws.

———. 2007a. "Dr Aamir Liaquat Resigns." May 7, 2007. http://www.dawn.com/news/254908/dr-aamir-liaquat-resigns.

———. 2007b. "Sweeping Curbs on Media: Amended Ordinance Empowers PEMRA to Seal Premises, Seize Equipment. Protests by Journalists, Rights Activists." June 5, 2007. http://www.dawn.com/news/250407/sweeping-curbs-on-media.

———. 2013. "'People Love Me,' Says Amir Liaquat Hussain." August 2, 2013. http://www.dawn.com/news/1033606.

———. 2014. "Sectarian Violence Increased in 2013, Says Report." January 6, 2014. http://www.dawn.com/news/1078664.

Dayan, Daniel. 2005. "The Pope at Reunion: Hagiography, Casting and Imagination." In *Media Anthropology*, edited by Eric W. Rothenbuhler and Mihai Coman, 165–75. Thousand Oaks, CA: SAGE.

Debevec, Liza. 2012. "Postponing Piety in Urban Burkina Faso: Discussing Ideas on When to Start Acting as Pious Muslims." In *Ordinary Lives and Grand*

Schemes: An Anthropology of Everyday Religion, edited by Samuli Schielke and Liza Debevec, 33–47. New York: Berghahn Books.

Derrida, Jacques. 1978. "Structure, Sign, and Play in the Discourse of the Human Science." In *Writing and Difference*, translated by Alan Bass, 2nd ed., 278–93. Chicago: University of Chicago Press.

de Witte, Marleen. 2015. "Media Afrikania: Styles and Strategies of Representing 'Afrikan Traditional Religion' in Ghana." In *New Media and Religious Transformations in Africa*, edited by Rosalind I. J. Hackett and Benjamin F. Soares, 207–26. Bloomington: Indiana University Press.

Eaton, Richard M. 2003. *India's Islamic Traditions, 711–1750*. New Delhi, India: Oxford University Press.

Echchaibi, Nabil. 2011. "From Audio Tapes to Video Blogs: The Delocalisation of Authority in Islam." *Nations and Nationalism* 17 (1): 25–44. https://doi.org/10.1111/j.1469-8129.2010.00468.x.

Economist. 2011. "Holy Smoke." October 29, 2011. https://www.economist.com/international/2011/10/29/holy-smoke.

Eickelman, Dale F. 1985. *Knowledge and Power in Morocco: The Education of a Twentieth-Century Notable*. Princeton, NJ: Princeton University Press.

———. 2002. Foreword to *The Public Sphere in Muslim Societies*, edited by Miriam Hoexter, Samuel N. Eisenstadt, and Nehemia Levtzion, 1–8. Albany: State University of New York Press.

———. 2018. "'Mainstreaming' Islam in the Digital Age." Research Center for Islamic Legislation and Ethics. September 13, 2018. https://www.cilecenter.org/resources/articles-essays/mainstreaming-islam-digital-age-pr-dale-f-eickelman.

Eickelman, Dale F., and Jon W. Anderson. 1997. "Print, Islam, and the Prospects for Civic Pluralism: New Religious Writings and Their Audiences." *Journal of Islamic Studies* 8 (i): 43–62.

———. 2003. *New Media in the Muslim World: The Emerging Public Sphere*. Bloomington: Indiana University Press.

Eickelman, Dale F., and James P. Piscatori. 2004. *Muslim Politics*. 2nd ed. Princeton, NJ: Princeton University Press.

El Fadl, Khaled Abou. 2002. "The Place of Tolerance in Islam." In *The Place of Tolerance in Islam: Khaled Abou El Fadl*, edited by Joshua Cohen and Ian Lague, 3–26. Boston: Beacon.

Eltantawi, Sarah. 2017. *Shari'ah on Trial: Northern Nigeria's Islamic Revolution*. Oakland, CA: University of California Press.

el-Zein, Abdul Hamid. 1977. "Beyond Ideology and Theology: The Search for the Anthropology of Islam." *Annual Review of Anthropology* 6 (1): 227–54. https://doi.org/10.1146/annurev.an.06.100177.001303.

Express Tribune. 2015. "For the Third Time: Aamir Liaquat among 500 Influential Muslims." October 4, 2015. https://tribune.com.pk/story/966965/for-the-third-time-dr-aamir-liaquat-among-500-influential-muslims/.

Faruqi, Ijaz. 1991. *Pakistan: A Crisis in the Renaissance of Islam*. Lahore: Sang-e-Meel.

Fischer, Michael M. J., and Mehdi Abedi. 1990. *Debating Muslims: Cultural Dialogues in Postmodernity and Tradition*. Madison: University of Wisconsin Press.

Foucault, Michel. 1984. "What Is Enlightenment?" In *The Foucault Reader*, edited by Paul Rabinow, translated by Catherine Porter, 32–50. London: Pantheon Books.

———. 1988. *Technologies of the Self: A Seminar with Michel Foucault*. Amherst: University of Massachusetts Press.

Fraser, Nancy. 1990. "Rethinking the Public Sphere: A Contribution to the Critique of Actually Existing Democracy." *Social Text*, no. 25/26, 56–80. https://doi.org/10.2307/466240.

Galal, Ehab. 2009. "Yusuf Al Qaradawi and the New Islamic TV." In *Global Mufti: The Phenomenon of Yūsuf Al-Qaraḍāwī*, edited by Bettina Gräf and Jakob Skovgaard-Petersen, 149–80. London: C. Hurst.

Ganti, Tejaswini. 2002. "'And Yet My Heart Is Still Indian': The Bombay Film Industry and the (H)Indianization of Hollywood." In *Media Worlds: Anthropology on New Terrain*, edited by Faye D. Ginsburg, Lila Abu-Lughod, and Brian Larkin, 281–300. Berkeley: University of California Press.

PEMRA (Amendment) Act No. II. 2007. Pakistan Electronic Media Regulatory Authority Ordinance-2002. http://www.site.pemra.gov.pk/pemgov/wp-content/uploads/2015/08/Ordinance_2002.pdf.

Geertz, Clifford. 1971. *Islam Observed: Religious Development in Morocco and Indonesia*. Chicago: University of Chicago Press.

Geo Television Network. 2016a. "Fact Sheet Addressing Allegations on Jang Group." Accessed July 31, 2016. http://web.archive.org/web/20140525042924/http://www.geo.tv/response/.

———. 2016b. "Ghamidi." Accessed July 31, 2016. http://web.archive.org/web/20130401200812/http://www.geo.tv/geonews/program.asp?pid=530.

———. 2019. "Ghamidi." Accessed November 6, 2019. http://web.archive.org/web/20130401200812/http://www.geo.tv/geonews/program.asp?pid=530.

Gibbins, John R. 1989. "Contemporary Political Culture: An Introduction." In *Contemporary Political Culture: Politics in a Postmodern Age*, edited by John R. Gibbins, 1–30. London: SAGE.

Gilsenan, Michael. 1982. *Recognizing Islam: An Anthropologist's Introduction*. London: Croom Helm.

Goffman, Erving. 1959. *The Presentation of Self in Everyday Life*. Garden City, NJ: Double Day Anchor.

———. 1976. "Gender Advertisements." *Studies in the Anthropology of Visual Communication* 3 (2): 69–154.
Gole, Nilufer. 2002. "Islam in Public: New Visibilities and New Imaginaries." *Public Culture* 14 (1): 173–90.
Government of Pakistan, Ministry of Law and Parliamentary Affairs. 1979. Martial Law Regulation No. 49.
Grimes, Ronald L. 2002. "Ritual and the Media." In *Practicing Religion in the Age of the Media: Explorations in Media, Religion, and Culture*, edited by Stewart M. Hoover and Lynn S. Clark, 219–36. New York: Columbia University Press.
Habermas, Jürgen. 1991. *The Structural Transformation of the Public Sphere: An Inquiry into a Category of Bourgeois Society*. Translated by Thomas Burger and Frederick Lawrence. Cambridge, MA: MIT Press.
———. 1994. *The Structural Transformation of the Public Sphere: An Inquiry into a Category of Bourgeois Society*. Cambridge, MA: MIT Press.
Hackett, Rosalind I. J., and Benjamin F. Soares. 2015. Introduction to *New Media and Religious Transformations in Africa*, edited by Rosalind I. J. Hackett and Benjamin F. Soares, 1–16. Bloomington: Indiana University Press.
Hadden, Jeffrey K., and Charles E. Swann. 1981. *Prime Time Preachers: The Rising Power of Televangelism*. Reading, MA: Addison-Wesley.
Haj, Samira. 2002. "Reordering Islamic Orthodoxy: Muhammad Ibn 'Abdul Wahhāb." *Muslim World* 92 (3–4): 333–70. https://doi.org/10.1111/j.1478-1913.2002.tb03747.x.
Hall, Stuart. 2003. "Encoding/Decoding." In *Culture, Media, Language: Working Papers in Cultural Studies, 1972–79*, edited by Stuart Hall, Dorothy Hobson, Andrew Lowe, and Paul Willis, 117–27. London: Routledge.
Haque, Abdul, and S. M. Hafeez Zaidi. 1981. "The Fall of American Skylab: A Study of Pakistani Students' Reactions." *Political Psychology* 3 (3–4): 162–69. https://doi.org/10.2307/3791145.
Hasan, Burhanuddin. 2000. *Uncensored: An Eyewitness Account of Abuse of Power and Media in Pakistan*. Karachi, Pakistan: Royal Book.
Hassan, Riaz. 1985. "Islamization: An Analysis of Religious, Political and Social Change in Pakistan." *Middle Eastern Studies* 21 (3): 263–84.
Hefner, Robert W. 2005. *Remaking Muslim Politics: Pluralism, Contestation, Democratization*. Woodstock, UK: Princeton University Press.
———. 2007. "Introduction: The Culture, Politics, and Future of Muslim Education." In *Schooling Islam: The Culture and Politics of Modern Muslim Education*, edited by Robert W. Hefner and Muhammad Q. Zaman, 1–39. Princeton, NJ: Princeton University Press.
Henry, Marsha Giselle. 2003. "'Where Are You Really From?': Representation, Identity and Power in the Fieldwork Experiences of a South Asian Diasporic." *Qualitative Research* 3 (2): 229–42.

Herman, Edward S., and Noam Chomsky. 2010. *Manufacturing Consent: The Political Economy of the Mass Media*. London: Random House.
Hirschkind, Charles. 1996. "Heresy or Hermeneutics: The Case of Nasr Hamid Abu Zayd." *Stanford Humanities Review* 5 (1): 35–49.
———. 2001. "Civic Virtue and Religious Reason: An Islamic Counterpublic." *Cultural Anthropology* 16 (1): 3–34.
———. 2006. *The Ethical Soundscape: Cassette Sermons and Islamic Counterpublics*. New York: Columbia University Press.
Hobsbawm, Eric, and Terence O. Ranger. 1992. *The Invention of Tradition*. Cambridge: Cambridge University Press.
Hoesterey, James B. 2016. *Rebranding Islam: Piety, Prosperity, and a Self-Help Guru*. Stanford, CA: Stanford University Press.
Hoodbhoy, Pervez. 2006. "Waiting for Enlightenment." *Economic and Political Weekly* 41 (29): 3136–38.
———. 2007. "Jinnah and the Islamic State: Setting the Record Straight." *Economic and Political Weekly* 42 (32): 3300–303.
Hoover, Stewart M. 2002. "Introduction: The Cultural Construction of Religion in the Media Age." In *Practicing Religion in the Age of the Media: Explorations in Media, Religion, and Culture*, edited by Stewart M. Hoover and Lynn S. Clark, 1–6. New York: Columbia University Press.
———. 2003. "Religion, Media and Identity: Theory and Method in Audience Research on Religion and Media." In *Mediating Religion: Studies in Media, Religion, and Culture*, edited by Jolyon P. Mitchell and Sophia Marriage, 9–20. London: T and T Clark.
———. 2008. "Audiences." In *Key Words in Religion, Media and Culture*, edited by David Morgan, 31–43. New York: Routledge.
Hoover, Stewart M., and Lynn Schofield Clark. 2002. "Introduction to Part 2: The Mediation of Religion in the Public Sphere." In *Practicing Religion in the Age of the Media: Explorations in Media, Religion, and Culture*, edited by Stewart M. Hoover and Lynn Schofield Clark, 87–89. New York: Columbia University Press.
Horkheimer, Max, and Theodor W. Adorno. 1972. *Dialectic of Enlightenment*. New York: Continuum.
———. 2002. "The Culture Industry: Enlightenment as Mass Deception." In *Dialectic of Enlightenment: Philosophical Fragments*, edited by Gunzelin Schmid Noerr, translated by Edmund Jephcott, 94–136. Stanford, CA: Stanford University Press.
Horsfield, Peter G. 1984. *Religious Television: The American Experience*. New York: Longman.
Howaydi, Fahmi. 1993. "Hadhar Min Al-La`ab Bil Nar." *Al-Ahram*, April 20, 1993.

Hughes, Stephen P. 2011. "Anthropology and the Problem of Audience Reception." In *Made to Be Seen: Perspectives on the History of Visual Anthropology*, edited by Marcus Banks and Jay Ruby, 288–312. Chicago: University of Chicago Press.
Hughes-Freeland, Felicia. 1998. *Ritual, Performance, Media*. New York: Routledge.
Ilahi, Manzoor. 2011. "(Spreading Deen through TV) تبلیغ کی دین ذریعہ کے وی ٹی." *Darul Iftaa, Al Jamia Al Binoria Al Almiya*, May 30, 2011. Page no longer available.
International Crisis Group. 2005. *The State of Sectarianism in Pakistan*. Asia Report No. 95. April 18, 2005. https://www.crisisgroup.org/asia/south-asia/pakistan/state-sectarianism-pakistan.
Iqbal, Afzal. 1984. *Islamisation of Pakistan*. Lahore: Vanguard Books.
Iqtidar, Humeira. 2012. "State Management of Religion in Pakistan and Dilemmas of Citizenship." *Citizenship Studies* 16 (viii): 1013–28.
Ismail, Salwa. 2003. *Rethinking Islamist Politics: Culture, the State and Islamism*. London: I. B. Tauris.
———. 2007. "Islamism, Re-Islamization and the Fashioning of Muslim Selves: Refiguring the Public Sphere." *Muslim World Journal of Human Rights* 4 (i): 1–21.
Jackson, Michael. 1996. *Things as They Are: New Directions in Phenomenological Anthropology*. Bloomington: Indiana University Press.
———. 1998. *Minima Ethnographica: Intersubjectivity and the Anthropological Project*. Chicago: University of Chicago Press.
———. 2005. *Existential Anthropology: Events, Exigencies and Effects*. Oxford: Berghahn Books.
Kant, Immanuel. 1983. "An Answer to the Question: What Is Enlightenment?" In *Perpetual Peace and Other Essays on Politics, History and Morals*, translated by Ted Humphrey, 41–48. Indianapolis, IN: Hackett.
Kazi, Taha. 2016. "The Changing Dynamics of Religious Authority on Pakistani Religious Television." *Culture and Religion* 17 (4): 468–85. https://doi.org/10.1080/14755610.2017.1296011.
———. 2018. "Religious Television and Contesting Piety in Karachi, Pakistan." *American Anthropologist* 120 (3): 523–34. https://doi.org/10.1111/aman.13061.
Khabeer, Su'ad Abdul. 2016. *Muslim Cool: Race, Religion, and Hip Hop in the United States*. New York: New York University Press.
Khan, Naveeda A. 2003. "Grounding Sectarianism: Islamic Ideology and Muslim Everyday Life in Lahore, Pakistan, Circa 1920s/1990s." New York: Columbia University.
———. 2012. *Muslim Becoming: Aspiration and Skepticism in Pakistan*. Durham, NC: Duke University Press.
Kondo, Dorinne K. 1986. "Dissolution and Reconstitution of Self: Implications for Anthropological Epistemology." *Cultural Anthropology* 1 (1): 74–88.

Korson, J. Henry, and Michelle Maskiell. 1985. "Islamization and Social Policy in Pakistan: The Constitutional Crisis and the Status of Women." *Asian Survey* 25 (6): 589–612.

Kraidy, Marwan M. 2010. *Reality Television and Arab Politics: Contention in Public Life*. Cambridge: Cambridge University Press.

Laclau, Ernesto, and Chantal Mouffe. 1985. *Hegemony and Socialist Strategy: Towards a Radical Democratic Politics*. London: Verso.

Larkin, Brian. 2008. "Ahmed Deedat and the Form of Islamic Evangelism." *Social Text* 26 (3 (96)): 101–21. https://doi.org/10.1215/01642472-2008-006.

———. 2015. "Binary Islam: Media and Religious Movements in Nigeria." In *New Media and Religious Transformations in Africa*, edited by Rosalind I. J. Hackett and Benjamin F. Soares, 63–81. Bloomington: Indiana University Press.

Larkin, Brian, and Birgit Meyer. 2006. "Pentecostalism, Islam and Culture: New Religious Movements in West Africa." In *Themes in West Africa's History*, edited by Emmanuel Kwaku Akyeampong, 286–312. Oxford: James Currey.

Launay, Robert. 1992. *Beyond the Stream: Islam and Society in a West African Town*. Berkeley: University of California Press.

Lehikoinen, Taisto. 2003. *Religious Media Theory: Understanding Mediated Faith and Christian Applications of Modern Media*. Jyväskylä: Jyväskylä University Press.

Lewis, Justin. 2007. "Television and Public Opinion." In *A Companion to Television*, edited by Janet Wasko, 433–48. Oxford, UK: John Wiley and Sons. https://doi.org/10.1002/9780470997130.ch24.

Lindsey, Ursula. 2006. "The New Muslim TV: Media-Savvy, Modern, and Moderate." *Christian Science Monitor*, May 2, 2006. http://www.csmonitor.com/2006/0502/p01s04-wome.html.

Lukens-Bull, Ronald. 1999. "Between Text and Practice: Considerations in the Anthropological Study of Islam." *Marburg Journal of Religion* 4 (2): 1–21.

Lule, Jack. 2005. "News as Myth: Daily News and Eternal Stories." In *Media Anthropology*, edited by Eric W. Rothenbuhler and Mihai Coman, 101–10. Thousand Oaks, CA: SAGE.

MacIntyre, Alasdair. 1988. *Whose Justice? Which Rationality?* Notre Dame, IN: University of Notre Dame Press.

Mahan, Jeffrey H. 2012. "Religion and Media." *Religion Compass* 6 (1): 14–25.

Mahmood, Saba. 2001. "Rehearsed Spontaneity and the Conventionality of Ritual: Disciplines of Salat." *American Ethnologist* 28 (4): 827–53.

———. 2005. *Politics of Piety: The Islamic Revival and the Feminist Subject*. Princeton, NJ: Princeton University Press.

———. 2006. "Secularism, Hermeneutics, and Empire: The Politics of Islamic Reformation." *Public Culture* 18 (ii): 323–47.

Makdisi, George. 1984. *The Rise of Colleges: Institutions of Learning in Islam and the West*. Edinburgh: Edinburgh University Press.

Mamdani, Mahmood. 2005. *Good Muslim, Bad Muslim: America, the Cold War, and the Roots of Terror*. New York: Potter/TenSpeed/Harmony.

Mandaville, Peter G. 2007. *Global Political Islam*. New York: Routledge.

Mankekar, Purnima. 1999. *Screening Culture, Viewing Politics: An Ethnography of Television, Womanhood, and Nation in Postcolonial India*. Durham, NC: Duke University Press.

Marsden, Magnus. 2005. *Living Islam: Muslim Religious Experience in Pakistan's North-West Frontier*. Cambridge: Cambridge University Press. http://ebooks.cambridge.org/ref/id/CBO9780511489549.

———. 2008. "Women, Politics and Islamism in Northern Pakistan." *Modern Asian Studies* 42 (2–3): 405–29.

———. 2010. "Introduction: Anthropology, Islam, and Pakistan." In *Islam and Society in Pakistan: Anthropological Perspectives*, edited by Magnus Marsden, xi–xxxiv. Karachi, Pakistan: Oxford University Press.

Masood, Salman. 2018. "Top Pakistani News Channel Is Forced Off Air, and Eyes Are on the Military." *New York Times*, April 6, 2018. https://www.nytimes.com/2018/04/06/world/asia/pakistan-geo-military-censorship.html.

McLuhan, Marshall. 1964. *Understanding Media: The Extensions of Man*. London: McGraw-Hill.

McLuhan, Marshall, W. Terrence Gordon, Barrington Nevitt, and Harold A. Innis. 2005. *Marshall McLuhan: The Medium Is the Message*. Corte Madera, CA: Gingko.

Messick, Brinkley Morris. 1993. *The Calligraphic State: Textual Domination and History in a Muslim Society*. Berkeley: University of California Press.

———. 1996. "Media Muftis: Radio Fatwas in Yemen." In *Islamic Legal Interpretation: Muftis and Their Fatwas*, edited by Muhammad Khalid Masud, Brinkley M. Messick, and David S. Powers, 311–20. Cambridge, MA: Harvard University Press.

Metcalf, Barbara D. 2004. *Islamic Contestations: Essays on Muslims in India and Pakistan*. New Delhi: Oxford University Press.

———. 2007. "Islamic Revival in British India: Deoband 1860–1900." In *India's Muslims: An Omnibus*, 87–315. New Delhi: Oxford University Press.

Meyer, Birgit. 1998. "'Make a Complete Break with the Past': Memory and Postcolonial Modernity in Ghanaian Pentecostalist Discourse." *Journal of Religion in Africa* 28 (3): 316–49.

———. 2006. "Impossible Representations: Pentacostalism, Vision, and Video Technology in Ghana." In *Religion, Media, and the Public Sphere*, edited by Birgit Meyer and Annelies Moors, 290–312. Bloomington: Indiana University Press.

———. 2011. "Mediation and Immediacy: Sensational Forms, Semiotic Ideologies and the Question of the Medium." *Social Anthropology/Anthropologie Sociale* 19 (1): 23–39.

Meyer, Birgit, and Annelies Moors. 2006. Introduction to *Religion, Media, and the Public Sphere*, edited by Birgit Meyer and Annelies Moors, 1–25. Bloomington: Indiana University Press.

Mir Khalil ur Rahman Foundation. 2016. "Zara Sochiye." *Zara Sochiye*. Accessed August 4, 2016. Page no longer available.

Moll, Yasmin. 2010. "Islamic Televangelism: Religion, Media and Visuality in Contemporary Egypt." *Arab Media and Society* 10:1–27.

———. 2012. "Storytelling, Sincerity, and Islamic Televangelism in Egypt." In *Global and Local Televangelism*, edited by Pradip N. Thomas and Philip Lee, 21–44. New York: Palgrave Macmillan.

Morgan, David. 2008. "Introduction: Religion, Media, Culture: The Shape of the Field." In *Key Words in Religion, Media and Culture*, edited by David Morgan, 1–19. New York: Routledge.

Morley, David. 1980. *The Nationwide Audience: Structure and Decoding*. London: British Film Institute.

———. 1992. *Television, Audiences and Cultural Studies*. London: Routledge.

Mufti, Shahan. 2007. "The Fundamentalist Moderate." *Boston Globe*, July 22, 2007. http://www.boston.com/news/globe/ideas/articles/2007/07/22/the_fundamentalist_moderate/.

Mulvey, Laura. 1989. *Visual and Other Pleasures*. Hampshire, UK: Macmillan.

Murdock, Graham, and Peter Golding. 1977. "Capitalism, Communication and Class Relations." In *Mass Communication and Society*, edited by James Curran, Michael Gurevitch, and Janet Woollacott, 12–43. London: Edward Arnold.

Murphy, Patrick D., and Marwan M. Kraidy. 2003. "Towards an Ethnographic Approach to Global Media Studies." In *Global Media Studies: Ethnographic Perspectives*, edited by Patrick D. Murphy and Marwan M. Kraidy, 3–19. London: Routledge.

Murthy, Gayatri. 2010. "Religious Media Content: A Cable TV Phenomenon." *AudienceScapes*. http://pas.org.pk/religious-media-content-a-cable-tv-phenomenon/.

Mustarshid, Al Kamaluddin. n.d. *Tasweer Ki Sharaee Haisiyat* [The position of tasweer under Shariah]. Karachi, Pakistan: Qadeemi Kutab Khana.

Naggar, Shaimaa El. 2018. "'But I Did Not Do Anything!': Analysing the YouTube Videos of the American Muslim Televangelist Baba Ali: Delineating the Complexity of a Novel Genre." *Critical Discourse Studies* 15 (3): 303–19. https://doi.org/10.1080/17405904.2017.1408477.

Naqvi, Tahir H. 2010. "Private Satellite Media and the Geo-politics of Moderation in Pakistan." In *South Asian Media Cultures: Audiences, Representations, Contexts*, edited by Shakuntala Banaji, 109–22. London: Anthem.

Nasr, Vali. R. 2006. *The Shia Revival: How Conflicts within Islam Will Shape the Future*. New York: W. W. Norton.

———. 2010. "The Rise of Sunni Militancy in Pakistan: The Changing Role of Islamism and the Ulama in Society and Politics." In *Islam and Society in Pakistan: Anthropological Perspectives*, edited by Magnus Marsden, 327–66. Karachi, Pakistan: Oxford University Press.

Nelson, Matthew J. 2009. "Dealing With Difference: Religious Education and the Challenge of Democracy in Pakistan." *Modern Asian Studies* 43 (3): 591–618.

———. 2014. "Ilm and the Individual: Islamic Education and the Production of Political Ideas in Pakistan." In *Being Muslim in South Asia: Diversity and Daily Life*, edited by Robin Jeffrey and Ronojoy Sen, 161–80. Delhi: Oxford University Press.

News. 2013. "Dr Amir Liaquat Included among 500 Most Influential Muslim Personalities." http://www.aamirliaquat.com/post/press_release/800.

Niazi, Zamir. 1994. *The Web of Censorship*. Karachi, Pakistan: Oxford University Press.

Norris, Pippa, and Ronald Inglehart. 2004. *Sacred and Secular: Religion and Politics Worldwide*. Cambridge: Cambridge University Press.

Nyamnjoh, Francis B. 2015. Foreword to *New Media and Religious Transformations in Africa*, edited by Rosalind I. J. Hackett and Benjamin F. Soares, 1–16. Bloomington: Indiana University Press.

Orsi, Robert A. 2005. *Between Heaven and Earth: The Religious Worlds People Make and the Scholars Who Study Them*. Princeton, NJ: Princeton University Press.

———. 2012. "Afterword: Everyday Religion and the Contemporary World; The Un-modern, or What Was Supposed to Have Disappeared but Did Not." In *Ordinary Lives and Grand Schemes: An Anthropology of Everyday Religion*, edited by Samuli Schielke and Liza Debevec, 146–61. New York: Berghahn.

Page, David, and William Crawley. 2005a. *Satellites over South Asia: Broadcasting, Culture, and the Public Interest*. New Delhi: SAGE.

———. 2005b. "The Transnational and the National: Changing Patterns of Cultural Influence in the South Asian TV Market." In *Transnational Television Worldwide: Towards a New Media Order*, edited by Jean K. Chalaby, 128–55. London: I. B. Tauris.

Paracha, Nadeem F. 2010. "It Fell from the Heavens." *Pakistan Defence*, September 28, 2010. http://defence.pk/threads/it-fell-from-the-heavens.74468/.

———. 2013. "Catch 79." *DAWN*, June 20, 2013. http://www.dawn.com/news/1019332.

Pink, Sarah. 1998. "From Ritual Sacrifice to Media Commodity: Anthropological and Media Constructions of the Spanish Bullfight and the Rise of Women Performers." In *Ritual, Performance, Media*, edited by Felicia Hughes-Freeland, 123–42. London: Routledge.

Postman, Neil. 2006. *Amusing Ourselves to Death: Public Discourse in the Age of Show Business*. New York: Penguin.

Powdermaker, Hortense. 2002. "Hollywood and the USA." In *The Anthropology of Media: A Reader*, edited by Kelly M. Askew and Richard R. Wilk, 161–71. Malden, MA: Blackwell.

Qadri, Shahid H., and Ahsan S. Anjum. 2015. *Pakistan Penal Code: XLV of 1860 with New Islamic Laws, 1979*. Lahore: Mansoor Book House.

Radway, Janice. 1996. "The Hegemony of 'Specificity' and the Impasse in Audience Research: Cultural Studies and the Problem of Ethnography." In *The Audience and Its Landscape*, edited by James Hay, Lawrence Grossberg, and Ellen Wartella, 235–45. Boulder, CO: Westview.

Rajagopal, Arvind. 2001. *Politics after Television: Hindu Nationalism and the Reshaping of the Public in India*. Cambridge: Cambridge University Press.

Redfield, Robert. 1956. *Peasant Society and Culture*. Chicago: University of Chicago Press.

Robinson, Francis. 1993. "Technology and Religious Change: Islam and the Impact of Print." *Modern Asian Studies* 27 (1): 229–51.

———. 2013. "Strategies of Authority in Muslim South Asia in the Nineteenth and Twentieth Centuries." *Modern Asian Studies* 47 (1): 1–21. https://doi.org/10.1017/S0026749X12000248.

Rothenbuhler, Eric W. 2005. "The Church of the Cult of the Individual." In *Media Anthropology*, edited by Eric W. Rothenbuhler and Mihai Coman, 91–100. Thousand Oaks, CA: SAGE.

Roy, Olivier. 2004. *Globalized Islam: The Search for a New Ummah*. New York: Columbia University Press.

Salvatore, Armando. 1998. "Staging Virtue: The Disembodiment of Self-Correctness and the Making of Islam as Public Norm." In *Islam, Motor or Challenge of Modernity*, edited by Georg Stauth, 87–120. Hamburg: LIT.

Salvatore, Armando, and Dale F. Eickelman. 2004. Preface to *Public Islam and the Common Good*, edited by Armando Salvatore and Dale F. Eickelman, xi–xxv. Leiden: BRILL.

Sanyal, Usha. 1996. *Devotional Islam and Politics in British India: Ahmad Riza Khan Barelwi and His Movement, 1870–1920*. Delhi: Oxford University Press.

Scannell, Paddy. 2003. "Benjamin Contextualized: On 'The Work of Art in the Age of Mechanical Reproduction.'" In *Canonic Texts in Media Research: Are There Any? Should There Be? How About These?*, edited by Elihu Katz, John D. Peters, Tamar Liebes, and Avril Orloff. Cambridge: Polity. Distributed by Blackwell.

Schielke, Samuli. 2009. "Being Good in Ramadan: Ambivalence, Fragmentation, and the Moral Self in the Lives of Young Egyptians." *Journal of the Royal Anthropological Institute* 15 (May): S24–S40. https://doi.org/10.1111/j.1467-9655.2009.01540.x.

———. 2010. "Second Thoughts about the Anthropology of Islam, or How to Make Sense of Grand Schemes in Everyday Life." ZMO Working Papers 2, Berlin: Zentrum Moderner Orient. http://www.zmo.de/publikationen/WorkingPapers/schielke_2010.pdf.

———. 2012. "Capitalist Ethics and the Spirit of Islamization in Egypt." In *Ordinary Lives and Grand Schemes: An Anthropology of Everyday Religion*, edited by Samuli Schielke and Liza Debevec, 131–45. New York: Berghahn Books.

Schielke, Samuli, and Liza Debevec. 2012. Introduction to *Ordinary Lives and Grand Schemes: An Anthropology of Everyday Religion*, edited by Samuli Schielke and Liza Debevec, 1–16. New York: Berghahn Books.

Schleifer, Abdallah. 2004. "Interview with Sheikh Yusuf Al-Qaradawi." *Transnational Broadcasting Studies Journal*, 13 (Fall). https://www.arabmediasociety.com/interview-with-sheikh-yusuf-al-qaradawi/.

Schulz, Dorothea E. 2003. "'Charisma and Brotherhood' Revisited: Mass-Mediated Forms of Spirituality in Urban Mali." *Journal of Religion in Africa* 33 (2): 146–71.

———. 2006a. "Morality, Community, Publicness: Shifting Terms of Public Debate in Mali." In *Religion, Media, and the Public Sphere*, edited by Birgit Meyer and Annelies Moors, 132–51. Bloomington: Indiana University Press.

———. 2006b. "Promises of (Im)Mediate Salvation: Islam, Broadcast Media, and the Remaking of Religious Experience in Mali." *American Ethnologist* 33 (2): 210–29.

Shaikh, Muhammed Ali. 2007. *Satellite Television and Social Change in Pakistan: A Case Study of Rural Sindh*. Karachi, Pakistan: Orient Books.

Silverstone, Roger. 1994. *Television and Everyday Life*. London: Routledge.

Simon, Gregory M. 2009. "The Soul Freed of Cares? Islamic Prayer, Subjectivity, and the Contradictions of Moral Selfhood in Minangkabau, Indonesia." *American Ethnologist* 36 (2): 258–75. https://doi.org/10.1111/j.1548-1425.2009.01134.x.

———. 2014. *Caged In on the Outside: Moral Subjectivity, Selfhood, and Islam in Minangkabau, Indonesia*. Honolulu: University of Hawaii Press.

Skovgaard-Petersen, Jakob. 1997. *Defining Islam for the Egyptian State: Muftis and Fatwas of the Dār Al-Iftā*. Leiden: BRILL.

Soares, Benjamin F. 1999. "Muslim Proselytization as Purification: Religious Pluralism and Conflict in Contemporary Mali." In *Proselytization and Communal Self-Determination in Africa*, edited by Abdullahi A. An-Na'im, 228–45. Maryknoll, NY: Orbis Books.

———. 2004a. "An African Muslim Saint and His Followers in France." *Journal of Ethnic and Migration Studies* 30 (5): 913–27. https://doi.org/10.1080/1369183042000245615.

———. 2004b. "Islam and Public Piety in Mali." In *Public Islam and the Common Good*, edited by Armando Salvatore and Dale F. Eickelman, 205–26. Leiden: BRILL.

———. 2005. *Islam and the Prayer Economy: History and Authority in a Malian Town*. Ann Arbor: University of Michigan Press.

Starrett, Gregory. 1998. *Putting Islam to Work: Education, Politics, and Religious Transformation in Egypt*. Berkeley: University of California Press.

Stout, Daniel A. 2012. *Media and Religion: Foundations of an Emerging Field*. New York: Routledge.

Stowasser, Barbara F. 1994. *Women in the Qur'an, Traditions, and Interpretation*. New York: Oxford University Press.

Taylor, Charles. 1989. *Sources of the Self: The Making of the Modern Identity*. Cambridge, MA: Harvard University Press.

Thomas, Günter. 2005. "The Emergence of Religious Forms on Television." In *Media Anthropology*, edited by Eric W. Rothenbuhler and Mihai Coman, 79–90. Thousand Oaks, CA: SAGE.

Turner, Victor W. 1969. *The Ritual Process: Structure and Anti-structure*. New York: Aldine.

———. 1990. "Are There Universals of Performance in Myth, Ritual, and Drama?" In *By Means of Performance: Intercultural Studies of Theatre and Ritual*, edited by Richard Schechner and Willa Appel, 8–18. Cambridge: Cambridge University Press.

Usmani, Hazrat Allama Shabbir Ahmad. n.d. *Taleef e Usmani: Minhadad Darul Ulum Ke Aham Ilmi Aur Deeni Masail Ka Tarjuma* [Book of Usmani: A translation of important educational and religious issues]. Lahore: Institute of Islamiat.

Walsh, Declan. 2011. "Islamic Scholar Attacks Pakistan's Blasphemy Laws." *Guardian*, January 20, 2011. https://www.theguardian.com/world/2011/jan/20/islam-ghamidi-pakistan-blasphemy-laws.

———. 2012. "A Star Televangelist in Pakistan Divides, Then Repents." *New York Times*, August 31, 2012. http://www.nytimes.com/2012/09/01/world/asia/a-star-televangelist-in-pakistan-divides-then-repents.html?_r=0.

Warner, Michael. 1992. "The Mass Public and the Mass Subject." In *Habermas and the Public Sphere*, edited by Craig J. Calhoun, 377–401. Cambridge, MA: MIT Press.

Wickham, Carrie R. 2004. "Interests, Ideas, and Islamist Outreach in Egypt." In *Islamic Activism: A Social Movement Theory Approach*, edited by Quintan Wiktorowicz, 231–49. Bloomington: Indiana University Press.

Wilk, Richard R. 2002. "'It's Destroying a Whole Generation': Television and Moral Discourse in Belize." In *The Anthropology of Media: A Reader*, edited by Kelly Michelle Askew and Richard R. Wilk, 286–98. Malden, MA: Blackwell.

Williams, Raymond. 1974. *Television: Technology and Cultural Form*. London: Fontana.

———. 1980. "Means of Communication as Means of Production." In *Problems in Materialism and Culture: Selected Essays*, edited by Raymond Williams, 50–63. London: Verso.

Willis, Paul E. 1977. *Learning to Labor: How Working Class Kids Get Working Class Jobs*. New York: Columbia University Press.

Winston, Diane. 2002. "All The World's a Stage: The Performed Religion of the Salvation Army, 1880–1920." In *Practicing Religion in the Age of the Media: Explorations in Media, Religion, and Culture*, edited by Stewart M. Hoover and Lynn S. Clark, 113–37. New York: Columbia University Press.

Wise, Lindsay. 2005. "Whose Reality Is Real? Ethical Reality TV Trend Offers 'Culturally Authentic' Alternative to Western Formats." *Transnational Broadcasting Studies Journal*, 15. https://www.arabmediasociety.com/whose-reality-is-real-ethical-reality-tv-trend-offers-culturally-authentic-alternative-to-western-formats/.

Wuthnow, Robert. 1990. "The Social Significance of Religious Television." In *Religious Television: Controversies and Conclusions*, edited by Robert Ableman and Steward M. Hoover, 87–130. Norwood, NJ: Ablex.

Yusuf, Huma, and Emrys Schoemaker. 2013. *The Media of Pakistan: Fostering Inclusion in a Fragile Democracy*. BBC Media Action, Policy Briefing 9. http://www.truevaluemetrics.org/DBpdfs/Countries/Pakistan/bbc_media_action_pakistan_policy_briefing-Jan-2014.pdf.

Zaman, Muhammad Q. 1998. "Sectarianism in Pakistan: The Radicalization of Shi'i and Sunni Identities." *Modern Asian Studies* 32 (3): 689–716.

———. 2002. *The Ulama in Contemporary Islam: Custodians of Change*. Princeton, NJ: Princeton University Press.

———. 2005. "Pluralism, Democracy and the 'Ulama." In *Remaking Muslim Politics: Pluralism, Contestation, Democratization*, edited by Robert W. Hefner, 60–86. Woodstock, UK: Princeton University Press.

———. 2009. "The Ulama and Contestations on Religious Authority." In *Islam and Modernity: Key Issues and Debates*, edited by Muhammad K. Masud, Armando Salvatore, and Martin van Bruinessen, 206–36. Edinburgh: Edinburgh University Press.

———. 2010. "Religious Education and the Rhetoric of Reform: The Madrassahs in British India and Pakistan." In *Islam and Society in Pakistan: Anthropological Perspectives*, edited by Magnus Marsden, 76–110. Karachi, Pakistan: Oxford University Press.

Zappa, Francesco. 2015. "Between Standardization and Pluralism: The Islamic Printing Market and Its Social Spaces in Bamako, Mali." In *New Media and Religious Transformations in Africa*, edited by Rosalind I. J. Hackett and Benjamin F. Soares, 39–62. Bloomington: Indiana University Press.

Zeghal, Malika. 1999. "Religion and Politics in Egypt: The Ulema of al-Azhar, Radical Islam, and the State (1952–94)." *International Journal of Middle East Studies* 31 (3): 371–99.

Zubaida, Sami. 1993. *Islam, the People and the State: Political Ideas and Movements in the Middle East*. London: I. B. Tauris.

———. 2009. "Political Modernity." In *Islam and Modernity: Key Issues and Debates*, edited by Muhammad K. Masud, Armando Salvatore, and Martin van Bruinessen, 57–90. Edinburgh: Edinburgh University Press.

INDEX

Aalim Online, vii, 1, 4, 7–8, 45–46, 48–50, 53–54, 57–58, 63–64, 78, 102, 114, 119, 131–32, 135, 147, 151, 156, 177, 186
'*abāya*, 80, 83
'*abd. See* slave
Abedi, Mehdi, 17n1, 86, 92, 140n1
Abu-Haiba, 108
Abu-Lughod, Lila, 8, 14, 19nn10–11, 20n11, 20n15, 115, 145, 186
accommodation: of competing claims to religious authority, 147, 149–50; of non-religious preferences, concerns, and interests, 42, 57, 175–77; of religious diversity, 2, 4, 59, 63–64, 67–69, 72, 95–96, 138, 140, 147, 149–51, 157, 162, 187–89, 101–2
activism: Ahl-i Hadīth, 89, 92–94; Barelwi, 84, 89–92, 94–95; constraints on, 72, 92, 94–95 Deobandi, 77, 79–80, 82, 86, 94–95, 151; doctrinal, 15, 42, 57, 64, 72–73, 81–82, 89, 94, 101, 145, 147; religious, 149, 188; sectarian, 139, 151
advertising, 35–37, 39–40, 54, 60, 187
affinity, 3, 144, 157, 161
agency, 172, 175, 180, 185n2, 185n6; audience, 9, 18–19n7, 135; of lay practitioners, 160, 162; agentive capacities, 85; agentive engagement, 107, 124, 162–63, 176
agenda, 46, 53, 58; political, 21–23, 25–26, 32, 36, 42–43, 52, 66–67, 69, 81, 119, 140; programming, 7, 47; secular, 42–43; setting, 50, 52–53, 62–64. *See also* commercialization, agendas; production, agendas
Ahl-i Hadīth, 2, 9, 19n8, 50, 72, 75, 93–94, 96nn3–4, 103, 114, 125, 127, 132–33, 138, 154. *See also* activism, Ahl-i Hadīth
Ahmad, Sadaf, 12, 19n11, 20n11, 104, 106, 129, 159, 172, 192
Ahmadis, 7, 59, 113, 131–32, 157
Ahmadīyā, 7, 18n5, 59, 156–57
Ahmed, Israr, 73, 81, 97n7, 125, 145, 156
airtime, 27, 49, 58
Al Huda, 104, 106, 129, 159, 169, 172
Al Jazeera, 47, 60, 132, 135
Al Mawrid, 119
Alif, 48, 51, 63, 119
Amaan Ramazan, 4, 48, 58, 65–66, 142, 149–50
Amber, 148–50, 152–55, 157–58
ambivalence, 15, 17, 149, 152, 155, 161
Amir *Sahib*, 74–75
appearance, 29, 124, 145, 157–60. *See also* attire; dress
anchors: religious, 48, 54, 131–37, 109, 140. *See also* control, by religious anchors
anxiety, 15, 109, 152–55, 162, 185n4, 189
'*aql* (intellect), 126–28, 181. See also *naql*
argumentation, 15, 105, 170
ARY (Network), 40, 48–49, 52, 54, 65, 168

219

Asad, Talal, 14–15, 80, 82, 86, 88–89, 97n9, 98n14, 105, 130–31, 137, 141n5, 164, 166, 191
Asif, 81
Aslam, Imran, 34–35, 40–41
ASWJ (Ahle Sunna wa Jamāʿat), 75, 78, 83
attire, 35, 83, 145, 159. *See also* appearance; dress; sartorial choices
audience: call-in, 50; intended, 52–53; participation, 27, 50, 62–63; reception, 47, 145; religious, 2, 9, 47, 49, 51, 63–64, 67–68, 76, 93, 102, 112–13, 116, 117n3, 117n5, 118, 134–35, 137–39, 141n6, 163, 171, 187; studio, 50, 59, 63, 65–66, 79, 111, 114–15, 133. *See also* agency, audience
authenticity, vii, 20n11, 48, 60–61, 79, 87–90, 98n15, 116, 121, 162–63, 168–69, 173, 175, 180, 188, 190. *See also* legitimacy
autonomy: individual, 17, 130, 179, 190, 192; media, 24, 28, 31, 38, 41, 70n7
ʿawrah (public visibility of women, covering up), 11, 19n9, 77, 80, 159
Ayra, 173–79
Ayza, 102–3
azad khyali. (free thinking), 130

backlash, 59, 81–82
banāt, 83, 133
Barelwi: authority, 82, 126, 133; belief and practice, 74, 75, 82, 93, 96n4, 114; position on *taṣwīr*, 84, 86–88; representation on television, 79, 93, 133. *See also* activism, Barelwi; Deobandi, and Barelwi
Baseerat, 25
behind-the-scenes, 54, 132, 156
Berkey, Jonathan P., 99–101
betrayal, 5, 160, 162
Bhutto, Benazir, 34–38
Bhutto, Zulfiqar Ali, 21, 24, 26–27, 30–31
bidʿa, 75, 96n4
Bina, 156
blasphemy, 51–52, 120, 131, 179, 193
broadcasting: decisions, 28, 38, 49, 57–59, 61; industry, 40; time, 146. *See also* Ministry of Information and Broadcasting; Pakistan Broadcasting Corporation
Burkina Faso, 176
burqa, 11, 128. *See also hijāb; niqab; purdah;* veiling

cable: channels, 37; penetration, 44n3; television, 36–39
Caldwell, John T., 47, 60–61
casting, 53
censorship, 30, 43, 90
channel ownership, 38, 41–42, 46, 48–49, 51, 59, 79, 81, 108, 157, 187
choice: enabling, 38, 177; exercise of, 176; liberal, 176–77, 189. *See also* sartorial choices
commercialization, 9, 39, 42, 47, 53, 55–58, 64, 79–80, 89, 108, 110, 142, 147, 187, 194n2; agendas, 3, 169; interests, 55, 57, 68–70, 129, 147. *See also* sponsorship
commodification, 55, 108, 139
competition: media, 1, 36, 39–40, 53, 65, 69, 108, 118, 137, 142, 187; religious, 56, 58, 62–64, 67–69, 72, 86, 89–90, 95, 109, 113, 139, 148–49, 151, 163, 168, 177, 184, 188, 191, 193; for religious authority, 72, 79–80, 86, 89, 143, 147–48
comportment, 160, 174, 193; female, 13; Islamic, 2, 133, 173–74
compromise, 73, 76, 79, 112, 182
concern: corporeal, 55, 89; everyday, 60, 176; existential, 12, 166, 177, 182, 190–91; for piety, 15–16, 163, 175–76, 179, 181, 191
conduct: ethical and moral, 8; female, 46, 174; of hosts, 7, 132–34; individual, 17; religious, 2, 8, 10, 14, 189; religious, rules of, 107, 124, 190, 195n4; scholarly, 47, 77, 84, 110, 148; social, 115. *See also Sharīʿa*
conflict: internal, 175–77; intra-Muslim, 50, 59, 64, 96n3, 149–50, 153; Kargil, 37; religious, 49–50, 187
confusion, 68, 90, 143, 147–48, 155–56, 162
conservatism, 5, 8, 16, 78, 81, 100, 108, 117, 120, 126, 133, 145, 153, 171, 174, 182–84, 195n3. *See also* liberalism
consensus, 94; scholarly (*ijmā*) 62, 84, 97n4, 113, 115, 122, 126–27, 130, 167, 177
contestation, 4, 16, 62, 67, 89, 92, 114–15, 123, 125, 166, 179–80
contract, 56, 131; contractual obligation, 49, 55–57
control: editorial, 47–59; programming, 7, 28, 69; by religious anchors, 137–40; over religious knowledge; 48, 99, 101, 103,

106–7, 124–25; state, 22–26, 28–30, 38, 40, 42–43, 51, 118, 139
conventionalism, 3, 42, 54, 107, 118, 125, 129, 145
Council of Islamic Ideology (CII), 26, 79, 119, 140, 193
critical deliberation, 16, 93, 127, 163–64, 166–67, 172, 179–83, 190
curbs, 24, 26, 41–42

dār al iftāʾ (center for Islamic rulings), 62
Dār al-ʿUlūm (Korangi), 9, 46, 77, 121
daʿwā (invitation to accept Islam), 77, 164, 172
Daʿwat i Islamī, 87, 97n10
DAWN (newspaper), 36, 41, 52, 131–32, 149
debating skills, 132, 138
Debevec, Lisa, 15, 166, 176–77
Deedat, Ahmed, 144, 170
demeanor, 157–58
Deobandi (Sunni): and Barelwi, 74, 78–79, 87–88, 93; belief and practice, 19n8, 46, 75, 93, 127; influence, 77–79 (*see also* activism, Deobandi); position on *taṣwīr*, 83–86; representation on television, 2, 74, 76–77
discourse, 5, 16, 20n11, 22, 42; authoritative, 47, 49, 130, 183–84; discursive dominance, 79, 86, 97n9, 121; discursive foundation, 86, 164; discursive space, 67, 122–23; discursive strategy, 89–94, 130; discursive tradition, 15, 88, 191, 194n2; Judeo-Christian, 130–31, 164; religious, 68, 92, 94, 101, 123, 149–50, 153, 175, 183; religious, pluralistic, 166; religious, televised, 93, 127, 163, 167; traditional, 67–68, 130, 138, 165;
diversity: doctrinal, 16, 138, 145, 155; Muslim, 67, 151–53, 155, 175; religious, 2, 5, 12, 63–64, 69, 95, 151–53, 161; of religious representation on television, 23, 39, 73, 133, 143–44, 153, 160–61, 166, 187, 190; of religious show engagement, 14, 142, 145, 183; viewership, 40, 81, 101–2, 139, 145, 147, 187
doctrine: Islamic, 90, 127, 164; doctrinal affiliation, 9, 64, 73, 94, 96, 113–14, 145, 147, 150, 155, 160; doctrinal assertions of authority, 72, 89, 94, 145–48, 161, 188; doctrinal debate, 86, 89, 113, 123, 149, 151, 154, 191; doctrinal difference, 62, 92, 145, 161, 188–89 (*see also* religious difference); doctrinal identities, 74, 154, 161, 188; doctrinal ideologies, 76, 147, 150, 169; doctrinal representation of television, 56, 58, 62–64, 68, 72, 81, 93, 105, 112–15, 137, 147–48, 151, 153, 188; doctrinal variations, 11, 45. *See also* activism, doctrinal; diversity, doctrinal; politics, doctrinal
doubt, vii, 110, 128, 143, 152, 177, 188. *See also* uncertainty
dress, 11, 29, 45–46, 66, 106, 124, 145, 158–59, 174, 179. *See also* appearance; sartorial choices
dupatta (scarf), 35, 45

edification, 48, 66, 108, 119, 133; edificatory benefits, 6, 101
Egypt, 3, 16, 19n11, 54–55, 66, 85, 88, 108, 117nn2–3, 132, 137–38, 144, 158, 172, 180, 186, 194n1, 195n3
Eickelman, Dale, 2–3, 46, 61, 90, 99, 101, 123–25, 141n6, 151–52, 159, 171, 184, 194, 195n4
el-Zein, Abdul Hamid, 87–88, 97–98n13
entertainment, 26, 33, 38, 40; channels, 36, 65, 108; and fun, 66, 107, 109; oriented religious shows, 65–67, 107–10, 116–17, 142, 155; programming content, 29–31, 36, 48, 55, 116; and religion, 7, 22, 65, 70n3, 107–10; secular, 6, 65–66, 76, 108, 116. *See also* format, entertainment
erudition, 10–11, 54, 111–12, 127, 133–34, 136, 138, 140n4, 144, 150, 158, 170
ethics, 4, 7, 8, 11, 65, 117, 130, 152, 165, 172–73, 180, 185n3, 185n5; ethical impulse of religious programming, 55, 66, 108; ethical subject, 172, 185n3
exegesis, 17n1, 127, 137; Qurʾānic, 126–27, 137; exegete, 119, 122, 132; exegetical method, 88, 129, 171. *See also* interpretation; *tafsīr*
expediency, 4, 84, 86, 162, 173, 181, 183, 190
expertise, 9–11, 16, 62, 111, 122, 124, 126, 132, 144, 148, 171, 194
extremism, 13, 42, 49–50, 67, 75, 78, 83, 104, 138, 153

Fahm ul Quran, 27, 90
Farman-e-Elahi, 27
Fatima, 146–48, 152

fatwā, 2, 17n1, 60, 82, 85–89; orientation, 116, 189, 193; programs, 59–62
fiqh (jurisprudence), 10, 99, 180
FM (*Mawlānā*), 75–77, 79–80
forbidden (*ḥarām*), 60, 83–85, 114
format, 1–2, 27, 37, 53, 59, 67, 107, 111, 116, 133, 135–36, 138, 169, 189–90; commercialized, 79, 80, 89; and content, 9, 46, 138, 186; entertainment, 107–9, 116, 142; pluralistic, 6, 80, 96, 102, 113–14, 173, 189; polemical, 68, 113, 149; transformations in, 47, 59–67, 73, 95, 165
Foucault, Michel, 80, 180, 185n3
France, 162n3
freedom, 30, 31, 40, 130, 164
fundamentalism, 97n7, 124, 153

Galal, Ehab, 47, 50, 60, 101, 103, 135, 137
Geertz, Clifford, 87, 101, 97n11
gender, 3, 11–13, 20n11, 145, 167, 174, 192; interactions, 11, 80, 174, 177; parity, 17, 191; segregation, 77, 79–80, 179
Geo Television, 1, 7, 34, 40–41, 48–49, 51–52, 55, 63, 65, 119, 131, 156–57
Ghamidi, Javed Ahmed, 42, 48–49, 53, 63, 73, 109, 119–26, 128–30, 138–40, 145, 156, 158, 165, 170–73, 175–76, 181–82, 184
Ghana, 46, 194–95n3
Goffman, Irving, 60, 112
Graham, Billy, 57, 158
Gumi, Abubakar, 106, 121, 136, 138

Habermas, Jürgen, 122, 138, 194, 195n4
ḥadīth, 19n8, 83–84, 92–93, 98n15, 121. See also *muḥaddith*; Prophetic tradition
Hall, Stuart, 12, 47, 60
Haq, Ziaul, 5–6, 21–22, 24–36, 42–43, 51, 56, 78
Haidara, Chérif, 123, 140n4, 162n1
Hasan, Burhanuddin, 22–28, 31–34
Hashmi, Farhat, 77, 159
hijāb (head covering), 11, 80, 83, 133, 171, 173–76, 182. See also *burqa*; *niqāb*; *purdah*; veiling
Hirschkind, Charles, 2, 15, 60, 85–86, 98n14, 115, 164, 166, 171–73, 176, 182, 192

Hudood Ordinances, 51, 124
Husain, Aamir Liaquat, vii-ix, 1, 5, 7, 14, 45–46, 48–51, 53–54, 58–59, 63–64, 79, 107–8, 115, 131–36, 138, 140, 145–47, 149, 150–51, 156–59
hypocrisy, 84, 91, 162

idolatry, 75, 94, 154
ijmā (consensus), 97n4, 127, 137
ijtihād, 93, 118, 127, 130–31, 164–65, 181. See also critical deliberation; reasoning, opinioned
ikhlās, 164. See also sincerity
ʿilm (knowledge), 10; *ilm-i ghayb* (unseen knowledge), 91
image; camera, 84; mirror, 87; scholarly, 79, 105, 109–13, 189 (see also impression management); television, 84, 87. See also *taṣwīr*
impression management, 112
India, 18n6, 19n8, 57, 63, 104, 154
Indonesia, 3, 97n11, 185n4
insecurity, 15, 18n4, 123, 187. See also anxiety
interpretation, 15, 42, 60, 67, 86, 92, 106, 119–20, 127–29, 144, 152–53, 163, 171, 176–77, 181, 184, 188, 190; Qurʾānic, 59–60, 122, 126–28, 137, 171; subversive, 123–27; interpretative differences, 129, 166; interpretative expertise, 111, 122–23; interpretative style, 120, 128–29, 165, 171. See also exegesis; exegesis, Qurʾānic
Iqraa, 108
Islamic code, 122, 193. See also *Sharīʿa*
Islamization, 5–6, 17n3, 21–22, 26, 28–32, 35, 42–43, 72

Jamāʿat-i-Islamī, 30, 72, 97n7, 119
Jameel, Tariq, 77, 83, 97n6, 102, 126
Jāmīʿat i ʿUlamā e Islam (JUI), 79, 96n1
Jāmīʿa ʿUlūm-ul Islāmīā (Banori Town), 9, 46, 78, 80, 83, 85
jihād, 124, 128
Jinnah, Muhammad Ali, 22, 32
Junejo, Muhammad Khan, 31–32
jurisprudence, 10, 19n8, 93, 127. See also *fiqh*

INDEX

Kargil, 35, 37
Kazi, Taha, 3, 124, 190–91
Khabarnama, 25, 27
Khaled, Amr, 3, 132, 138, 144, 158
Khalid, 155–56
Khalid, Malik Miraj, 38
Khan, Ayub, 23–25, 30, 33
Khan, Naveeda, 11, 24, 33, 75, 104–5
khauf (fear of God), 164
khushu (humility), 164
Kraidy, Marwan M., 18n7, 190, 194

Larkin, Brian, 106, 121, 124, 136, 138, 144, 170
Lashkar e Jhangvi (Army of Jhangvi), 83, 97n5
legitimacy, 16, 31, 41, 61, 85, 92, 95–96, 100, 103, 121, 127, 154, 162–64, 167–69, 175, 180, 188, 191
liberalism, 42, 49, 67–68, 82, 130–31, 153, 159, 171–72, 174, 178, 182–84, 189, 193; liberalization, media, 1, 22, 36, 38–43, 59–60, 63, 119, 144. *See also* choice, liberal; conservatism
licensing, 38, 40–41
lifestyle, 4, 7, 107, 174, 179, 190
literalism, 120, 124, 126–27, 130, 137, 171
lived experience, 16, 143, 165, 177

MacIntyre, Alasdair, 88
Mahmood, Saba, 15, 20n11, 43, 89, 109, 115, 144, 164, 172, 174–76, 192
Mali, 90, 94, 123, 154, 158, 189
Malik, Ghulam Murtaza, 125, 145
Mansoora, 159
Mariam, 167–68, 173
Marsden, Magnus, 15, 158–59, 164, 181–82, 185n5, 191–93
Masoud, Moez, 3, 138, 158
Maududi, Syed Abul A'la, 73, 97n7, 119
maulvī, 33, 104, 158
media deregulation, 36, 38, 41
memorization, 9, 20n12, 99–100, 111
Metcalf, Barbara D., 22, 24, 87
Meyer, Birgit, 2, 106, 149, 192, 194, 195nn3–4
Ministry of Information and Broadcasting, 26, 28, 30
Mi'rāj (Prophet's [PBUH] ascension), 111, 181

moderation: Enlightened, 42–43, 52, 119, 139; religious, 3, 5, 7, 8, 43, 52, 66–67, 104–5, 117–18, 124, 131, 133, 138–40, 145, 152–53, 158, 171, 187
modernity, 20n11, 105–6, 180, 190, 193
Mohsin, 126
Moin Sahib, 91–92
Moll, Yasmin, 3, 47, 51, 54–55, 66, 105, 108, 136, 138, 144
Momin, 153–55, 161
muftī (Islamic juris consult), 10, 88, 121, 136; *Muftī* Manzoor Illahi, 85; *Muftī* Muneeb ur Rahman, 91–92; *Muftī* Naeem, 78; *Muftī* Qadir, 83, 89; *Muftī* Rafi Uthmani, 77, 95; *Muftī* Umair, 54–57
muḥaddith (expert on *ḥadīth*), 10
mullah (religious cleric), 30, 104–5, 158–59
Muqabal Hai Aaina, 34
Musharraf, Pervez, 1, 5, 19n8, 22, 37–38, 40–43, 51–52, 76, 97n5, 119, 139–40
Muslim: being, 14, 67, 130, 160, 169, 175; belief, 16, 68, 87, 129, 131, 178–79; life, 15, 17, 29, 109, 165–66, 174–76, 191–92; religiosity, 12, 14, 15, 17, 166, 175, 179–80; subjectivity, 136, 171; viewership, 16, 59, 65–66, 158, 187, 190. *See also* conflict, intra-Muslim; diversity, Muslim; politics, Muslim
mustanid (authentic, established), 115, 121–22, 126–27
Mustarshid, Kamaluddin (*Mawlānā*), 84–85, 107, 122–23, 126–29
muta'abbid, 131. *See also* slave

Nadia, 150–52, 155, 157
Naik, Zakir, 154, 170, 172
naql (mimicry), 126, 128. See also *'aql*
Naqvi, Tahir H., 39–42, 140
Nasr, Vali R., 78, 97n7, 151
National News Bureau, 25
negotiation, 11, 62, 73, 89, 92, 116–17, 166, 175
Nelson, Mathew J., viii, 74, 90, 95, 155, 188
Nigeria, 106, 121, 136, 138
niqāb (veiling), 11, 80, 83, 159, 173–76, 182. See also *burqa*; *hijāb*; *purdah*; veiling
Noorani, Kokab (Okarvi), ix, 5, 14, 24–28, 35, 63, 86, 159

INDEX

norms, 11, 16, 17n2, 117, 124–25, 133, 158–60, 165, 172, 175, 180, 190; normative, ix, 17, 29, 43, 80, 101, 120, 125, 130, 134, 138–40, 172, 177, 184, 191
NTM, 35

objectification, 101, 117n1, 172
opinion: personal, 16, 126–28, 130, 135, 165, 181–83, 190. See also *fatwā*; *ijtihād*; reasoning, opinioned; *tafsīr, tafsīr bi-l-rai*
orthodoxy, 2, 15, 42–43, 78, 87–88, 100, 122, 192

Pakistan Broadcasting Corporation, 24
Pakistan Electronic Media Regulatory Authority (PEMRA), 38, 40–42, 55, 57, 187
Pakistan People's Party (PPP), 34, 78
Pakistan Tehreek-i- Insaf (PTI), 52, 131
Pakistan Telecommunication Authority (PTA), 36
Pakistan Television Corporation. *See* PTV
Paracha, Nadeem F., 21–22, 27, 30, 33
pedagogy, 39; pedagogical attributes, 3; pedagogical content, 27; pedagogical orientation, 129; pedagogical style, 109, 119
permissible (*ḥalāl*), 60, 127–128, 130, 136, 164, 177
personhood, 166, 180, 188, 191
piety: female, 124, 128, 159, 172–75, 182; ideas about, 29, 66, 189, 191–93; individual, 3; popular forms of, 13; selective, 176–81; transformations in, 13, 192. *See also* concern, for piety
Piscatori, James, 2, 46, 61, 125, 151–52, 159, 171, 184
polarization, 5, 6, 182, 192
politics: doctrinal, 9, 149–50, 169; Muslim, 2, 9, 15, 64, 72, 77–78, 89–90, 116–17, 123, 125, 144, 149–50, 153, 182, 187; sectarian, 73, 82, 95, 139, 143, 148, 151, 154
preachers: celebrity, 2–3, 7, 9, 16, 42, 48, 49, 53, 59, 61, 63–64, 69, 118, 120, 123, 131–32, 136, 140, 144, 160, 165; Christian, 57, 158, 170; female, 77, 159; preaching style, 105–6, 125; self-styled, 10, 61, 122, 128, 132, 136, 145, 173

production: agendas, 47, 59, 64, 133, 140; considerations, 9, 47, 108, 187; control, 27, 49, 53, 55, 58, 69, 105; decisions, 51, 63, 68–69, 186; interests, 54, 187. *See also* studio, production
Production Control Room (PCR), 49
proficiency, 11, 124, 144, 162n1
prohibition, 30, 42–43, 57, 76–77, 79, 82–83, 87–88, 120, 165
propaganda, 22, 33, 36–37, 56–57
Prophetic tradition, 85–88, 92, 144. *See also ḥadīth*
PTV, 1, 21–25, 27–38, 40, 42, 59–60, 63, 70n1, 125, 140, 144–45
public sphere, 3, 94, 122, 138, 144, 170
purdah, 171, 182. See also *niqab*; veiling

Qadri, Tahirul, 125
Qaradawi, Yusuf al, 132, 135, 137
Qatar, 47, 60
qiyās (precedent), 97–98n4, 127
QTV, 48, 54–57, 79, 89, 105, 146
Qur'ān, 16, 19n8, 31, 58, 90–91, 93, 95, 97n4, 102, 129, 144, 154, 164, 167, 174, 178, 182; Qur'ānic discourse, 152; Qur'ānic injunctions, 60; Qur'ānic study, 9, 99, 102, 111, 129, 169; Qur'ānic verses, 1, 25, 27, 111, 122, 170–71. *See also* interpretation, Qur'ānic

radicalization, 5–6, 8, 13–14, 56–57, 64, 69, 72, 81, 94, 105, 138, 167, 174
Rahman (Professor), 56, 86, 105–6, 110, 112
Rahman, Mir Shakilur, 157
rationality, 105–6, 129, 164, 170–73, 181, 192
reasoning, 15, 105, 126, 163–64, 171, 178; individual, 93, 172; opinioned, 126–28, 130; rules of, 15, 164–65, 170, 173, 182. *See also ijtihād*
reflexivity, 2, 87–88, 163–64, 172–73, 180, 184
reform: media, 1, 24, 29, 33, 38, 41–42, 106; political, 72; reformist, 10, 19n8, 106; religious, 19n8, 42, 78, 88, 100, 119, 152
religious credentials, 2, 53, 93, 118, 121, 125, 132, 136, 145, 171. *See also* religious education

religious credibility, 25, 28, 36, 38, 58, 103, 109, 113, 157, 169
religious debate, 2, 13, 15, 46, 51, 61, 67, 69, 73, 89–90, 94–95, 115, 120–23, 130, 135, 137, 140, 149, 105, 118, 126, 162, 183, 186, 194: televised, 53, 90, 103, 115, 125, 128, 165; terms of, 16, 47, 115, 122, 125–26, 128–29, 134, 137, 140, 162, 164–65, 170–71, 173, 179, 182, 184. *See also* doctrine, doctrinal debate
religious difference, 3, 46, 59, 67–69, 90, 92–93, 95, 113–14, 130, 147, 150–51, 155, 187–88
religious education, 29, 100–101, 103, 105, 111, 122–23, 125, 127, 131, 133
religious game shows, 7, 48, 58–59, 65–67, 69, 107–10, 116, 134, 150
religious obligation, 2–3, 28, 62, 114, 128, 173–74, 176, 178
resistance, 13, 19n11, 62, 88–89, 92, 143, 145, 172, 175, 179–80, 193–94
ribā (financial interest), 103, 128
ritual, 2, 70n4; practice, 19n8, 75, 90, 96n4, 115, 174; ritualized viewers, 70n6
Robinson, Francis, 72, 122, 140n2, 143, 185n7
roshan khyali (enlightened thinking), 130–31
Royal Islamic Strategic Studies Center, 157

Salman, 147, 158–59, 181
Sania, 181–82
Sanyal, Usha, 19n8, 75, 93, 96n4
sartorial choices, 83, 144, 174–75. *See also* appearance; attire; dress
Schielke, Samuli, 15–16, 166, 176–77, 180
scrutiny, 10, 61, 112, 116, 151, 189
sectarianism, 5–7, 13, 42, 50, 67–69, 72, 74, 78, 95, 113–14, 145, 149, 151, 154–55, 162, 187, 192. *See also* activism, sectarian; politics, sectarian
secularism, 16–17, 32, 65, 124, 138, 144, 164, 170, 172, 192–93. *See also* agenda, secular; entertainment, secular
sensationalism, 21, 58, 134, 146
Sharī'a (Islamic code of conduct), 5, 10, 32, 103, 124, 163, 165, 180; *Sharī'a wa'l ḥayāt*, 60, 135, 137

Sharif, Nawaz, 34–38
Salafi (Shaykh), 125–26, 130, 132, 134, 138
Shi'a (Ithna Ashari) belief and practice, 75, 81–82, 96n3, 151; representation on television, 89, 92–94, 113–15, 168–69
sincerity, 79, 84, 86, 95, 109–10, 126, 132, 147, 156, 164–65
Sipah Sahaba Pakistan (SSP), 19n8, 78, 97n5
skepticism, 23, 66, 81, 109–10
slave, 130–31. *See also muta'abbid*
Soares, Benjamin F., 3, 94, 101, 103, 115, 158, 162n3, 189
South Africa, 144, 170
sponsorship, 39–40, 47–48, 54–55, 187
Star TV, 36–37
status: celebrity, 116, 155–61; of religious authorities, 10, 105, 118, 122–23, 131, 138, 140, 184; of television, 82–86; of women, 11–12, 50, 178–79
studio: audience, 50, 59, 63, 65–66, 79, 111, 114–15, 133; production, 8, 45–46, 49, 186–87
Subhe Pakistan, 53
subjectivity, 115, 143, 175, 177. *See also* Muslim, subjectivity
subordination: female, 178–79; of religious authority, 68–69, 123
subversion, 14, 30, 48, 109, 116, 123–26, 134, 155, 163, 172, 175, 190
sutra, 167
Swaggart, Jimmy, 57, 64

Tablīghī Jamā'at, 77–78, 83, 97n6, 126
Tafheem-e-Deen, 27, 90
tafsīr (exegetical commentary), 1, 10, 27, 60; *tafsīr bi-l-rai*, 125–30. *See also* exegesis; exegesis, Qur'ānic
taqlīd, 93, 100, 126–28, 137, 170
taṣawwuf (intercessionary practice), 75, 96n4
taṣwīr (picture image, pl. *taṣāwīr*), 83, 85, 87, 89. *See also* image, camera; image, mirror; image, television
televangelism, 3, 47, 57, 64, 66, 108, 125, 138, 144, 158, 170
tolerance, 66, 134, 148–53, 155, 157, 161, 188, 191
Turkey, 11

uncertainty, 61, 155, 167–68, 173, 188. *See also* doubt
United States, 5–6, 35, 42, 52, 57, 64–66
Usman, Safdar (*Mawlānā*), 93, 125
Usmani, Shabbir Ahmad (*Allama*), 127, 182

values, 16, 18n7, 20n11, 38, 64, 175, 178–79, 192; Islamic, 16, 27, 68, 78, 101, 108, 116, 133–34, 166, 172, 176, 178, 180, 187, 190, 193–94; secular, 17, 164, 179, 191, 193. *See also* norms

veiling, 13, 19n9, 124, 128, 167, 173, 175, 192. See also *burqa*; *hijāb*; *niqāb*; *purdah*

Women's Protection Bill, 52

Zainab, 176–77, 179
Zaman, Muhammad Q., 19n8, 85, 96n2, 101, 106, 117n3, 151, 162n2, 164
Zara Sochiye, 51–52
Zee TV, 36–37
Zina Ordinance, 51–52

TAHA KAZI earned a PhD in social anthropology from SOAS University of London. Her research interests include anthropology of Islam, sectarian politics, religious authority, television, popular culture, and social media. She has published papers on religious media and their implications in the journals *American Anthropologist* and *Culture and Religion*.

www.ingramcontent.com/pod-product-compliance
Lightning Source LLC
Chambersburg PA
CBHW030620230426

43661CB00053B/2084